36 75

ROOM ADDITIONS

Other Books in McGraw-Hill's Complete Construction Series

Dodge Cost Guides ++ Series

All from McGraw-Hill and Marshall & Swift

ROOM ADDITIONS

Paul Bianchina

McGraw-Hill

New York   San Francisco   Washington, D.C.   Auckland   Bogotá
Caracas   Lisbon   London   Madrid   Mexico City   Milan
Montreal   New Delhi   San Juan   Singapore
Sydney   Tokyo   Toronto

Library of Congress Cataloging-in-Publication Data

Bianchina, Paul.
    Room additions / Paul Bianchina.
      p. cm.
    Includes bibliographical references.
    ISBN 0-07-006939-5
    1. Buildings—Additions.   2. Construction contracts.   I. Title.
TH4816.2.B53   1999
690'.24—dc21   99-19647
                                          CIP

McGraw-Hill

*A Division of The **McGraw·Hill** Companies*

1 2 3 4 5 6 7 8 9 0 DOC/DOC 9 0 4 3 2 1 0 9

ISBN 0-07-006939-5

The sponsoring editor for this book was Zoe Foundotos, the editing supervisor was Christine Furry, the editing liaison was Patricia V. Amoroso, and the production supervisor was Pamela A. Pelton. It was set in Melior by North Market Street Graphics.

Printed and bound by R. R. Donnelley & Sons Company.

 This book is printed on recycled, acid-free paper containing a minimum of 50 percent recycled de-inked fiber.

To Rose, as always,
with my love and gratitude for 22 incredible years

CONTENTS

ACKNOWLEDGMENTS

I would like to express my deep appreciation to the following individuals and companies who assisted me with material for the preparation of this book: Beth Hunt of Trus Joist MacMillan; Suzi Grundahl of the Wood Truss Council of America; Paul Mackey of the Western Red Cedar Lumber Association; Libby Woods of Velux-America; Mike Schmaltz of Sive/Young & Rubicam (Senco); the Cedar Shake & Shingle Bureau.

INTRODUCTION

For any contractor, one of the most demanding, satisfying—and potentially profitable—construction projects is the room addition. From simple single-room bump-outs to complete second-story expansions, the room addition presents a unique set of challenges for the builder of any level. Transitions between one room and another need to be seamless. Bearing walls need to be removed and loads transferred safely to new supports. Materials from the 1990s need to match up and blend in with materials from the 1930s. And in the end, the finished addition needs to be so carefully crafted as to be completely unobtrusive, a natural extension of the original house that looks in every way as if it's been there forever.

Craftsmanship of this quality and complexity is only one of the challenges facing the builder who undertakes an addition. There is the client consultation and bidding process, the preparation and presentation of the estimate, the need to sell your services to the homeowner in the face of stiff competition (even when you're not the low bidder).

There are contracts and change orders, lien notices and permits, sketches and specifications, and a hundred and one other paperwork considerations. There is the stress of dealing with the day-to-day realities of tearing open someone's home and then putting it back together again. And along with all of that comes the explaining, cajoling, coaxing, hand-holding, and occasional arguing that comes with a project of this magnitude.

For the professional builder who is serious about entering the interesting and lucrative arena of room additions, *Room Additions* is the perfect book. For the beginning contractor, there is enough basic information to provide a very thorough learning experience, while the experienced contractor will benefit from a variety of new ideas, new materials, and more advanced concepts.

Divided into two basic sections—Part 1, The Paperwork Side, and Part 2, The Building Side—*Room Additions* explains everything you need to know in order to enter this rewarding area of remodeling:

- In The Paperwork Side, you'll walk through the entire meeting, design, and presentation process, from initial consultations through bidding and selling. You'll have a chance to take a long, hard look at the realities of additions, from contracts and conflicts to weather protection and the responsibilities inherent in becoming a temporary member of the homeowner's family.

- In The Building Side, you'll see the practical aspects of the actual construction process—how to make it all come together. The transition process between the new addition and the existing house. Demolition and safety issues. The latest in engineered lumber products. Roofing and siding. Windows and doors. In short, *Room Additions* provides *every* mental and physical tool the builder needs to design, estimate, sell, and construct a top-quality room addition.

When you undertake a room addition, you'll find yourself as part builder, part designer and decorator, part financial adviser and real estate consultant, part friend and counselor. It's fun, it's interesting, and it's one of the biggest challenges you'll face as a builder. It's the best opportunity you'll find to blend craftsmanship and creativity with a financially solid business you can be proud of.

Room Additions will show you how it's done.

ROOM ADDITIONS

The Paperwork Side

An Overview of Room Additions

Room additions present a set of unique challenges to the contractor, and that's what makes them such an interesting part of the construction field. Every addition is different, with diverse problems and opportunities, and every one will push you to perform at the highest levels that you and your crew are capable of.

There's the intellectual challenge of designing an addition that fits aesthetically and structurally with the house while at the same time meeting the specific needs and preferences of your clients. There's a sales challenge in convincing the homeowners what you already know—that you're the best contractor for the job. There's the business challenge of making this a job that's profitable for your company and that also paves the way for future work and referrals. And there's the challenge—and the satisfaction—that comes from mustering all of your carpentry skills into creating an addition that is fully functional and at the same time completely indistinguishable from the original house.

Why Do People Add On?

As you'll see from Chapters 2 and 3, there are dozens upon dozens of reasons that people need more space. Families grow and need more room, or space for additional privacy. Growing families also need more bathroom space, more kitchen space—more of just about everything. People develop new hobbies and interests, or they choose to work out of their homes. Others want a guest room for out-of-town friends and family, while others may want a shop, another stall in the garage, or even just an organized pantry or a big walk-in closet.

But why they want the space is only part of the picture—after all, if you need a bigger house, why not just sell the one you have and buy or build one that's large enough to suit your needs? You need to know the answers to that question if you're going to sell and construct additions, because it helps you to better understand your clients. The reasons for adding on instead of buying another home are varied, and here are some of the most common ones.

"I like the neighborhood." This is probably the single most important reason why people choose to expand a home rather trade up to something larger. Over the years, many people form an attachment to a particular neighborhood, from their friends across the street to the shady park down the road. There is the issue of familiar schools for the children, favorite restaurants and shopping areas, local medical care and other services, perhaps even the proximity to other family members.

Being attached to a particular neighborhood is an emotional thing, and it's important that you understand this reasoning and motivation.

"I like this house." Many people have a very strong attachment to the house itself. Perhaps they grew up there or acquired it through an inheritance from a loved one. There may be other sentimental reasons at work—it's their first home, or the home where their first child was born.

For a lot of people, "I like the house" means exactly that—they like this particular house. It could have an architectural style that is unique or pleasing. It could have a sunny south exposure that they enjoy in the winter or early morning light that's great for painting. They could be attached to that big oak tree in the front yard, the lush lawn they've spent five years nursing along, a yardful of beautifully established landscaping, or the fruit trees out back that are just now beginning to bear fruit.

"They don't build 'em like this anymore." This is kind of an offshoot of "I like this house," but it's an important distinction to recognize. Many people who own older homes and who have checked out

the market for new construction don't particularly like the quality of construction in some of today's new homes. We all know that the lumber is not of the same quality that it was a few years ago, and rising labor and material costs across the board have made it necessary for builders in entry-level and some midlevel housing markets to cut costs wherever possible in order to maintain an affordable edge.

"I can have exactly what I want." For people with specific needs (a particular hobby, for example, or the need to create an accessible space for someone who is handicapped or elderly) a room addition presents the opportunity to construct a custom-designed area that meets their exact criteria.

Since it's highly unlikely that they will be able to find an existing home with all of the things they specifically need, the only alternative other than an addition would be to custom-build a home, which is not an economically feasible option for most people. One of the most important things for you to stress when working on the sale of an addition is that you can create a custom space that's just what the customer is looking for.

"I'm doing it for the resale value." Resale value—the opportunity to improve the house and have its value increase when it's time to sell—is an important motivator for many people. You'll want to help your clients determine what will and won't add value to their home (see Chapter 3).

For example, a three-bedroom, one-bath house will benefit tremendously from the addition of a second bathroom. Several studies have shown that bathroom additions—when it's the second bathroom in a home that previously had only one—will pay back more than the invested cost. In other words, investing $10,000 in a new bathroom might increase the resale value of the house by $12,000 to $15,000, depending on the neighborhood.

Another example would be that of a 1500-square-foot house in a neighborhood where the homes range in size from 2500 to 3000 square feet. A well-planned and well-executed addition might pay back more than was invested in the construction costs.

If you intend to build room additions in a particular area, it pays to take the time to talk with a knowledgeable real estate agent, or at the very least to study the real estate section of the local paper. Learn which houses are selling best in the area, and find out a little bit about them—

size and style, number of bedrooms, number of bathrooms, and other rooms or amenities that make them desirable. As will be stressed over and over in this book, the more knowledgeable you are about your profession, the better chance you'll have of beating out your competition.

"I can do some sweat equity." Many do-it-yourselfers look at remodeling projects as a chance to gain value in their homes, and doing some things themselves is the only way they can afford what they want. In a case where they need additional space, building an addition where they are able to do part of the work themselves may be much more practical and affordable than having to go out and purchase another home.

For you as a contractor, this leads to the obvious question of whether you wish to work with homeowners who also want to do some of the work themselves. Remember that this is a very common occurrence, and while it does create some additional work and occasional headaches for you, bear in mind that you'll probably lose some volume of work if you're not willing to accommodate the home handyperson.

"I just refuse to move." For some people, the reason for building an addition is simply that moving is an absolute nightmare. The packing, the unpacking, the disruption in routine—all of this can be more than some folks want to deal with.

The Differences Between Room Additions and Other Types of Remodeling

Every remodeling project has challenges and problems, but there are some definite differences between a room addition and other types of remodeling, such as redoing a kitchen. If you have done remodeling work before and now intend to undertake room additions, there are some important differences to be aware of.

More structural considerations: One of the biggest and most important aspects of room-addition construction is the need to remove load-bearing construction to open up the existing house to the addition. This may, depending on the project, involve foundation, footing, and slab alterations; removal or alteration of large portions of wall and floor framing; load transfers between old framing and new framing; and complicated roof tie-ins.

Room additions typically require some slow, methodical, and very precise framing. You'll encounter a lot of "head-scratching" situations in which you need to stop, measure, calculate, sketch, and generally work through a framing problem to be sure that you've moved and supported a load correctly before moving on.

More aesthetic considerations: Nothing is more satisfying than a room addition that takes on the characteristics of the original house and extends out from it as though the original carpenters built it when the house was new (Figure 1.1). Conversely, few things look worse than an addition that is clearly that—an addition.

Room additions have more aesthetic considerations than any other type of remodeling. For an addition to blend in properly, you have to match existing windows, doors, siding, roofing, trim, drywall, and much, much more. In those instances where a match is completely impossible—a stone house where the stone is no longer available, for example—then the addition must be carefully crafted to blend with and complement the original materials in a manner that's consistent and harmonious.

FIGURE 1.1

Room additions require a very careful blending of new (left) with original (right).

Heavier financial burdens: Room additions, typically, are the most expensive types of remodeling, and it's not unusual to have the cost of an addition equal or exceed the cost of many new homes. You will be dealing with clients who have invested a lot of money in their homes—and in you—and you'll have to deal with all of the responsibilities that accompany that.

To deal with large and expensive jobs, you will have cash-flow needs that must be carefully planned for. As you'll see in later chapters, it is important to plan for regular draws from your clients—and to know how to work with them to ensure that the money continues to flow. Delays on draws can seriously impede your ability to do your work and run your company—and in extreme cases have driven contractors out of business.

Longer job duration: It's not unusual for a room addition to require three or four months from beginning to end—much more of your time than any other type of remodeling—and this long duration of work has several ramifications. This will be discussed in more detail in subsequent chapters, but an overview here will get your thought processes started off in the right direction:

- Depending on the size of your crew and the financial strength of your company, a project of this size may limit your ability to take on other clients.

- It's all too easy to see a long job stretching out ahead of you and become overconfident of ongoing employment. Too many contractors get wrapped up in one room-addition project and wait until it's almost over before starting to look for other new clients and new jobs, which often results in periods of little or no work.

- On a project of this length in a house that is typically occupied, you will become a temporary member of the family, requiring a lot of patience on your part and on the part of your clients to maintain a positive relationship.

- If you live in a large city or town, having a project on one side of town may pose logistical problems for supervision and scheduling if you simultaneously have jobs on the other side of town.

A larger work force: A room addition, by virtue of its size and complexity, will require a greater number of people to complete in a timely manner than will a simpler remodeling project. For most additions, running a one-person shop is simply not possible unless you intend to subcontract most of the work. The amount of demolition and structural work makes at least two full-time people a physical necessity, and given the time frames imposed by banks, building departments, and the clients themselves, more than two people are usually required to complete the work within a reasonable period.

Given the number of systems being impacted (plumbing, heating, electrical, etc.), a number of subcontractors are required, all of whom must be skilled in remodeling. More materials are required, and they must be kept flowing to the job site. You'll need to order many items that require long lead times—doors, windows, cabinets, flooring, and much more.

All of this requires spending a greater amount of your time in supervision and scheduling—and less time with a hammer in your hand. In something of a Catch-22 situation, the bigger the project, the less time you'll usually have to physically work on it, requiring that more of it be turned over to others, which in turn requires even more of your time for supervision.

Increased red tape: Room additions have more attendant red tape than do other types of remodeling. Other types of remodeling, such as converting a bedroom into a home office or redoing a bathroom, typically do not entail enough structural, plumbing, or electrical work to require a building permit. Room additions typically require several.

With remodeling that is contained within the original boundaries of the home, there are no problems with zoning or setback requirements. Nor are there problems with the neighbors. Not so for room additions, where you need to pay serious attention to property lines and setbacks, zoning and neighborhood use restrictions, the requirements of homeowner's associations, and possibly complaints from neighbors who object to you expanding closer to their property.

Room additions, unlike any other form of residential remodeling, will require that a sizable chunk of your time be spent with city and county building and planning departments, engineering departments, utility departments, sewer and water departments, and many municipal and bureaucratic entities. Get used to this now—it's part of the job, and your patience and good nature are the best weapons you have for getting through it all.

A Look at Some Important New Trends

Trends change, and it's no different in the building industry than it is in any other field. Certain things become popular, and those are the types of additions your clients will likely want. So, as mentioned earlier, if you're going to sell room additions, you've got to know your market and keep up with what people are looking for.

One recent survey of homeowners, conducted in April of 1998, showed the following:

- About 60 percent of families currently live in single-family homes. This is your market for room additions, and it represents a good number of potential clients.

- Approximately 47 percent of homeowners do not have children at home. In considering your marketing strategies, this is an interesting statistic, indicating that you'll probably find more work building home offices and media rooms than adding on extra bedrooms.

- In creating second and third bedrooms, many people who looked at new homes felt these rooms were too small. If your client's room-addition plans call for an extra bedroom, keep it as large as practical.

- "Flex" space is currently very popular. Flex rooms are essentially large, open rooms with the flexibility to change uses as the family's needs change. Common uses for flex space include offices, workshops, storage areas, exercise rooms, guest rooms, or hobby areas.

- An offshoot of the flex space idea worth considering if your addition plans call for adding or renovating a garage: build a three-car garage, with the third stall left open for alternative uses. Make this space as flexible as possible by having it dry-walled and painted; insulating it well; having good natural lighting; installing adequate electrical wiring, including plugs and overhead lighting; and providing adequate storage areas.

- Media rooms for television, VCR, stereo, video games, and often a computer are very popular rooms. When looking at this type of room, remember to allow for as much prewiring as possible.

- Fireplaces have declined somewhat in popularity because of the mess of dealing with firewood and the rising cost and declining availability of good fireplace wood. Gaining popularity in their place is the new generation of gas fireplaces, which offer much of the ambiance of wood-burning fireplaces, but with better fuel efficiency, less mess, and better temperature control.

- Natural gas remains the fuel of choice for most people, preferred by 75 to 80 percent of the people surveyed. If your addition plans call for extensive reworking of the home's fuel supply or the addition of new appliances, consider natural gas as the fuel source.

- The concept of the "bonus room" is very important in new construction, and this represents a desirable and underutilized sales opportunity for room additions as well. Bonus rooms are extra, unfinished rooms that can be framed at a reasonable cost while construction is under way, then converted to living space at a later date as the need arises and the financing is available. You might consider creating a bonus room over a garage or shop addition or over other rooms where the roof pitch is sufficient to create the necessary headroom. If the style of the house is consistent with the use of dormers, this is a good way to gain some extra headroom for increasing living space—you can frame them in, set the windows, and then leave them unfinished for later use. When designing and constructing bonus rooms, remember to provide all the necessary structural components, the windows, access to a heat duct or other heat source, and at least one electrical circuit stubbed into the room.

- Home offices are very popular at the moment, with 73 percent of homeowners stating that they would like one. A rather astounding statistic is that 86 percent of the survey respondents have a home computer, and 32 percent have two of them. Again, when designing a home office, you'll want to take a hard look at prewiring phone and data transmission lines.

- When working with clients on additions that will contain flex space or bonus rooms, it's important to be able to show them how the rooms can be used and why the addition of these spaces is cost-effective. These types of rooms may not have been considered during preliminary discussions of what the client wants in the addition, but they present an additional sales opportunity for you and a practical money-saving idea for the your client.

■ People who were surveyed expressed overwhelmingly that poor-quality workmanship was the biggest turnoff to buying a new home. They will be turning to you to create a quality addition to a home that they view as having been solidly constructed in the first place. Supply them with an addition that meets or even exceeds their expectations, and you'll have referrals coming in at a very steady rate.

What Types of Contractors Build Room Additions?

In two words—good ones! Room additions require a tremendous amount of skill to design and construct, and in many ways they represent the peak of the remodeling field.

You may hear a little scoffing over the years from new-home builders who somehow look down on remodelers, but in truth, a good room addition is considerably more difficult to construct than a new home. Room additions encompass virtually all aspects of construction that a new-home builder faces, with the added difficulties of structural transitions, material transitions, and the challenges of working in an occupied home.

Being a contractor—of any type—means being professional in your business conduct, being honest and consistent in your client relations, and being skilled in everything from your estimating to your finished product. It means feeling good about yourself and about the company that you own and operate.

As a remodeler specializing in room additions, your sense of pride should come easily. You can walk away from any addition you build with a tremendous amount of client contentment and personal satisfaction, which translates into a company that you're proud to own and a field of construction that can and will earn you a very good living.

Your Initial Client Contacts

The telephone rings in your office one afternoon. Mrs. Smith is calling, and she got your name from a friend that you did a sizable remodeling job for a year or so ago. She's interested in getting an estimate for a master bedroom suite addition, but she's not at all sure how big the room should be or what she wants it to look like.

She has only a vague idea of how much she'd like to spend, and she's already gotten preliminary approval for a loan from her credit union. She works during the week, and she'd like to know if you would be willing to come out to her house on Saturday to talk about the addition.

Which of the following responses sounds the most like yours?

Response Number 1: The Lazy Approach

"Well, I'll tell you what Mrs. Smith—let me save us both a lot of time. All of my room additions average around 90 bucks a square foot. So just figure out how big the new room's gonna be, multiply by 90 bucks, and there's my price, give or take ten thousand. Unless you want a lot of fancy stuff."

"But that's just the problem. I don't know exactly how big I want the room, or what I want in it. That's where I thought you could help."

"Well, there's really not too much I can do for you until you know what you're looking to have done. Why don't you get some plans drawn up, then drop 'em by my office. In the meantime, figure a hundred dollars a square foot to be on the safe side."

Response Number 2: The Obnoxious-but-Unemployed Approach

"A master suite, huh? I remember when they used to just call 'em bedrooms—I gotta tell you, I really hate all these trendy, yuppie terms. I don't even do additions all that often. I like those big, new houses—that's where the real money is. But what the hell, I'm outta work right now, so I guess I gotta bid whatever's out there."

Response Number 3: The You're-Fortunate-to-Have-Me Approach

"Well Mrs. Smith, actually, I rarely do remodeling any more. I find it too dirty, and quite honestly, most people don't really have houses that are even worth adding on to. However, I do have an opening in my schedule four months from now, and it would give the crew something small and simple to work on."

"Uh, okay. But I'd need you to come out and take a look at the house and give me some ideas. And I also need an estimate that I can take to my credit union."

"For me to come out and discuss the project with you would be $45 an hour, and that's nonrefundable. Also, I don't do bids—they're too time-consuming. My jobs are strictly time and materials. Take it or leave it."

Response Number 4: The Professional Approach

"Certainly, Mrs. Smith. That's exactly the type of remodeling project I specialize in, and I'd be delighted to come out and discuss it with you in detail. I'd like to have at least two hours available for the first meeting, so I can hear what you have in mind and take a close look at the house. Is 10 o'clock Saturday morning convenient?"

If some variation of response 1, 2, or 3 sounds like you, you're not alone. You're not exactly right, but at least you're not alone. Bidding *is* time-consuming and doesn't directly produce income—not until the job becomes reality, which is not at all a sure thing.

But—no bids, no work. So the reality of it is, if response 1, 2, or 3 was your answer to this lady's call, it's probably time to be thinking about getting into another line of work—you're setting yourself up to be one more statistic on the growing list of failed construction companies.

If, on the other hand, you can honestly say you're more likely to use response 4, congratulations! You're among the rare breed of professional contractors who know how to deal with people and who understand the importance of the estimating process in securing new clients.

Client Screening

So does that mean you need to rush out and look at every job you get a call on? The first inclination for most contractors (myself included not that long ago) is to say, "Yes, you go see every job, because you never know for sure what will and won't turn into work."

It's true that every job call has some potential for turning into an actual job, but realistically, most don't. Bidding—good, accurate bidding—requires a lot of time and effort and tends to be very tedious. And if one out of every three of those bids you prepare turns into work, you're doing pretty well. So, quite often, the natural tendency for a busy contractor answering Mrs. Smith's call might be to hear only that she wants you out on a Saturday to look at a project that is extremely vague and short on details.

But let's look again at Mrs. Smith. First, she's been referred to you by a previous satisfied customer for whom you did a large job. Second, she has arranged financing, so you know that she's serious about having the work done and that she has the money available to pay for it. Just looking at these two aspects of her call gives you important clues to the fact that Mrs. Smith is very much worth pursuing as a potential client.

This is the process called *screening*, which most contractors haven't heard of and don't practice. Screening is a simple process performed by you, your estimator, your secretary, or whoever takes the original call. Through the use of few extra questions and a simple checklist, you can prequalify many of your callers and decide on the spot whether to take the time for a site visit and estimate.

One contractor began employing the screening process about two years ago. Prior to screening, he estimated every job he got a call on, and if the bid resulted in a request that his company do the work, he undertook the job no matter how busy his company was. For three straight years, his company did between $900,000 and $1 million worth of gross sales, but he noticed that many of the jobs he was doing were not particularly profitable, or else they became major headaches.

After learning of the screening process, as outlined in this chapter, he began implementing it in his business. He began turning away certain jobs, and his gross sales dropped to between $750,000 and $800,000. But a close examination of his books revealed an interesting thing—his net profits were rising steadily each quarter! By using a little more care in selecting his clients, he was spending less time estimating and had fewer callbacks and client problems. Both the contractor and all of his staff were much happier, and on top of it all he was making more money.

The Screening Checklist

If you've been in business as a contractor for any length of time, you've no doubt noticed that you have better luck with certain types of clients. They are good people to work with, financially responsible, and realistic in their goals and expectations. Certain others are the proverbial "clients from hell"—uncooperative and arrogant, constantly changing their job specifications (and expecting you to do it for free), and unwilling (or unable) to pay you on time. You know the type. So how can you get more of the first type of client and less of the second type? *Screening.*

To develop a screening list, begin by taking a look at your "good" clients and your "bad" clients, and identify the traits of each group. How did the people in each group come to call you in the first place? Were they referrals from past clients or suppliers? Did they find you via advertising or in the Yellow Pages? Do they own expensive houses or inexpensive ones? Did the job entail full room additions or minor repairs? Were you the only bidder, or one of three or more? Pull as much information as you can from your files and from your memories about the experiences you had with each client.

From your own notes, and from the suggestions that follow, develop a checklist of those things you feel make for a desirable client; then use that checklist as a guide when you or others in your office take a call about a prospective job. You can list the most desirable traits at the top of your list or assign a number to each one. For example, say you've found that referrals from past clients make the best new clients—put that at the top of the list, or give it a rating of 10 out of 10.

CHECKLIST SUGGESTIONS

- *Referral from past client:* We all know that no matter how much we advertise, most of our work still comes from referrals by previous clients. A prospective client referred by a previous satisfied customer will already be predisposed to use you. Calls such as this should be given top priority.

- *Architect and designer referrals:* These are typically excellent referrals as well. If you get a call from prospective clients who are working with an architect or a designer on the plans for their addition, you have several things going for you: They're serious about the project, and they're already willing to invest some money in it; they have a professional preparing the plans, which makes it much easier on you to estimate and ultimately construct the addition; they have established a relationship with the designer already, so any recommendation from him or her about which contractors are good will carry a lot of weight.

- *Referral from a supplier:* If the lumberyard where you do most of your shopping gave your name to someone who asked about reputable contractors in the area, this is probably a good lead to follow up on as well.

- *Home and trade shows:* If you participate in home shows or trade shows, you should be getting calls from people who saw you at the show. These are usually good leads to follow up on, especially if you remember talking with the person at the show.

- *Referral from a manufacturer:* If you use a lot of products from particular manufacturers (windows, for example), they may give your name to people who prefer to use those particular products (i.e., brand names) in their room addition.

- *Referral from the building department:* If you have a good reputation around town for quality workmanship, building inspectors who are aware of it may direct people to you.

- *Yellow Pages and other advertising:* Advertising is something of a mixed bag. We want to do it to generate leads, but on the other hand we often end up with people who are just curious about prices, or even do-it-yourselfers who are hoping for a little free advice. You pay good money to advertise, whether it's in the Yellow Pages or with you local newspaper or radio or TV station, so you obviously don't want to disregard leads that come to you from these sources, but this is where a little savvy questioning can help you weed out the time wasters from the legitimate leads.

■ *The "angry shopper"*: You will occasionally get a call from someone who's had a bad experience with some other contractor in the past and can't wait to tell you all about it. They don't quite trust contractors now. They need one, but they're skeptical about hiring one. That's not to say that this couldn't potentially be a very good client for you—just be aware that you'll have some initial distrust to overcome first.

Taking the Initial Phone Call

We've all heard the saying that "you only get one chance to make a first impression," and it's advice that's certainly as important to remember in the construction field as in any other profession. That first impression, positive or negative, begins with the initial phone call.

Whether you're a one-person shop that handles everything from phone calls to construction work or a larger operation with a receptionist to take the calls, telephone etiquette is a crucial part of being a successful contractor. If you (or anyone else in your operation) can't handle yourself professionally on the phone, then either get some training or have someone else take the calls—it's that important.

As you read the following suggestions, one thought that may cross the minds of some of you is, "Yeah, but I can't afford an answering service or a cellular phone." Put bluntly—if that's the case, then you shouldn't be in business for yourself. Every business has a certain number of start-up expenses and ongoing overhead expenses, and while small-business owners obviously can't afford to be extravagant with expenditures, they can't ignore the basic equipment that's needed to run the company, either.

You certainly wouldn't attempt to frame a major room addition with only a handsaw—you couldn't work fast enough to be competitive, and your finished product would suffer from the irregular cutting. In the same way, your company will suffer from an unprofessional image, and I guarantee you that you'll lose work as a result of it. Here are some alternative ways to keep in touch with your customers.

Secretaries and receptionists: First of all, whenever possible it should be a live person who answers the phone, not a machine. Studies have repeatedly shown that people greatly prefer dealing with companies who have a receptionist or other person who takes their call, as opposed to having to leave a message on an answering machine.

When hiring a secretary or receptionist, screen your candidates well. Emphasize phone duties as well as whatever other qualifications you're seeking (typing, bookkeeping, etc.). Ask business owners in any trade—and their customers—and they'll all tell you that the most important element in a good first impression is how the clients are treated on the phone.

Answering services: If you're a small operation and cannot afford to have a secretary or receptionist, then use an answering service. Even if you have a secretary or receptionist during normal business hours, you should use an answering service instead of an answering machine to take all of your after-hours calls.

Interview the answering service in person, and understand what services it provides and how much it will cost. Most services have a flat monthly fee for a certain number of calls, then charge so much per call in excess of that minimum number.

Make certain the service understands the nature of your business, the type of work you do, and exactly how you would like your phone to be answered—"Jones Construction," or "This is Jones Construction, may I help you," or whatever you prefer.

Pagers: In addition to the answering service, you should wear a pager. Direct the service to ask incoming callers if they would like to leave a message for you or if they would prefer to have you paged—most good answering services know how to weed out the salespeople to avoid bothering you with unnecessary pages. It is, however, very important that a client be able to get in touch with you when needed, and the pager is the next best thing to being there to take the call yourself.

Cellular phones: You might as well face it, this is the age of instant communication. And though that may be irritating when you're trying to frame a roof or even just finish your lunch, it's what today's customers have come to expect from the people they hire. If you've instructed your secretary or your answering service to page you for client calls, then you need to respond to those calls right away. Having a cell phone with you or in your truck makes that possible with minimum delay.

Home phones and answering machines: One of the biggest mistakes the small contractor can make is to use his or her home phone number. A client with $150,000 who's looking for a professional contractor to do a room addition doesn't want to get a busy signal for two hours while you chat on the phone with a friend, or to hear an answering machine say, "Hi, this is Dave and Debbie's house and Jones Construction. We're out playing with the dog, so leave a message."

As much as you may love your children, your client doesn't want to have his or her call answered by a four-year-old who burbles and giggles into the phone before screaming for Daddy, or by a teenager who lacks the energy to complete a coherent sentence and who may or may not deliver the message.

Another thing about home phones—you don't want to be married to your business 24 hours a day, and your family doesn't want that, either. Clients who know they have access to you at night will tend to take advantage of that privilege, interrupting your chance to relax or, more likely, work on the paperwork you didn't do during the day. Let the answering service screen the calls for you.

Screening the Phone Call

How well you screen the initial phone call is going to give you a lot of good information about this person and help you make a judgment call about the potential for a job:

- Listen to clients carefully, and give them a chance to talk. Let them explain a little about their project, and ask them a few questions along the way. Try and get a feel for how serious they are about the project, how much thought they've already put into it, and whether it's the type of project you're competent to work on.

- Get all of the basic client information. This includes address, phone number, fax number, directions, and so forth. This is obviously necessary information, but it also tells you a little about the people and the neighborhood. How willing people are to give you this information and how cooperative they are on the phone also tells you something about their personality.

■ Ask how they heard about you. This is crucial information to tie into many of the categories on your screening sheet. If they were referred to you by someone, be sure and find out exactly who so you can follow up later with a thank-you (see Chapter 10).

■ Ask if they've had plans and specifications drawn up for the addition. As mentioned previously, this helps you to know how far they are in the planning process, and it may give you a better feel for how serious they are. Remember, however, that it's not unusual for people to begin seeking out a contractor before they have plans ready. If they do have plans available, ask who their designer or architect is—if you know the designers, you can give them a call later and get a little more information about the project and the clients.

■ Try to determine how many contractors are bidding on the work. You might simply ask if they've had any other estimates yet, or ask if all of the bidders will be provided with plans and specifications. Listen for other clues: "I was told that additions are about $80 a square foot in this area." "Someone else said I'd probably need to reinforce the foundation, so I want you to take a look at that." "I know we have some structural problems with the floor joists that need to be repaired." This kind of technical wording or pricing usually comes from another contractor rather than a friend or neighbor.

An Estimator's Checklist

Here's a simple checklist you can post on the wall above the phone in your office. Use it as a guide to deal with—and win—clients.

__ **Respond in a timely manner.** Set a policy for yourself that you will respond to an estimate request within a given time period—say one to two days. Nothing starts you off on a worse footing with potential clients than not calling them back in a timely manner, or creating a situation where they have to call you a second or third time before they can set up an appointment.

As the second part of your timely response, set a goal that you'll have the estimate prepared and in the client's hands within another three to four days after your initial visit. This makes a great impression, and it definitely gives you an advantage over the contractor who doesn't respond for weeks.

___ **Be prepared.**   When you go out for the estimate, be prepared with everything you need, from a ladder and a measuring tape to your clipboard and company brochures. If the client wants to talk bathrooms, have a few fixture brochures with you and some photographs of other bathroom additions you've done.

___ **Be prompt.**   Make it a point to be on time for your appointments. Studies show that most people consider you on time if you arrive within 7 minutes either way of your scheduled appointment time. If you're going to be more than 10 minutes late, be sure to call and let the client know. If you're hung up somewhere and are going to be more than 30 minutes late, give the client the option of rescheduling the appointment for another time.

___ **Learn to listen.**   While you're meeting with the clients, pay close attention to what you're being told. Listen to their needs and their concerns, and allow them adequate time to explain what they want. Teach yourself to listen for clues about the type of people they are, and learn to separate the good clients from the potential headaches.

Take the time to answer any questions they have, about you or about their project. Wherever possible—and only if it's welcome—offer suggestions and alternatives for their project that could help with their planning. Be honest in your opinions—if you don't think something will work well, or if you really feel it won't look right, tell them.

___ **Do all estimates in writing.**   Never give a verbal estimate for anything. It's too vague and unsubstantiated and will almost always come back to haunt you. You may be able to write up small projects on the spot, but take the large ones back to your office and spend some time doing it right.

___ **The estimate makes an impression.**   How you prepare and present your estimate goes a long way toward establishing your credibility. Estimates should be typed on your letterhead. They should be clearly laid out, clean, organized, and easy to read and understand. If you present a sloppy estimate, can your clients expect your workmanship to be any better?

__ **Details now avoid confusion later.**   Be detailed in your estimates. It avoids confusion and misunderstanding and will save you innumerable headaches later on. Clearly explain what your bid includes, and spell out what items the client will be doing or providing on their own. Whenever possible, specify brand names, model numbers, colors, sizes, types of wood, and so on.

__ **Use the estimate as a marketing tool.**   Never miss an opportunity to market and promote yourself. When you submit the estimate, include a business card, a professionally printed brochure about your company, a list of references the client can call, testimonials from previous clients, and a list with the numbers of your contractor's license, bond, and insurance.

__ **Be sure of your paperwork.**   These are lawsuit-happy times we live in, and a solid paper trail is your first and strongest line of defense. Use a written contract and written change orders. Have clearly defined start and completion dates, a detailed payment schedule, and a place for you and your client to sign and date everything.

__ **Above all, be professional.**   Always represent yourself as a true professional who takes pride in his or her profession. Set a standard for yourself and your company that clearly places you apart from—and above—your competition. Stand behind your word and stand behind your work, and you'll build a solid reputation and a lucrative business that you'll be proud to call your own.

Client Meetings and Design Considerations

How you handle yourself, from the first phone call through the first in-person meeting, goes a long, long way toward whether you'll end up as the successful bidder on the project. It also sets the tone for your relationship with your clients throughout the entire job.

At your initial meetings, you will be meeting your clients for the first time, discussing their plans and hopes for the addition, and touring and evaluating their home. Your role here is twofold—to guide them into an addition project that makes good structural, aesthetic, and economic sense and to convince them that you are the best contractor to hire for the job.

There's a lot to do in the first meetings, and it's time-consuming and even a little stressful. You're trying to figure out how the addition can meet their needs for new, effective space within a given budget, while at the same time trying to get a handle on their personalities and figure how best to sell them your services. Something of a tall order, but the suggestions in this chapter should help you through all the necessary steps.

The Initial Client Meeting

When you meet with clients for the first time, try to have all of the decision makers at the meeting. If you're dealing with a married couple, set your meeting time so both husband and wife can be there. If you are meeting with a property manager or an agent for an estate, try to have the home's owner there as well, or establish that the agent has the authority to act on the owner's behalf. Don't ever deal with renters unless the owner of the home is present or unless you have spoken to the owner and have a set of very explicit instructions.

My Place or Yours?

If you are working out of your home, then meeting a client there is probably not a particularly good idea unless you have a separate office area at your house that can be accessed without having to walk through your personal living areas.

If you have an office away from your home, you may want to have your first visit with the client there. This makes it a little easier on you and wastes a minimum of your time should this turn out to be a project you do not wish to bid on. Meeting at your office is also a good idea if you have a showroom of products (cabinets, windows, etc.), or at least a number of product samples to show the client.

If you are meeting at your office, remember that first impressions are important here as well. Look at it from the client's perspective: Would you want to hire a person to work on your home whose office is a complete mess, with overflowing ashtrays, stacks of things all over, lights that don't work, doors that don't latch, and a desk chair that's missing a wheel?

You will, of course, need to see the client's house at some point, so most remodeling contractors simply have the first meeting there. This gives them the best opportunity to view the house, get a feel for the clients and their lifestyle, and work through some preliminary design ideas. Many subsequent meetings can then be held in your office.

Appearance Matters

Let's face it, jeans and work boots are practically a uniform for most contractors. Clients expect to see you in work clothes, and that's not going to bother most people. That is not, however, an excuse to be a slob.

Keeping the whole first impression concept in mind, you need to be neat, clean, and presentable when you visit someone's home, as you would expect them to be if they were to come to your home. That means that your jeans are clean and minus holes in the knees, your work boots don't track mud into the house, your shirt is clean, and you've washed up since leaving your last framing job.

If your business is such that you're often going directly from a job site to an estimate, then keep a change of clothes with you at all times. Leave the job early enough to change and wash up.

Opening Discussions

Every successful room-addition project, as with any remodeling, begins with good planning. You and your clients need to decide what they want and what they need—not always the same thing—and how much they would like to spend. You also need to get a feel for them as people and as potential clients, and give them the same opportunity to get to know you, a process that will hopefully lead ultimately to a successful and mutually enjoyable project.

Establish a comfortable place to talk. If you're meeting at your office, sit at a table with enough room to spread out papers and take notes. Avoid having clients sit in front of your desk, which often sets up too much of an adversarial feeling. If you're at their house, suggest the kitchen or dining room table as opposed to sitting on the living room couch. Spend a little bit of time talking before beginning a tour of the house.

Let the owners walk you through their ideas first. Get a feel for what they hope to accomplish with the addition, and try to determine their likes and dislikes. Find out who else lives in the house (children, elderly parents, etc.), and determine how the remodeling will affect their needs as well. Talk with your clients about developing a wish list (see page 31). If you've had them work on that beforehand, now is a good time to go over it with them.

Once you have a feel for what they want to accomplish, take a moment to talk about yourself and your company—but only a moment. Tell them how long you've been in business, how many employees you have, and what types of work you specialize in if it relates to their project. Emphasize your professionalism and your skills, but don't drone on—this is their moment to share their house with you, not your moment to brag about how wonderful you are.

You might want to describe a little about what types of additions you've done in the past and how they relate to this client's addition. You may be very proud of a $250,000 second-floor addition you did in an upscale neighborhood a few months ago, but it may not relate at all to the small guest room these clients want to add to the back of their starter home. You can mention the big addition to help demonstrate your experience and skill level, but once again, don't brag.

Establishing What Your Clients Hope to Achieve

During these initial client meetings, you need to really get a handle on what the clients wish to accomplish with their addition. Some people have been planning the addition for years, and you'll be presented with a surprising quantity of ideas, notes, sketches, magazine clippings, photos of other houses, and whatever else they've collected. Others are coming into this process blind, knowing only that they have a growing family or a new hobby that they'd like room to accommodate.

Either way, your job at this point is to collate those ideas into a realistic plan. This discussion period is important in a number of ways: it helps clients clarify their goals; it helps you to understand them as people and as potential clients; it allows you the opportunity to make suggestions and let them see that you genuinely care about their project; and it establishes common ground on which you can base a working relationship.

What Do They Need?

As basic as this question seems, it's necessary to take a really hard look at what your clients want out of their room addition. The answers can ensure that their real needs are being met while at the same time eliminating costly, unneeded space. Since they are considering adding space to their home, they probably already have specific needs in mind, and now is the time to discuss them.

Here are some of the more common reasons for adding onto an existing home.

A GROWING FAMILY

If the addition will serve the needs of a family that is outgrowing their existing space, are they hoping to add one or more bedrooms? Will they also need one or more additional bathrooms? Bathrooms are the second-costliest room to add to a house, but on the other hand, nothing is more inconvenient than a house without enough bathrooms, and bathroom additions statistically show the greatest return on investment dollars at the time the house is sold.

A NEW KITCHEN

Perhaps the addition will serve to accommodate a larger kitchen. On a price-per-square-foot basis, kitchens are typically the most expensive rooms to add or remodel because of the amount of wiring, plumbing, cabinetry, and other equipment the room has to accommodate.

If a new kitchen is your clients' goal, you'll need to look closely at what they need. Do they need more counter space? If so, how much? Do they need room for specific work areas, such as a baking center? Are they looking for more storage space, such as a walk-in pantry?

Do they have their eyes on new appliances that require a large amount of space or special hookups, such as some of the commercial fixtures now finding their way into more and more residential kitchens? Will the new kitchen require plumbing changes, gas lines, or new electrical circuits?

FAMILY, HOBBY, AND MEDIA ROOMS

Another popular reason for adding space is the desire for a family, game, or hobby room. If this is the goal, there are several things to take into consideration. Will the room be serving a special purpose, such as housing a pool table, and therefore need to be a certain size? Will it contain a wet bar, cooking or refrigeration facilities, or other appliances or fixtures that require special areas or connections?

Hobby areas may require a built-in desk, specialized worktables, shelving, or other work areas. Specific hobbies may have special needs. A photographer may be looking to add a darkroom, which requires a light-tight area with running water. An artist may want a painting studio flooded with natural light. The potter wants an easy-to-clean floor and a 240-volt outlet for the potter's wheel and kiln.

For today's very popular media rooms, special provisions may need to be made for stereo, television, or other electronic hookups. Many of the new entertainment systems are fully integrated with one another (television, VCR, stereo, surround-sound speaker systems, video games) and require quite a bit of prewiring.

HOME OFFICES

Creating an office for working at home is another very popular reason for adding on. Primary considerations here, as with the media room, are prewiring for telephone, fax, data links, cable and satellite television, and other electronic needs. Other considerations for the home office should be adequate storage space, especially for heavy, concentrated loads such as books, paperwork, and file cabinets; privacy and good soundproofing to isolate the office from the rest of the home; and good natural light through windows or skylights.

SHOPS AND GARAGES

Other add-on spaces with their own special requirements would be a garage, a workshop, or a combination of both. How many cars will need to be accommodated? What about an RV or a boat? Will the shop require special electrical hookups for machinery, welding equipment, or an air compressor? How about storage for lumber or metal stock? Once again, worktables and assembly tables, space for painting, or other special use areas might be desirable.

If the shop area is to be used for any sort of commercial enterprise, do any city, county, or state restrictions apply? Also, are there any special requirements for ventilation, sanitation, or fire safety that you need to include in your plans?

SUNROOMS

There are a variety of sunspace addition options to consider, from add-on kits to site-built rooms. Are your clients looking for a two- or three-season room with glass and some seating areas, or are they hoping for a full-blown solar addition that will help reduce their heating bills? Can you get the necessary solar orientation? What special ventilation needs must be met, both for getting heat into the house in winter and out of the sunroom in summer? Will you need special window coverings or landscaping to shade the room against excess summer-heat buildup?

The Wish List

A simple method for helping your clients focus in on what they really want and need is to have them establish a wish list. The wish list is simply a list of absolutely everything they can think of that they want in the addition, broken down into three categories:

1. *Must have.* In the must-have category, they should list everything they absolutely must accomplish with the construction of the addition. If, for example, one of the main goals of the addition is a new bathroom with two sinks, a tub/shower, and a big, well-lighted mirror and makeup area, it should go in this list.

2. *Would like if possible.* These are items that are secondary to the main goal, to be included only when all of the must-have goals have been accomplished. In the bathroom addition example, a "would like if possible" might be to make the bathtub a whirlpool tub.

3. *Can live without.* The third category includes those items that will be done only if the budget allows. Realistically, virtually all of this list will fall by the wayside quickly. For the bathroom, an example might be a bidet or a steam bath, or even something simpler such as brass fixtures instead of chrome.

Counsel your clients that if it's important, it goes in the first list. An addition that doesn't accomplish all or virtually all of the primary goals of the homeowner will be a disappointment no matter how well constructed it is. So if that bidet or steam bath is *really* important, it goes on the must-have list, and some other item may have to fall by the wayside in order to meet the budget.

Concurrent Remodeling and Repairs

In addition to the many considerations about the addition itself, now is a good time to discuss other remodeling or repair needs with your clients. Perhaps the house is due for a new roof—you can provide them with a better price if you're doing the job in conjunction with the addition, while your crew or subcontractors are already roofing the addition. Maybe the insulation needs to be beefed up, the wiring and plumbing systems need updating, or the carpet and paint could use some freshening up.

Whatever the home needs, it's wise to get it all done at once, if possible. You can offer the clients a better price on the extra work than you could if you had to come out for that job alone; you save them quite a bit of additional mess and inconvenience later; and if they're borrowing money to build the addition, the other work often can be covered under the same loan.

One word of caution. If you have been asked to come out to bid the addition and notice other work that needs doing, it's okay to mention it during your first visit. If the clients don't seem responsive, don't overwhelm them with other choices and decisions—and the expenditure of additional money—that they aren't prepared to discuss. You can always revisit the subject later, after all of the details on the addition have been ironed out.

A Look at Lifestyles

An important aspect in planning for an addition—or any remodeling—that is overlooked by many contractors and homeowners alike is the lifestyle of the home's occupants. During your initial discussions of the project, this topic is worth discussing—it can make a big difference in achieving the addition the clients want at a cost they can afford.

For example, does the family entertain a lot? If the answer is yes, you might consider the need for extra kitchen facilities, such as a built-in barbecue, a wet bar, or a second sink. Maybe an expanded dining area would be helpful, or a kitchen eating area for the children to use when adults are being entertained in the dining room. If your clients have a lot of out-of-town guests, a guest room with its own bath might be ideal.

If adding a swimming pool or spa is in the plans, then adding a separate shower and dressing area can save a lot of wear and tear on the bathrooms in the house. Some other considerations for the avid entertainer might be outdoor lighting, backyard seating and table space, a gazebo, a patio enclosure, or a built-in video entertainment center.

On the other hand, if entertaining is fairly rare and you're working with an on-the-go couple that doesn't spend that much time at home, the expense of a formal dining room or an extra guest bedroom might be a total waste. You may instead want to work up some ideas for an efficient kitchen layout with a small eating area, or a hobby room that can double as temporary sleeping quarters for the occasional out-of-town guest.

If the home environment is especially important and entertainment needs are few, consider a whole wall to house all of your client's audio and video equipment. In one convenient area, you can group your television, stereo, VCR, video games—the works! You might suggest an expanded master bedroom suite, complete with a lavish bathroom. A home sauna, a steam room, a whirlpool spa—all this and much more might be just what you need to suit a predominantly stay-at-home lifestyle.

How about teenagers or perhaps small children? Specialized game and entertainment rooms for them and their friends might be well worth considering. This is also the time to take another look at your client's needs for an extra bathroom, an expanded kitchen, a practical laundry room, and even small, easily overlooked items like extra telephone, stereo, and television jacks.

Taking the time to study and honestly evaluate lifestyles can go a long way toward making any expanded living space practical and enjoyable for everyone. Remember, at this early planning stage, no consideration is too small or unimportant.

Establishing a Budget

Money. On the one hand it's a subject that no one really likes to talk about, yet on the other hand, it's at the heart of all plans and negotiations that you and your clients will be discussing.

Sometime during your initial conversations and discussions, you will need to establish a budget. Unless you stumble upon clients with a "money's no object" attitude—I haven't had one yet—then you need to talk about how much they would like to spend to accomplish what they want.

While some people are very open about what they would like to spend, you'll find that many others are very reluctant to share their budgets with you. I've had several clients over the years who haven't wanted to tell me how much they have to spend because they're afraid I'll increase my estimate to the top limit of their budget.

When you encounter clients such as these, you need to immediately take the time to start setting the tone of your relationship—it's an excellent time to begin establishing the trust and confidence you'll all need to have a successful working relationship.

You need to explain that your role is to help them determine the type of addition they want and need and whether it will work with their existing house. Once you've established the parameters of the remodeling, you will write a detailed estimate that explains what you'll be doing and how much it will cost, so it will be clear how you arrived at your price and what they'll be getting for their money.

Beyond that, your clients need to show you the trust you deserve. You are a reputable professional, and your price for their room addition will be based on what is necessary to achieve their goals, *not* on what is necessary to take every dime they have available. Just as clients would be wasting everyone's time to walk into a Ferrari dealership if all they could afford was a Geo, it's a waste of your time and theirs to be discussing an addition that you know will cost at least $75,000 if all they want to spend is $40,000.

You need to establish this budget early in the discussions so you know and they know if they're being realistic. If they're not, it's your job to tell them so—gently and diplomatically—and then to help them adjust their thinking or their budget to bring the project and the finances more into line with one another.

Touring the House

Next, take a tour of the house. Let your clients walk you through the affected areas, both inside and outside. Take notes as you go, and pay particular attention to the style of the house, the types of materials used in the original construction, any other remodeling that has been done, and the general quality and condition of the original house.

As you go, ask to see any areas you feel are important to you. Ask their permission before entering any rooms or opening any closets. Ask to see the basement and attic areas if they affect your estimate. You may need to climb up on the roof or wiggle through the crawl space, so have some coveralls with you just in case.

If the job is complicated and you feel that you have a good shot at being hired for the project, consider taking pictures as you go. Again, ask the client's permission first. Use a good-quality 35mm camera—a simple point-and-shoot type is fine—and shoot color prints. Many people are very impressed that you take pictures, and you can use the pictures later to help with your estimating. These "before" pictures are also great for showing other clients and for use in advertising.

Except for a simple addition, you probably won't need to take measurements the first time you visit. You're there to discuss the project with the clients, see the home, and get an overall feel for things. Explain that you will need to return later for more complete measurements, perhaps with a designer or architect if the project is quite large.

Structural Considerations

As you tour the house, pay particular attention to potential problem areas, especially in older houses (Figure 3.1). These areas might include the following:

FIGURE 3.1

- *Structural problems.* Structural problems abound in many homes, especially older ones. Undersized framing, dry rot, insect damage, inadequate clearances, illegal masonry, lack of proper drainage, and many other problem areas can seriously affect your ability to construct a room addition without first making repairs to the existing house, which can add considerably to the overall cost.

- *Electrical panel.* Is the electrical service adequate for additional circuits that may be required by the remodeling? Are the wiring, main service panel, and panel disconnects up to code?

- *Plumbing.* How good is the water pressure? Is the house on city sewer or on a septic system? If it's a septic system, is it big enough to handle the additional plumbing fixtures

Structural considerations on this addition required a jog in one wall in order to maintain access to the only egress window in one of the existing bedrooms (right).

being added, and is the drain field in a location away from the proposed addition site?

- *Plaster.* Many older homes were originally constructed with plaster walls and ceilings. Do the owners want the addition done in plaster as well? If you're going to use drywall, will areas of transition between the two materials present a problem?

- *Roofing and siding materials.* Does the home have roofing or siding that can no longer be matched? If so, how will you make the transition between the addition and the existing house?

- *Rocks.* In rocky areas, will the ground conditions make siting the addition more difficult or more costly? (The same applies to additions built on a hillside.)

FIGURE 3.2

A small breakfast nook is one possibility when adding outward from the back of the house.

Up or Out?

As you begin the process of consolidating your ideas with your clients' and finalizing the design, the obvious first decision is what part of the house to add on to. You might be looking at extending out from the existing house (Figure 3.2) or up from it (Figure 3.3), either adding to an existing second floor or creating an entirely new one. It might even be a combination of both.

Depending on the existing house and the intended addition, where and how to add on might be obvious. In other cases, both options (extending out or up) might be open to you. Each has its own pros and cons, and your first consideration is to decide which one is best.

If you choose to extend out, the first question is one of space. Is there enough room for the intended addition? Most areas have specific setback requirements

FIGURE 3.3

Adding upward is a possibility with some types of houses.

that limit how close you come to your property lines. These setbacks are typically 15 to 25 feet in front and back and 5 to 10 feet on the sides, but they can vary widely among locales. Be sure to check with your local building department or planning division to confirm the setback requirements for this particular neighborhood.

When extending out, the addition will require a new foundation. You will also need to determine how the roof of the addition will intersect and tie in with the existing roof. Continuing the siding at the point where the walls intersect is another consideration.

If you decide to extend up, the floor of the addition is the biggest problem. If you are considering an entirely new second floor, you might encounter two problems. First of all, one- and two-story houses need different-size foundations and footings because of the greater load that the foundation on a two-story house must bear. If the existing foundation is undersized for a second story, it might be necessary to reinforce it. If this appears to be a problem for your addition, it's best to consult with the building officials or an engineer before you proceed with the plans.

The second problem is the size of the existing ceiling joists. In a one-story house, the ceiling joists need be only large enough to support the finished ceiling material that is attached to them, and they're usually too small to handle the additional load imposed on them if they must act as floor joists for the second story. This problem is usually solved by adding new floor joists of the proper size next to the old ceiling joists, but you'll want to take a close look at the existing framing to make sure this is possible.

Evaluating the Existing House

As the ideas and needs begin to become clearer, the next step is to determine what's realistic for the house. Some homes lend themselves quite naturally to extending out, while some, either because of space limitations or architectural design, are best served by extending up. Still other types of homes easily encompass both types of additions.

First among your considerations at this point is the type of house you are working with. Is it a sprawling one-story ranch house that would look awkward with a second story? Is it a two-story home that could be added to on one or both levels? Do you think you have enough land to add out? Does the house have a particular architectural style, such as Tudor or Colonial, that must be accurately matched in order for the addition to blend in? Are there natural jogs in the home's contour or in the relationship between the floors that would lend themselves to being filled in with new rooms?

Next consider how the interior of the home is laid out. Are there hallways that serve various rooms? What are the traffic patterns in the house—that is, how does traffic flow between various rooms and areas? How would the addition tie into the existing house to provide access to the new rooms?

This is a very important aspect of the planning at this stage. The usefulness of the new space could be diminished greatly if access is awkward (e.g., a new guest room that can be reached only by going through another bedroom, or a dining room that doesn't have a direct connection to the kitchen).

Evaluating the Neighborhood

One often-ignored aspect of adding on to an existing home is the possibility of "overbuilding" for the neighborhood. Overbuilding occurs when the proposed value of the work being done would necessitate a selling price for the house that is way out of line for the area, virtually ensuring a financial loss when the house is sold (Figure 3.4).

Although the primary reason for adding on is to create needed space, a room addition is also an investment in the home, and as a professional contractor you have an obligation to discuss this with your clients if your think it might present a future problem. Some clients don't care—they want and need the space, and they have no intention of selling the house and moving. Others have dreams that are not very practical, and a gentle reality check is sometimes in order.

First, the owners need to determine the fair market value of the house—that is, the approximate amount that the home could actually be sold for today, given the cost of similar homes in the area that recently have been sold. (The fair market value might vary consider-

FIGURE 3.4

In subdivisions where all the houses are similar, care must be taken not to overbuild for the area.

ably from the appraised value for tax purposes.) It may be necessary for the homeowners to consult with a real estate agent who specializes in their area, or at least to follow the real estate advertisements in the local newspaper for several weeks to determine the selling price of comparable homes in the same area.

Next, the clients will need an approximation of what the addition will cost. Adding this cost to the fair market value of the home will give them a pretty good idea of what the home would have to sell for in order to realize a return on their investment.

Finally, look at the selling price of homes in the area that would compare to the house after the addition. If the estimated value of the house with the addition is roughly in line with similar homes in the area (or would be in a relatively short time), then the plans are realistic and your clients are probably not overbuilding for the area.

Deciding on Sizes

As your ideas and needs for specific rooms and areas become clearer, it's important to begin thinking in terms of sizes. Bear in mind that adding a room that's too small to serve its intended use, now or in the future, isn't much better than not having the room at all.

On the other hand, creating excessively large rooms is a financial drain for a number of reasons. The larger the addition, the more expensive the initial construction costs will be, and the more the owners will pay for heating and cooling, taxes and insurance, and even furnishings. Try to keep these two things in mind when considering room sizes, and attempt to strike a happy medium between an addition that's too small to be useful and one that's too large to be practical.

If a room will house an object of a specific size (a pool table, for example), you will have a good basis from which to determine the room's ultimate dimensions. Look at the actual size of the table, and consider how much room is needed around it in order to play comfortably. Add space for other furnishings, and you'll be assured of a room that will serve its purpose adequately.

Other rooms also have minimum size requirements. A bathroom, for example, typically requires a wall of at least 5 feet in length to accommodate a bathtub. Toilets and bidets each require approximately 3 by 3 feet of space and are usually set side by side for convenience in routing the plumbing. In planning a bathroom, it's usually best to ascertain what fixtures will be in the room and their sizes, and use those required spaces as a minimum. Additional room can then be allocated as space within the addition permits, helping you avoid a room that's too cramped.

A common mistake when planning the overall size of an addition is to simply add up the sizes of the rooms. This method overlooks two basic considerations that need to be planned for: storage space and access.

Say, for example, that you have decided the new guest bedroom will be 12 by 12 feet and that it will fit nicely next to a 12- by 16-foot game room. The bedroom will require a closet, perhaps 2 by 6 feet. To take 2 feet off the length of the room might make the bedroom too small. Taking the necessary 2 feet out of the game room might interfere with that room's intended use. Simply placing the 2 feet between the rooms makes the entire addition larger, which affects the building costs, the appearance of the addition, perhaps even the maximum space you have available in the yard.

A similar problem might arise with access. The bedroom might be a perfect size, and you might have allowed for the closet, but will the room need to be served by a hallway? How much of the room must be set aside for doorways or perhaps a stairwell? These seemingly minor considerations can upset the best-laid plans and need to be kept in mind at this stage of the planning process.

Kitchen Planning

The kitchen of today, far removed from its often-ignored predecessors, has achieved new status as a family meeting place, casual entertaining center, and pleasant, comfortable place for meal planning and preparation. If a new kitchen is part of the addition, the planning becomes somewhat more complicated and a little more critical. Many of the planning considerations for a kitchen will affect how efficient it is, and it's very important that this room in particular be laid out correctly. You might even wish to consult a designer who specializes in kitchens.

Once again, you should help your clients examine their lifestyle, and then honestly assess what's needed in a new kitchen. Are they gourmet cooks or avid bakers who require special equipment? Do they have a large collection of kitchenware? Do they stock up on food for future use? Is room for formal meals needed, or would a small eating counter be more practical? Is there more than one cook in the house? Does the family gather for meals, or does the house resemble a 24-hour cafeteria?

Ask your clients what they don't like about the existing kitchen. Too small? Poorly laid out? Not enough storage or counter space? Poor lighting or ventilation? Drab decorations? Outdated or inadequate appliances?

A typical kitchen requires about 100 to 160 square feet of floor space. Certain activity centers are basic to all kitchens, and understanding what they are is of prime importance to a good design:

- *The refrigerator center.* Your refrigerator should be located away from the range, dishwasher, or any other heat-producing appliance. It should have a minimum of 18 inches of counter space on the latch side of the door for setting groceries.

- *The preparation center.* The area where food is prepared for cooking should contain 36 to 48 inches of counter space, near the sink or refrigerator if possible. The area should allow ample storage space for pans, bowls, and dry ingredients, and adequate electrical outlets should be provided.

- *The cooking center.* The cooking center contains the cooktop and oven. If the oven is separate, it should be located near the cooktop. Allow a minimum of 24 inches of counter on one side and 12 inches on the other, and make sure one side is equipped with a permanent or portable heatproof surface for setting hot cookware. Provide ample storage for pots, utensils, spices, and canned goods. For safety, do not locate the cooktop near a window or at the very end of a counter.

- *The cleanup center.* The cleanup area handles the cleaning and trimming of food, cleanup of kitchenware, and disposal of waste. In addition to the sink, it contains the garbage disposal, dishwasher, and possibly a trash compactor. Provide at least 30 to 36 inches of counter on each side of the sink, plus storage for cleaning supplies and garbage pail. If a dishwasher will not be installed at this time, make provisions for one in the future by planning on a 24-inch cabinet next to the sink, which later can be removed.

■ *The work triangle.* The work triangle is the relationship between the kitchen's three major work areas, and a proper triangle is essential for an efficient kitchen. The three legs of the triangle should total between 12 and 22 feet, combined as follows: refrigerator to sink, 4 to 7 feet; sink to cooktop, 4 to 6 feet; cooktop to refrigerator, 4 to 9 feet. The distance between any two centers should never be less than 4 feet.

With these activity centers in mind, the next design step is to fit them efficiently into one of the following basic layouts:

■ *U-shaped layout.* The U-shaped layout (Figure 3.5) is considered by most designers to be the most desirable layout if space permits. It allows an effective traffic flow and work triangle and makes the most effective use out of a given space. It requires a minimum of 6 feet between the base cabinets and special corner cabinets, so it is usually the most expensive layout to construct.

■ *L-shaped layout.* The L-shaped layout (Figure 3.6) still allows good traffic flow, but less kitchen area is put to practical use than with the U-shaped layout. One leg of the L can be extended to create a room divider or eating/serving counter. Care must be taken in the placement of the cabinets to avoid a bad triangle, and the layout can be somewhat exhausting if either leg is too long.

■ *Corridor layout.* This economical layout, having unconnected cabinet runs on two parallel walls, creates a good work triangle (Figure 3.7). One end of the corridor should be blocked off to prevent inefficient

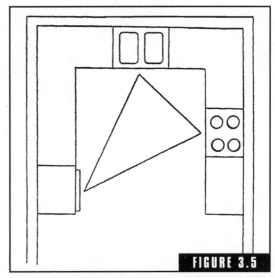

FIGURE 3.5

An example of a U-shaped kitchen, with the work triangle indicated.

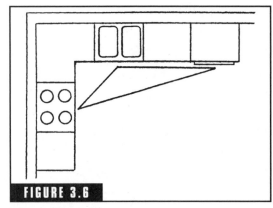

FIGURE 3.6

An L-shaped kitchen layout.

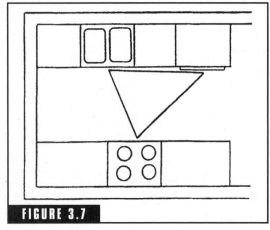

FIGURE 3.7

A corridor, or two-wall, kitchen.

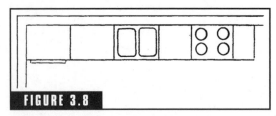

FIGURE 3.8

A one-wall kitchen. Note that no work triangle is possible.

traffic flow. About 5 feet should be allowed between the cabinet runs, and some space is wasted at the blind end of the corridor.

■ *One-wall layout.* The one-wall layout (Figure 3.8) is best for small spaces, usually opening to another room. The sink should be located in the middle, and the total run of counter should not exceed 22 feet. A triangle is not possible, so the appliance layout is somewhat poor.

■ *Island layout.* Used in conjunction with the U, L, or one-wall kitchen, a permanent or rolling island can add storage and counter space within the same square footage of area. The island is often used to house the sink or cooktop, thereby shortening the triangle.

Working with Do-It-Yourselfers

Remodeling is expensive, and one of the first questions you're likely to be asked is, "Can we do part of the work ourselves?" Your answer will depend on the skill of the homeowners, what aspects of the work they want to do themselves, and, to some degree, how patient you are.

When discussing do-it-yourself work with your clients, begin by inquiring what things they would like to do; then help them with a realistic assessment of the time and effort involved versus the potential financial gains.

■ Do they have the necessary skills to undertake the work? Do they have, or can they get, the necessary tools?

- What about the necessary time, especially if there is a loan in place for the addition that is costing them interest, or if the coming of winter weather makes a certain time frame imperative?

- Do they understand that any work they do will be subject to inspection by the building department, just as your work will be?

For some people, doing part of the work themselves is a matter of pride or even financial necessity, and if you're unwilling to accommodate them, you may not be chosen as their contractor. Taking the time early on for an honest look at this important aspect of contracting, however, can help avoid future problems and will go a long way toward good relations and the best possible finished product.

Plans and Specifications

Before your clients' room-addition project can move from the planning stages into the actual construction phase—and before you can even give them an accurate estimate—you'll need to transform the ideas you and your clients have developed into preliminary sketches, and from there into a complete working set of plans and specifications.

Preliminary Sketches

As room sizes begin to take shape, you will probably need to start getting some preliminary sketches down on paper. Sketches help to clarify your thoughts and your clients', help to strengthen good ideas and eliminate bad ones, and go a long way toward avoiding misunderstandings.

How much sketching you do and how detailed those sketches are is a matter of personal bidding and selling style, dictated in large part by how serious your clients are about the addition. You may feel that a quick layout on scratch paper is sufficient for one client, while another (who is perhaps more serious about the project or more financially able to undertake it) may require more detailed, to-scale sketches in order to evaluate your ability to construct the project.

You can make simple sketches of rooms or parts of rooms as you go. Try out various relationships between rooms, and consider how traffic patterns will develop, both within and between the rooms. Visualize window and door layouts, furniture arrangements, ceiling heights—anything you feel is important. The cheapest investment you can make in an addition is plenty of scratch paper. It's much easier to move a pencil line than it is to move a completed wall!

One simple method for arranging rooms on paper is to draw a series of circles, with each circle representing a specific room. The size of the circle should be in proportion to the size of the room (a small circle for a bathroom, a larger one for a bedroom, etc.), and the circles should touch where the rooms would join. This is a quick way of getting something down on paper, and it lets you compare and visualize a variety of room relationships and traffic patterns with a minimum of effort.

Sketching to Scale

When you are comfortable with the room sizes and layouts, the next step is to determine if they will "fit together." Quite often, although everything lays out quite neatly on your preliminary sketches, the relationship of the actual-size rooms may create problems. You may find that the 12-foot bedroom you penciled in next to the 13-foot kitchen leaves a 1-foot jog in the wall that you can't remove!

Ideally, you'd like to lay out the rooms full size and take a look at them. Since space considerations make this impractical, a scale drawing is the next best thing. All building plans are drawn to scale, making them accurate, easy to read, and enabling the actual dimensions and relationships of the rooms to be seen in true proportion.

Scale drawing is easy for your clients to understand. It is simply a matter of substituting one unit of measurement for another. Suppose you have a room that will be 12 feet wide by 14 feet long. Because drawing this room full size is obviously out of the question, a smaller but consistent unit of measurement is used to represent each foot in the room. This smaller unit could be any size you wish, governed primarily by the size of the paper on which you are drawing. For architectural drawings such as these, typical scales are ⅛ inch = 1 foot; ¼ inch = 1 foot; and ½ inch = 1 foot.

For example, consider your 12- by 14-foot room. If you choose a scale of ¼ inch = 1 foot, then ¼ inch on your drawing will equal 1 foot of actual size. This size is referred to simply as ¼-inch scale, since the scale size is always equal to 1 foot. Therefore, the 12-foot wall of your room would be 3 inches long (¼ in × 12), and the 14-foot wall would be drawn as 3½ inches long (¼ × 14). As long as you maintain the same scale for any one drawing, each of the room sizes you draw will be in correct relation to each other.

At the sketching stage, the simplest way of making a scale drawing is to use graph paper. This type of paper is laid out in a series of small squares and can be purchased in a variety of grid sizes (4 squares per inch, 8 squares per inch, 10 per inch, or 16 per inch). If you are using a paper with 4 squares per inch, each square will be ¼ by ¼ inch in size, which corresponds to a ¼-inch scale. Counting 12 squares in one direction and 14 squares in the other direction will allow you to quickly sketch out your 12- by 14-foot room. Graph paper eliminates the need for repeated measurements and allows you to quickly sketch a variety of room layouts, window and door arrangements, and even furniture placements.

Complete Working Plans

The next step is to prepare a complete set of working plans that shows all of the elements of the addition from the foundation to the roof. Depending on the size and complexity of the addition, working plans may consist of a single sheet, or a complete set may run to 10 or more pages.

These working plan sets will be used by just about everyone associated with the addition, including the bank, the building department, subcontractors, and material suppliers. Therefore, the plans need to be accurate, readable, and prepared according to certain standard guidelines.

Who Prepares the Plans?

The plans and specification sheets for the project can be prepared by the homeowners, by an architect, by an engineer, by a designer, by you as the contractor, or by a combination of all these people. Who's going to do what—and who's going to be responsible for the cost—is one of the first things you need to discuss and clarify.

Determining who prepares the plans is often a matter of what's required and what's expedient for a particular project. Following are some of the advantages and disadvantages of having the plans prepared by each of the various people involved, but for the most part, you will probably find that preparing the plans yourself or hiring a designer or draftsman to do them will prove to be the most time- and cost-effective method for most of your addition projects.

OWNER-PREPARED PLANS

- *Advantages:* Having the owners do their own plans allows them to be sure that they are incorporating everything they want in the addition. They can make changes, discuss various options, add or delete spaces, all at their own pace and without the worry of how much the design and drafting time is going to cost them. You as the contractor are spared the hassle of drawing the plans or hiring someone to draw them, and any discussions about who foots the bill is completely avoided.

- *Disadvantages:* The biggest disadvantage is that usually the homeowners are not qualified to make the drawings. They may be able to generate a usable to-scale floor plan, but unless they work in construction, drafting, or some related field, they're rarely able to produce all of the elevations, foundation plans, roof plans, and other necessary drawings.

ARCHITECT-PREPARED PLANS

- *Advantages:* Due to the amount of training and education that architects have, the plans they prepare are typically very complete and very accurate (Figure 4.1). All of the necessary drawings will be included, and all of the necessary specifications will be listed for the bidders to work from. Because of their training and their greater exposure to different types and styles of buildings, architects often have some of the best ideas for blending the aesthetics of the addition into the existing house. For more complex additions, the architect is also

FIGURE 4.1

Many architects, engineers, and designers work with computer-assisted drafting (CAD) software, making changes to the plans much easier. *(Courtesy of Trus Joist MacMillan.)*

trained to perform the necessary calculations for structural loads and is licensed to stamp and certify those calculations to the building department and other agencies (see Certified Plans, following).

- *Disadvantages:* For most people, the disadvantage is the cost. On a per-hour basis, using an architect is typically the most expensive way to acquire construction plans, and unless the addition is complex, the services of an architect may not be necessary.

ENGINEER-PREPARED PLANS

- *Advantages:* Structural engineers have the best overall training in the calculation of loads. They have a thorough knowledge and understanding of how loads act on a building, what is involved in altering or moving those loads, and what materials are available on the market or by special fabrication to handle all of the structural phases of your project. Like architects, they are also state-licensed to stamp and certify building plans regarding the accuracy of their calculations.

- *Disadvantages:* Again, like the architect, the disadvantage is primarily one of cost. Also, because engineers receive their training almost exclusively on the structural side of construction, they may not have the skills or the inclination to help design the aesthetics of the addition.

DESIGNER- OR DRAFTSMAN-PREPARED PLANS

- *Advantages:* Building designers and draftsmen are people who are skilled in the preparation of building plans. They are typically very well versed in the building codes for a specific area and are knowledgeable in construction techniques in general. They are usually very good at understanding what it takes to make an addition blend into an existing house and are typically very "real world" in their approach to design. They are also less expensive—often considerably so—than architects.

- *Disadvantages:* Designers and draftsmen, while often college-trained, lack the depth of education that architects have. They are not state-licensed, and they will not be able to certify any structural calculation on your plans if that should be necessary.

CONTRACTOR-PREPARED PLANS

- *Advantages:* Preparing a set of plans yourself has the advantage of your being able to work directly with your clients on the design of the addition. You can work with and alter certain structural connections between the house and the addition in a manner that makes it easier to frame, and you can better control certain material and framing costs to help make certain the addition stays within your clients' budget. As with anything you keep in-house at your company, doing the plans yourself speeds up the process and keeps the time frame for completion within your control. Furthermore, money that would otherwise be paid to a designer stays in your company. Doing your own plans may be another selling point for many clients, which may give you an edge in landing the job.

- *Disadvantages:* In order to do your plans, you need to have a certain skill level in drafting. If you do not, you may not be able to produce drawings that are accurate, complete, or acceptable to the building department. You also may not be able to do the work quickly enough to be profitable at it or neatly enough to make a favorable impression on your clients.

CERTIFIED PLANS

Certain types of additions require that the plans be stamped and certified by a licensed engineer or architect. This is often the case with commercial additions, especially if the space will be used by the public, or with residential additions where the design, size, or location of the addition presents special circumstances. Examples might be an addition built on a hillside, where a number of complicated cantilevers are required, or additions built in certain types of soil. Beams, footings, and other structural factors involved in additions that have extensive unsupported open spaces or large expanses of windows may also require certified plans.

If the building department or other agency requires certified plans, you will need to have an architect or engineer perform the necessary calculations to ensure that the materials selected and the construction methods proposed are correct for a given situation. In this case, you can hire the architect or engineer to draw the entire set of plans, which speeds the process and ensures accuracy and continuity.

If only a certain part of the addition needs calculations—a beam size, for example, or a structural connection between the addition and the house—another alternative is to prepare most of the plans yourself or with the help of a designer, and then hire an architect or engineer to do the necessary calculations, prepare any specialty drawings required, and certify that portion of the work.

Anytime you are working with certified plans, be sure to discuss the project with the building department first and understand exactly what you are required to provide.

Who Pays for the Plans

Who will be paying for the plans—and when—is a key detail to iron out with your clients before any drawing gets under way. As mentioned, a complete set of plans is essential to the bidding process and, obviously, to the construction itself. But the preparation of these plans can be time-consuming and relatively expensive, so some agreement on this needs to be worked out early.

There are two good, straightforward methods of handling this. You can meet with the homeowners, discuss their plans and ideas, walk through the house, and maybe even make a sketch or two. This is pretty standard for most contractors and should take about two to four hours of your time—more or less depending on the clients and scope of the project. Contractors cannot, unfortunately, charge for estimating time, so this initial visit will probably be on you.

At that time, you can discuss the need for complete plans and explain why the plans are necessary before you and any other contractors can make a complete and accurate "apples-to-apples" estimate of costs. Recommend a couple of good designers or architects that your clients can contact to get the drawings done.

If you feel this job has potential and you'd like to go a step further, you can offer to sit in on their first meeting with the designer and assist with ideas and input. But explain carefully that the designer will be working directly for them, and they will be responsible for paying this bill when the plans are completed. The plans, of course, are theirs to keep and use as desired once the bill has been paid.

A second alternative and a very good selling feature (especially if you typically prepare your own plans) is to first meet with the home-owners as outlined previously, then offer to provide them with all of the plans for the project. Explain that they will have to pay you a pre-arranged fee for the plan preparation, but that if you are chosen as the contractor for the project, you will give them a full credit for the money they spent on the plans. This simplifies their life and smoothes out the design process, while keeping you involved in the project's planning all the way along. It's an excellent way to stay a step ahead of your competition, and if worse comes to worst and you don't get the job, at least you'll be paid for your design and drawing time.

Choosing a Designer or an Architect

If you decide to leave the design aspect of the addition to someone else, there are a few simple guidelines to follow when choosing some-one to work with. An architect typically has a much broader formal education in design and structural calculations and is licensed by the state. Designers are typically not licensed (although some may be licensed contractors) and will therefore not be able to stamp and cer-tify your plans should that be required.

There are several types of designers, including those who special-ize in kitchens and bathrooms, those who deal mainly with interior design and decoration, and those who are skilled enough with struc-tural design to work on additions and entire houses. For an addition, you will typically be using a building designer who works primarily with residential and light commercial projects, both for new homes and remodeling. They are usually well versed in building codes, tech-niques, and materials, and can blend the creative with the practical.

The best way to choose a designer or an architect is through word of mouth. Knowing someone who has used a particular person and was pleased with the results is about the best recommendation you could ask for. Other sources for obtaining names are your city or county building department, contractors or material suppliers, a pro-fessional referral service, the Better Business Bureau, or the telephone Yellow Pages.

Initially, set up an informal meeting with potential designers at their office. Discuss your project in general, and find out if they have done similar work in the past. Some may specialize in areas other than what you have in mind and might not be suitable for your client's project. Try to get to know the designers a little and see if you—and, by extension, your clients—will feel comfortable working with them. You'll be working closely with them through what can, at times, be a difficult creative process, and you want someone who will listen to your ideas and those of your clients while offering their own. Finally, agree on a fee, either hourly or for the whole project, and be sure you know exactly what that price includes.

Once the designer or architect has been selected, he or she will need to make at least one visit to the house. Provide the designer with all the information you and the clients have put together from your initial meetings, and be as specific as possible about exactly what you want. This will help ensure that your clients get what they want and will avoid unnecessary hourly design costs. Discuss various options, and then take measurements of the house and lot.

Ask the designer to provide some preliminary sketches as soon as possible. There may be a small additional fee for the sketches, but it's better than paying for finished drawings that may not be exactly what you want. When you have agreed on all the design aspects, the designer will prepare a full set of finished drawings. Be sure to ask for at least four copies: one for yourself, one for subs or suppliers, one for the building department, and one for the clients. If the project is large and will have a number of subs and suppliers, or if bank financing is involved, ask for a couple of additional sets of plans so you have them available for other interested parties.

The Set of Working Drawings

No matter who is doing the actual design and drafting work, certain drawings are necessary to make up a working set that fully shows all the details of your project. These drawings are fairly standard in how they're prepared and what they need to contain, and therefore they can be read and understood by anyone who has to deal with them.

The actual number of drawings that make up a full set varies, depending on the complexity of the project. Following are descriptions of the basic drawings that are always necessary. A call to your local building department will tell you if any others are required.

Floor Plan

The floor plan (Figure 4.2) is the main drawing of the set, the one that usually will be referred to most often during construction. It is drawn in two dimensions as though you were looking directly down on the addition, which is known as a *plan view.* Width and length are the two dimensions drawn; height is not shown.

A floor plan shows the outside walls of the existing house, at least as far as they pertain to the addition—if you're adding on to the back of the house, for example, it's not necessary to show the front walls of

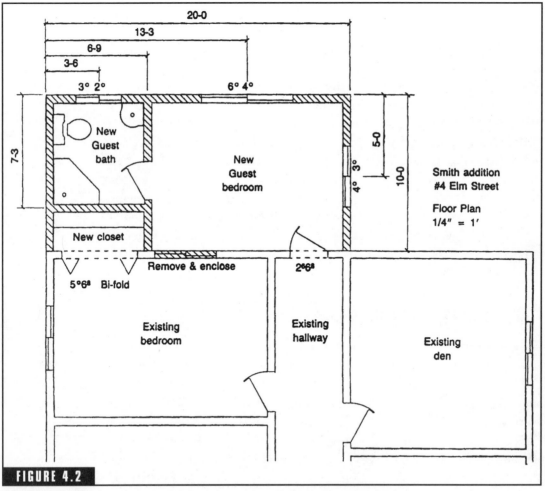

FIGURE 4.2

A typical floor plan, showing the addition and a portion of the existing house.

the existing house. The floor plan also shows the interior and exterior walls of the addition; window locations; door locations and swings; stairwells; plumbing fixtures; stationary electrical appliances; cabinet locations; the size, direction, and spacing of ceiling joists; and any other similar details relevant to the new rooms.

The floor plan also includes most of the important dimensions, including the overall outside length and width; the distance from fixed points, usually a corner, to the center of interior walls; the sizes of windows and doors and the distance from a fixed point to the center of each; the name and interior sizes of each room; and any other important sizes and dimensions.

General notes are also included on this drawing (wall insulation levels, floor-covering materials for each room area, etc.). The designer typically uses his or her judgment here, including any general information that is not noted anywhere else in the set of drawings. The scale of the drawing is always included here as well.

Elevations

Elevations (Figure 4.3) show what the outside walls, roof, windows, and doors of the addition will look like and how they tie into the exist-

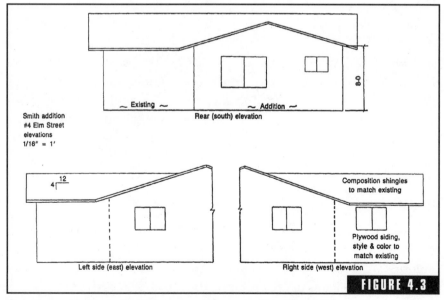

Elevations, only three of which were necessary to show this addition.

ing house. The drawings are again two-dimensional, this time showing width and height. They are drawn from the perspective of someone standing a short distance outside the addition and looking directly at each wall. Typically, one drawing is made for each major wall area of the addition (the north wall, the west wall, etc.). Each drawing is labeled to identify its location on the actual job site, either by compass direction (east elevation, south elevation) or by referring to it as the front elevation, rear elevation, or left or right side elevation.

The elevation drawings should provide a good visual look at the theoretical finished project and offer a valuable perspective on how the finished project will appear. These drawings are often of major importance if the addition is being checked by the local planning department, an architectural review board, or any kind of neighborhood standards committee.

In addition to the visual depiction of the addition, certain notes should be included on the elevation drawings: information on the type of siding; details of the roof-covering materials; wall heights and the heights of major features such as deck railings, usually measured from the ground up; door and window types and materials; and any other exterior details such as paint colors, chimney heights, or masonry work. Again, include any relevant information, and make note of the drawings' scale.

Foundation Plan

The foundation plan is devoted entirely to details of the foundation (Figure 4.4). It should show stem-wall locations; footing sizes and details; pier block locations; the size, direction, and spacing of girders and floor joists: slab details; and vent sizes and locations. The foundation plan is usually a simple plan-view drawing, with individual details, such as a cross section of the footings, included as needed.

Plot Plan

In order for the building department and other agencies to determine if the addition meets their setback requirements, a plot plan is required (Figure 4.5). This drawing, depicting the area as viewed from above, shows the boundaries of the property; the size of the existing house and

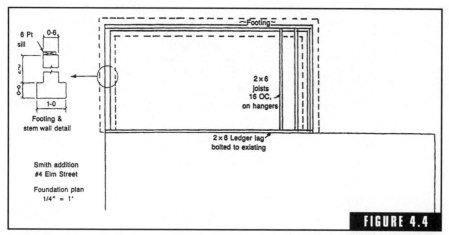

6 Pt sill
0-6

Footing

2 × 6 joists 16 OC, on hangers

1-0

Footing & stem wall detail

2 × 6 Ledger lag bolted to existing

Smith addition
#4 Elm Street

Foundation plan
1/4" = 1'

FIGURE 4.4

Foundation plan, including a footing and stem wall detail and details on the floor framing.

its location on the property; the size and location of the proposed addition; driveways and adjacent roads; other separate buildings on the property; parking areas, if needed; septic tank and drain field size and location; and any large trees, streams, ponds, or other major landscaping features.

Dimensioning is very important on this drawing. It needs to show the distance from the house to each adjacent property line and the distance from the addition to adjacent property lines. It also shows the distance from the addition to other buildings on the property and its location relative to the septic system. A simple arrow or other mark should be included to indicate north, and the drawing scale should be included.

Cross Section

Most building departments also require a cross-section drawing, which depicts the building as though it were cut in half. The drawing perspective is the same as for the elevations, showing the width and height. Details included in the cross section are the method(s) of framing; size and spacing of the wall studs; roof pitch; roof braces; amount of cornice; ceiling height; attic ventilation; bearing partitions; posts and beams; specific foundation-bearing details; finished grade; and any necessary excavations.

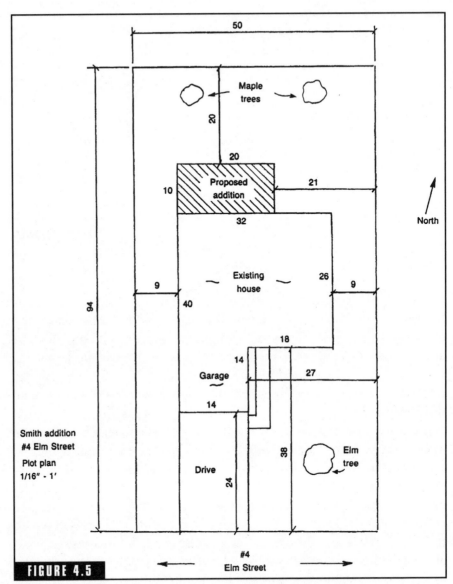

FIGURE 4.5

A plot plan, showing the location of the house and the addition on the lot.

Electrical Plan

This drawing is usually optional with most building departments, but it's an important tool in helping your clients design their electrical layout (Figure 4.6). It guides the electrician and eliminates a lot of miscommunication and misunderstandings later.

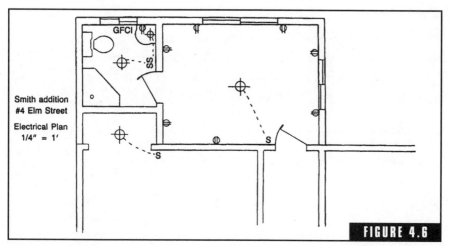

Smith addition
#4 Elm Street

Electrical Plan
1/4″ = 1′

FIGURE 4.6

Electrical plan.

The electrical plan shows the location of electrical outlets, switches, lights, and other wiring details. Standard electrical symbols are used to eliminate the need for cumbersome written notes. This drawing should also include the location of the electrical panel; any special-use wiring, such as circuits for large tools or appliances; low-voltage wiring for intercoms or alarms; and telephone, stereo, television, and other electronic wiring.

For most standard residential wiring, it is not necessary to show the actual wiring runs. It is assumed, for example, that all the outlets in the addition will be divided into the proper number of circuits, so only their locations within each room are shown on the drawing. The exception is the wiring for lights and switches. It is common practice to use a dotted line to connect each switch shown on the drawing with the location of the light fixture it controls, eliminating any confusion about which switch will operate which fixture. Written notes are used as necessary to provide complete information.

The electrical plan is prepared in plan view just like the floor plan, showing the walls, windows, and doors in addition to the electrical details. In many cases, electrical information can be placed directly on the floor plan, as long as sufficient detail can be provided without cluttering the drawing. If the addition is to contain a large amount of wiring, or if a lot of extra information must be provided, it's best to make a separate drawing in the same scale as the floor plan.

Roof Plan

The roof plan (Figure 4.7) shows the ridge and valley lines of the addition roof and how the addition will affect the roof lines of the existing house. This drawing is optional and needs to be included only if the elevations do not show the roof lines clearly.

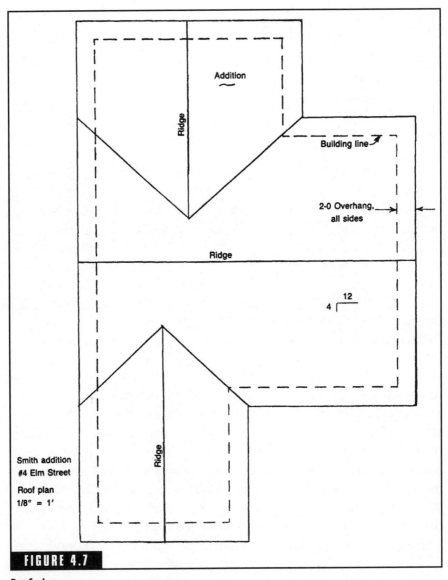

FIGURE 4.7

Roof plan.

Detail Drawings

Additional drawings are included as necessary to show important details, such as elevations and construction and material details for cabinets; perspectives, which show all or part of the project in three-dimensional form; unusual framing details, such as a cornice or bay; cross sections of special moldings or trim; or details of any built-ins.

Kitchen Cabinet Layouts

If your addition plans include a new or remodeled kitchen, a complete kitchen layout should be done as part of the plan set. Again, this clarifies things for you and the homeowners and ensures equivalent bidding between all the contractors.

The following guidelines are intended primarily for modular cabinets that are purchased individually, but they will help with the layout of custom cabinets also. Before you start, you'll need to obtain a copy of the manufacturer's specification catalog for the cabinets you'll be using, which shows the sizes and accessories available in that particular line.

Begin by making a scale drawing of the kitchen's floor plan. Work with as large a scale as possible, usually ½ inch to the foot. Make note of everything in the room that will affect the cabinets, including window and door sizes and locations, plumbing, and wall offsets. Also note all your dimensions on the drawing.

Now study the catalog. You'll notice three major product groupings, usually in the form of drawings: wall cabinets, base cabinets, and accessories and trim. After each cabinet, you'll see a series of numbers, which indicate the available sizes for that particular cabinet.

For wall cabinets, some manufacturers use numbers such as 1230, 1830, and so forth, indicating that the cabinet is available in sizes 12 inches wide by 30 inches high and 18 inches wide by 30 inches high, respectively. Other companies will simply denote "30-inch cabinet," indicating its height, followed by 12, 18, 24, and so on, indicating the available widths. Wall cabinets are offered in both 12- and 24-inch depths.

Base cabinets are offered in one standard height, usually 34½ inches, with a choice of widths from 9 inches up to 48 inches or more. In addition to the base and wall cabinets, most manufacturers also offer oven and pantry cabinets, which are 24 inches deep, 84 or 96 inches high, and 12 to 36 inches wide. Some companies offer island cabinets and special wall cabinets that enclose the range hood.

In the third group, accessories and trim, you'll find all the miscellaneous parts and optional add-ons you'll need to complete your installation. Items available will vary widely with the manufacturer, but you'll usually find wine racks, roll-out shelf kits, side and front panels for dishwashers and refrigerators, and moldings and fillers.

Begin laying out the various cabinets on your drawing, starting with the base cabinets. Start with the wall that houses the sink, because the sink is usually the one thing in the kitchen that cannot be easily relocated. Select a sink base cabinet—a cabinet with no shelves for use where the sink and related plumbing will be located—and center it where your sink will be. Work from the sink base to the nearest corner, using either a blind corner cabinet or an L-shaped lazy Susan cabinet in the corner.

Try the available corner, sink, and other base cabinets until you arrive at a combination that fits the available space. Note that blind corner cabinets will usually allow you 3 to 4 inches of "pull" away from the corner to let you make up for odd room dimensions. The gap behind the cabinet is later hidden with the countertop. Lazy Susan cabinets do not have these allowances, so odd inches need to be made up by shifting the sink base to one side or the other, keeping the plumbing locations in mind, or by adding filler strips between the cabinets. Continue around the room, first locating the major features (oven, pantry, cooktop, and dishwasher) and then filling in with applicable base cabinets.

Use the base cabinets as keys to the layout of the wall cabinets, maintaining a symmetry of appearance so that the room appears fairly well balanced. Shorter cabinets, usually 12 or 15 inches high, are used over cooktops, refrigerators, and other areas that require more clearance, so be sure to make your selections accordingly. A proper layout may require several attempts at shifting the available sizes of cabinets around before you have a cohesive appearance.

Computer Drawings

Virtually all custom cabinet shops and modular cabinet dealers have computer-assisted drafting (CAD) capabilities, which greatly simplifies laying out the cabinets. Make a rough drawing on paper using the preceding guidelines so that you and your clients can be sure you're in agreement on a layout, and then have the cabinet dealer or cabinet-maker visit the site to take the necessary measurements.

If the kitchen is to be part of the addition—so that there is no physical room to measure at the time you're preparing your plans and your estimate—the dealer or cabinetmaker can work from the plan dimensions to create a layout and price that's fairly accurate. Once the addition is framed, exact measurements can be taken prior to ordering or building the cabinets.

Using these measurements and a CAD program designed for cabinetwork, the designer can prepare a layout of the cabinets on the computer. Then, viewing a printed copy of the layout or working directly from the layout on the computer screen, alterations can be made quickly and easily. Best of all, the computer will then generate three-dimensional views of the room so that you and your clients can "walk" through the area to get a feeling for what the finished kitchen will look like.

Blueprints and Copyrights

During the process of constructing an addition, several people will need copies of the plans. The building department will usually require two or three sets for review. Material suppliers and subcontractors will need to see copies. Even lenders will require a set for their records. Therefore, you will need to have several copies of the plans, and the most accepted method of copying architectural drawings, especially large ones, is blueprinting.

In the blueprinting process, the original tracings are placed on a sheet of light-sensitive paper, and the two sheets are passed through a blueprinting machine. The machine exposes the sheets to intense light, causing the blueprint paper to fade to a light blue. Wherever the light was blocked by the lines on the tracing paper, the blueprint paper remains a much darker blue. The sheets are then developed in a chemical that fixes the colors. The result is a durable, easy-to-read copy. The process takes only a few minutes and is quite inexpensive.

Additional blueprints can be made only from the original tracings—you cannot make a blueprint from a blueprint. Some larger blueprint shops, however, have special photocopy machines that are large enough to make a copy of a blueprint.

If you have made the drawings or have arranged for someone else to prepare them on behalf of the owners, the drawings typically remain your property until your clients pay for them, at which time they become the property of the homeowners. For this reason, it is common practice to place a copyright notice on the drawings, with a warning not to blueprint, photocopy, or otherwise reproduce your drawings without your permission. Because this warning is permanently affixed to the drawing, after the homeowner has paid for the plans it is customary to give them a letter granting permission to copy the plans as desired.

The Estimate and Proposal

With the design work pretty much behind you and with a basic layout and set of specifications for the project established, it's time to prepare the estimate and sell the job. Chapters 5 and 6 will take a hard look at how the numbers come together and how to win the client.

If you've done remodeling work in the past, you know that there are a lot of tricks to estimating this kind of project. Room additions add their own twist to the remodeling estimate, and in many ways they are probably the most difficult of all types of residential construction work to bid accurately and correctly. The fact is, it's a virtual impossibility to get everything right on an estimate such as this, so you need to resolve as many basic costs as possible and then learn how to work with the unforeseen problems and hidden costs in a manner that is fair to you and your client alike.

Different Types of Estimates

There are four basic ways in which you can estimate the cost of a room addition. Each has certain advantages and disadvantages for both you and your client, and this is something you'll need to discussed and clarify before you actually get out your pencil and calculator.

Fixed-Cost Estimates

In a fixed-cost estimate, you propose to do a clearly specified amount of work for a clearly specified amount of money. Your estimate should be very clearly prepared and written and should specify as many materials and quantities as possible—"23 squares of medium cedar shake roofing," for example, or "500 linear feet of hemlock Colonial-style baseboard."

This fixed-cost proposal is the type of estimate that's preferred by most homeowners, since they have a very clear idea of how much the addition will cost and what they will be getting for that money. It makes it much easier for them to budget their financing, especially if a lender is involved, and this kind of closed-end financial agreement is definitely more comfortable for most homeowners.

For the contractor, however, this form of estimate is virtually impossible to do accurately, because there is no way to determine exactly what you're going to encounter once you begin opening up walls and tearing out floors. If you have agreed, for example, to "perform all necessary framing to complete the addition"—typical wording for a proposal of this sort—and you encounter structural problems that require a substantial amount of additional worker-hours and materials, you're going to have to absorb those costs out of your own pocket.

A common strategy for the contractor faced with an estimate of this type is to "pad" certain potential problem areas, such as the framing. If you calculate that the labor and materials required for your crew to do the framing will be $15,000 if everything goes well, you might estimate $18,000 or even more to cover potential problems. The downside to this approach is that it's still not very accurate for you or your client, and if other contractors bidding the job don't do it, you're almost certain to wind up as the high bidder.

Time-and-Materials Estimates

The second common estimating method is time-and-materials, also called a cost-plus estimate. In this form of estimate, your company is hired to construct the project at an agreed-upon hourly rate for any labor that you provide directly. For the materials you provide and the subcontractors that you hire and oversee, you are paid the actual cost you incur, plus an agreed-upon percentage of markup. In other words, if your plumber charges $5000 to do the work, and the markup you've agreed on with the homeowner is 10 percent, you would bill the client $5500 for the plumber.

Time-and-materials estimates are obviously preferable for the contractor because you know that you'll be paid a reasonable wage plus a reasonable markup for all of the work you actually perform. In this way, if you encounter an unexpected structural problem, you can go about fixing it with the security of knowing you can bill the client for the extra hours and materials.

Typically, clients are very leery of this type of estimate—and taken from their point of view, understandably so. They have very little control over what they're paying for and what the final cost of the project will be, and there is always the suspicion that they're being charged for your crew to eat lunch or for the time you spend on the cell phone at their job talking to other clients.

Time-and-materials estimates require an inordinate amount of trust on the part of the homeowner, and even though this method is the most fair to the contractor, you're unlikely to find a homeowner who will agree to it on a project the size of a room addition.

Square-Footage Estimates

For some types of projects, you may be able to simply do a square-footage estimate. This is simply a matter of calculating the size of the addition, then multiplying by your square-foot cost. If you have a 600-square-foot addition and you know that you can do it for $90 a square foot, then your estimate would be $54,000.

Square-footage estimates require that you know a lot about room-addition construction and the material and labor costs in your area. You can't just guess, "I should be able to do that for $90 a foot." If you make a mistake of just $2, you've eaten $1200 on that 600-square-foot addition. You have to be able to really look at the details of the addition and the construction of the existing house and know within $1 per square foot how much that addition will cost you to build.

This type of estimate also requires a proposal that clearly spells out the types and grades of materials you'll be using, so your clients know exactly what to expect. Without a clear understanding of the specifications, your clients won't be comfortable signing the contract—nor should they be—and you're setting yourself up for a multitude of mis-understandings, problems, and hard feelings down the road.

Allowances Estimates

A hybrid combination of the fixed-cost and time-and-materials esti-mates is the allowances estimate. This type of estimating is preferred by most experienced contractors and is acceptable to most homeown-ers, so it's the closest you'll come to a win-win situation in the ongo-ing financial battles between contractor and client.

In the allowances estimate, you begin by estimating as many hard costs as you can. For example, you should be able to figure quite accu-rately how much the foundation or the roofing will cost or how much it will cost to paint the exterior and to supply and install the windows and doors.

For the items you cannot figure precisely, make as accurate a cal-culation as you can and then put that in the bid as an allowance. For example, your estimate might say, "all necessary framing for the addi-tion, including floors, walls, roof, and structural tie-ins; framing allowance $15,000." During the course of construction, you need to track the actual time and materials spent doing the framing. If you encounter problems that take the cost over the $15,000 allowance, the client is billed for the additional amount. Conversely, if you come in under that allowance, the client receives a credit against the final billing.

Materials are also spelled out as allowances. You might have "lighting allowance, $1200," so the clients know how much they may spend on light fixtures, or "carpet allowance, labor and materials, $24 per square yard," so they know how much they have to spend on their carpets.

Discuss the details of this type of agreement with your clients beforehand. They need to understand exactly how the system works. It is also standard practice to have a change order signed when you are over or under your allowance by a substantial amount. This reciprocal agreement puts in writing the fact that you are owed an additional amount by the client or that the client will receive a credit.

It's important to keep in mind that you need to be realistic with your allowances. Trying to be the low bidder on a project by putting in $11 a yard for carpeting or $12,000 for framing that you know will cost

$15,000 will only lead to a lot of hard feelings. You might get paid on this job, but your reputation as a shady dealer will be difficult to overcome.

The Basics of Estimating

With the exception of the time-and-materials estimate—which is unlikely to occur with a room addition project—you'll need to prepare an estimate of costs that's as accurate as possible. Accurate and thorough estimating is the only way to ensure that you're competitive with the other contractors and that you can do a particular job for a particular amount of money and walk away with a profit.

What follows will help you with the basic estimating process for each stage. Every addition is different, and some have special requirements you won't find covered here, so you'll need to adjust your own estimates accordingly.

Terminology

First, acquaint yourself with the various terms used in estimating, and understand the simple mathematics behind them. This is basic stuff to any contractor who's been estimating for awhile, but if you're new to contracting or remodeling, this should help.

board foot (bf or bd ft) A common measurement for lumber, equal to an area 12 inches wide, 12 inches long, and 1 inch thick. To convert into board feet, multiply the board's thickness in inches by its width in inches by its length in feet, then divide by 12. For example, a 10-foot-long piece of 2×12 lumber would contain 20 board feet $(2 \times 12 \times 10 \div 12 = 20)$.

cubic yard (cy or cu yd) A measure of volume, equal to the length in yards times the width in yards times the height in yards. As an example, if a 12- by 15-foot area were 9 feet high, or 4 by 5 by 3 yards, it would contain 60 cubic yards. There are 27 cubic feet in a cubic yard, so in the preceding example you could also multiply the measurements in feet and then divide by 27 $(12 \times 15 \times 9 = 1620 \div 27 = 60$ cubic yards$)$. Materials such as concrete, sand, rock, gravel, and dirt are measured in cubic yards.

each (ea) The most basic unit of estimating, *each* refers to the cost of one item, regardless of size. Examples include plumbing and electrical fixtures and components, appliances, and specialty hardware.

linear foot (lf or lin ft)   Equal to 1 foot of distance measured in a straight line, regardless of height or width. For example, a 10-foot-long two-by-four is 10 linear feet, as is a 10-foot-long piece of molding. Linear-foot measurements are common for moldings, certain types of lumber, electrical wire, and pipe.

M, C   M and C are holdovers from Roman numerals and are common abbreviations used with a variety of building materials. M stands for 1000, and when it is placed in front of a unit designation, it indicates 1000 of that unit. MBF, for example, is an abbreviation for 1000 board feet, while MLF would be 1000 linear feet. Less commonly used is the abbreviation C, which indicates 100.

sheet (sht)   Similar to *each,* some building materials are sold by the sheet (e.g., plywood and drywall). Most sheets are 4 by 8 feet, but you will need to verify the size for the particular product you are ordering.

square (sq)   Equal to 100 square feet of area. Most types of roofing products are sold by the square.

square foot (sf or sq ft)   An area's width in feet times its length in feet. For example, an area 12 by 15 feet contains 180 square feet. Tile, screen, plastic, and wood veneers are commonly sold by the square foot.

square yard (sy or sq yd)   The length in yards times the width in yards. A 12- by 15-foot area would be 4 by 5 yards, or 20 square yards. Because there are 9 square feet in a square yard, you also can determine the square yardage of an area by dividing the square footage by 9. Fabrics and many types of floor coverings are measured in square yards.

A Sample Estimate

A comprehensive estimate is easier to do if you break it down into logical stages, then estimate each stage individually. Working from the ground up, you'll want to begin by estimating the cost of the foundation, then proceed through the floor, walls, and so on. You may wish to refer to later chapters of this book to be certain you understand what's involved in each stage and to help you determine whether that stage is something you will undertake yourself or have someone else do (and therefore estimate) for you.

For purposes of example in the following estimates, let's assume that two rooms are being added to the back of an existing house. The total size of the addition is 20 by 10 feet, with 8-foot-high walls and a gable roof with a 4/12 pitch and 2-foot overhangs.

Estimating the Foundation

First of all, are there any excavation costs? If the building site is level and you are hand-digging the footing trenches, then you need to figure the number of hours and the per-hour cost for your crew. If you need the services of an excavator or if you have to rent any equipment, list those costs.

The forms are next, and what you need is governed by how high and how long the forms need to be. For example, if you are building the forms out of ¾-inch plywood and they will be 2 feet high, you will get two 8-foot-long strips of 2-foot-high plywood out of each 4 × 8 sheet, or enough to build the inside and outside of 8 linear feet of forms. Add up the total linear footage you need, then divide by 8 to get the total number of sheets you need. In this case, the 40-linear-foot foundation will require five sheets of plywood (40 ÷ 8). Multiply this by the cost per sheet to determine material costs for the forms.

If your soil conditions are such that footing forms are also needed, which are usually constructed from 2 × 6 lumber, include the material cost for these, too. Add in the cost of stakes and other miscellaneous materials. Finally, figure how many hours it will take your crew to erect the forms, and multiply this by your per-hour labor cost. Add the labor and material together, and you have your form costs.

The second step is estimating concrete. A 6-inch-high by 12-inch-wide footing is ½ square foot, and a 6-inch-wide by 24-inch-high stem wall is 1 square foot. Together, they equal 1½ square feet. Since the foundation is three-dimensional, length must also be considered, so each linear foot of foundation would contain 1½ cubic feet of concrete (1 linear foot times 1½ square feet).

The foundation in the example is 40 linear feet in length. Multiply that by 1½, and you arrive at 60 cubic feet. Since concrete is ordered by the cubic yard, and there are 27 cubic feet in a cubic yard, divide 60 by 27 to arrive at the amount of concrete required, which in this case is the number of cubic feet in a cubic yard. This works out to approximately 2.3 cubic yards.

Allowing for waste, you would probably want to order 2½ cubic yards. Multiply the number of cubic yards by the cost per cubic yard, and you have the total cost of the concrete. To the concrete and form lumber prices you'll want to add an appropriate amount to cover the foundation vents, anchor bolts, stakes, and other miscellaneous materials.

Now figure the labor required for your crew to pour the concrete and later to remove the forms, add this to the cost of the concrete and the cost of the forms, and you'll know the total estimated cost for building the foundation.

Estimating Framing Costs

FLOOR COSTS

Again working from the ground up, begin by figuring your floor costs, starting with the joists. Suppose you intend to use 2 × 6 floor joists, spaced 16 inches on center (OC). This addition will require 16 joists (20 feet × 12 inches = 240 inches of length for the addition; 240 inches ÷ 16 inches OC = 15 joists, plus one to start). Each joist needs to be 10 feet in length (10 feet × 16 joists = 160 linear feet of lumber). You will also need 20 feet of lumber for the rim joists and 20 feet for the ledger, giving you a grand total of 200 linear feet. You also will need to figure in 40 linear feet of pressure-treated lumber for the sill plates.

The subfloor is the next consideration. If you intend to use plywood, you'll need to determine the total square footage of floor area you have to cover. A 10- by 20-foot addition has 200 square feet of floor area. One sheet of plywood covers 32 square feet (4 × 8), so divide 200 by 32 and you'll arrive at 6.25, which means you'll need seven sheets of plywood.

Finally, multiply the various types of lumber and plywood by the cost per foot or per sheet to arrive at your lumber costs. Add a small amount to cover nails, adhesive, sill sealer, and so forth. Then determine how long it will take your crew to frame the floor. Multiply by your per-hour charge, add the two together, and you have the cost for the floor framing.

WALL COSTS

To estimate the cost of the wall framing, the quickest and easiest method is to first determine the total number of linear feet of walls, both interior and exterior. Now simply figure one stud per linear foot of wall, which gives you enough extra lumber for trimmers, corners, intersections, and blocking. Next, take the total linear footage of the walls and multiply by 3, which will give you the amount of lumber needed for one bottom plate and two top plates.

For example, this addition has 17 linear feet of 8-foot-high 2 × 4 walls, so you will need approximately 17 two-by-four studs and 51 feet of two-by-four plates (3 × 17). This would be a total of 136 linear feet of lumber for the studs (17 studs × 8 feet long), giving you a total of 187 linear feet of two-by-fours (136 + 51).

The calculation is the same for the two-by-six exterior walls. Thus, 40 linear feet means 320 feet for the studs (40 studs × 8 feet), plus 120 feet of two-by-sixes for the three plates (3 × 40), for a total of 440 linear feet of two-by-sixes.

Multiply the linear footages by the cost per foot; add in the cost of any special lumber for beams or headers, plus the cost of your nails, hangers, and other hardware; add your labor cost; and you have the wall framing.

CEILING AND ROOF COSTS

Rafters and ceiling joists are calculated the same way as the floor joists. First determine the length of one rafter and one joist, then multiply these lengths by the number of each that you'll need.

From the scale drawings of the plans, measure along the slope of the roof from the ridge to the fascia. You will see that each side of the roof is approximately 12½ feet long, including the overhangs, so you'll need 14-foot material for your joists. In the other direction, along the ridge, the roof is 12 feet wide with the overhang, so you'll need a 14-foot board for the ridge. Determine the number of rafters you'll need, add in the fascias and barge rafters, multiply by the cost per foot, and you'll have the main roof-framing costs. Add 10 to 20 percent for lumber at the intersections and for blocking.

By multiplying 12½ by 12, you can determine that each side of the roof has an area of 150 square feet. Multiply by 2 (for both sides), and you arrive at a total of 300 square feet of roof area. You will also need to include the two triangular areas where the addition roof intersects with the existing roof. Measuring off the roof plan, you can determine that the two legs of the triangle are 9 and 11 feet. The formula for calculating the area of a triangle is ½ × base × height, which in this example would be ½ × 9 × 11, or 49.5 square feet. There are two equal areas at this intersection, so you have a total of 99 square feet of area at the intersection. Add this to the 300, and you have a total roof area of 399 square feet.

If you are using plywood or OSB for the roof sheathing (one sheet = 32 square feet), divide 399 by 32 and you'll see you need 13 sheets. If you have an open soffit, refer to your plans to determine how much of the total roof area will have to be a finished grade of plywood, such as C-C plugged, which is more expensive than the OSB or C-D-X grades used for the rest of the roof. If you have a closed soffit, remember to add in the cost of the plywood you'll be using to cover the soffits.

Again, add up all the lumber and plywood costs, then add in an amount for nails, eave and roof vents, and other miscellaneous materials. Add in your labor costs to come up with the total cost for the ceiling and roof framing.

Estimating Roofing Costs

Roofing is sold by the square (100 square feet). The roof is 399 square feet, so you'll need four squares of shingles. You'll also need extra shingles for the ridge, starter course, and waste at the intersections, so five squares of roofing would be safe. You'll also need felt paper under the shingles, which is usually sold in 3-square or 4-square rolls, so you'll need to figure on two 3-square rolls.

If you are planning to reroof the existing house at the same time the addition is being done, take your measurements directly from the roof itself for accuracy. Calculate the number of squares as just shown, then add in what you've calculated for the addition to determine the total number of shingles needed. Don't forget roof and plumbing vent flashings and new attic vents for the existing roof (to match those on the addition).

Calculate your labor costs next, which can be on a per-hour or a per-square basis. For the reroofing, don't forget the cost of tearing off the old shingles and preparing the sheathing for the new shingles, which typically runs about $30 per square and up, depending on the number of layers.

Estimating Windows and Doors

Windows and doors are easy. Simply make a list of the sizes and styles of each, and take them to your window supplier for a material estimate. Mark up the materials as appropriate—typically anywhere from 5 to 20 percent—to cover your time in ordering and overseeing delivery. Figure a per-door and a per-window labor rate for installation, and add the two together.

Estimating Siding

For this addition, plywood siding is being used. Because the walls are 8 feet in height, 9-foot-long sheets of siding will be needed to cover the walls and overlap the floor framing. The addition has 40 linear feet of exterior wall to be covered. Each sheet of plywood siding is 4 feet wide, so 10 sheets will be needed for the walls.

In addition to the walls, the gable end must be covered. Since the gable end forms a triangle, use the formula for calculating the area of a triangle to determine exactly how much area you need to cover. From the drawings, you can determine that the gable end is approximately 3½ feet high and 20 feet wide at the base. Applying the formula, you arrive at 35 square feet ($\frac{1}{2} \times 20 \times 3\frac{1}{2}$). This is just over one 4×8 sheet of siding, but because of the waste from the angled cuts, three sheets will probably be needed. For this addition, therefore, you will need 10 sheets of 4×9 siding and 3 sheets of 4×8 siding.

These types of simple square-footage calculations can be used regardless of what type of wood siding you are using. If you are using brick, stucco, or other types of masonry, use the square-foot figures to determine the quantity of these materials also. Don't forget an allowance for your tie-ins where the addition meets the existing house.

These exterior square-footage numbers can also be used to determine how much wall sheathing you'll need (if that's required for the type of siding you're using), the amount of house wrap required, and the amount of exterior paint or stain.

Estimating Electrical, Plumbing, and Heating Costs

ELECTRICAL COSTS

For most contractors, electrical, plumbing, and heating work is done by subcontractors, so estimating is simply a matter of giving the plans to the subs and allowing them to prepare the necessary estimates. If you are licensed in any of these fields, or if your state allows people with a general contractor's license to do work in these areas, you may need to do your own estimates.

Estimating your costs for electrical supplies is pretty straightforward. It is primarily a matter of counting the number of 110-volt receptacles shown on your plan, then multiplying this number by the combined cost of a receptacle, box, and cover plate. Repeat the process for all the 220-volt receptacles, all the switches, and all the lights that require a fixture box.

Electrical wire is sold by the foot or in boxes of 100 or 250 feet, so next you'll want to calculate the total feet of wire needed and multiply by the cost per foot. Different wire types will have different per-foot prices, so calculate separately how much of each wire type you'll need. If you are adding new circuits, add in the cost of new circuit breakers and any conduit or other fittings necessary to enter the panel box.

The rest of the electrical material costs are based on "each" prices. Add up the individual cost of each light fixture you need, along with appliances, fans, room heaters, and so forth. Adding an additional 10 percent to the electrical total should cover all your miscellaneous needs, such as staples, fittings, wire nuts, and waste. Finally, add in your labor costs.

PLUMBING COSTS

Accurately estimating plumbing costs is a little more tedious. Begin by dividing the plumbing into two separate systems: (1) hot- and cold-water lines and (2) drain, waste, and vent (DWV) lines. Study the plans to determine where each water and waste line will originate (at a sink, toilet, etc.). You'll also need to take a close look at the house to determine where each line will tie into the existing house plumbing.

Beginning with the water lines, sketch on paper where each line begins and where it goes. Follow it all the way to where it ties into another line, noting the approximate footage of each run, any changes of direction, and the size of pipe you'll be using. Do this for each water line, both hot and cold.

Add up the footages for the pipe, and multiply the total by the cost per foot of each pipe size. For the elbows, tees, and other fittings, it's easiest to just get an average cost per fitting and multiply it by the total number of fittings needed, regardless of size. For example, if most ½-inch fittings are 60 cents each and most ¾-inch fittings are 80 cents each, and you have a total of 40 fittings, multiply 40 by an average per-fitting cost of 70 cents to arrive at an approximate cost of $28 for fittings.

Repeat the procedure for the DWV lines, beginning with a separate sketch. Figure up the number of fittings and the total footages for the different sizes of pipe and multiply them by their respective costs. Add the water and DWV estimates together and, depending on how accurate you think your takeoffs were, add in another 10 to 25 percent to cover any unforeseen needs that always seem to arise.

Most of the finished plumbing is figured on the basis of individual needs. Add up the cost for sinks, toilets, bathtubs, and other kitchen and bath fixtures, along with the related needs of each fixture such as faucets and shutoff valves. Other specific needs, such as a new water heater, are also added in at this time. It's important that you take the time to visualize as many of your material needs as possible in order to avoid underestimating.

Now figure how long the plumbing will take you and your crew to perform, including rough-in and top-out, and multiply by your per-hour rate. Add this to the materials total for a fairly accurate cost for your rough plumbing materials.

HEATING COSTS

Finally, you'll need to ascertain what's required for heating, cooling, and ventilation materials and labor. If you are adding to an existing heating or cooling system, you'll need to figure the lengths of the duct runs, then multiply that total by the cost per foot. Remember to add in the necessary fittings.

If you're adding exhaust fans or any type of combustion appliances, you'll also want to determine the ventilation requirements of each and add in these costs as well. If you are adding an entire new heating and/or cooling system, your dealer can supply you with the costs for the unit and related accessories. Again, calculate and add in the costs for installation labor—and don't forget gas piping, flues, and electrical wiring.

Estimating Interior Costs

Using some of the preceding examples, you can next calculate the total square footage of four specific areas: the inside surface of all exterior walls, both surfaces of all interior walls, the surface of the ceiling, and the surface of the floor. These four figures, separately and together, will be used several times in calculating your material costs for finishing off the interior of your addition.

Insulation Costs

You will typically be using several different types of insulation in the addition, depending on the location and the desired R-value. These include the attic, vaulted ceilings, floor, exterior walls, interior walls (soundproofing), heating ducts, and water pipes. Most insulation is sold by the square foot, so determine the size of each area you need to insulate and the cost for each type of insulation. Then simply multiply each area's square footage by the appropriate cost. Finally, add in your labor costs.

Drywall

If you are applying drywall to the entire interior, add up the square footages of the ceiling and all the interior and exterior walls, then divide the total by 32 to determine the number of 4 × 8 sheets of drywall you'll need. In some areas it may be advantageous to use 4 × 12 sheets instead, so divide by 48 for these areas. Add in approximately 15 percent for waste, then multiply by the cost per sheet. Allow an additional 20 percent to cover nails, tape, and joint cement.

Wall Coverings

A wide variety of wall coverings are available to finish off the interior drywall, and most are sold by the square foot. Use your ceiling and wall calculations to determine how much paint, wallpaper, or other materials each area will require. You might need to consult your supplier to determine how much waste allowance to include for materials like wallpaper (where the waste created by pattern matching can often be substantial).

Floor Coverings

Most floor coverings are sold by the square yard, with the exception of wood and ceramic tile, which are sold by the square foot.

Carpet is sold only in 12-foot-wide rolls (except for some special-order commercial carpets), and sheet vinyl is sold in either 6- or 12-foot-wide rolls, so keep this in mind when you calculate your yardage needs. For example, if the room you want to carpet is 11 × 18, you will need to figure it as 12 × 18, since that's how you'll be buying the materials.

To calculate your needs for any material sold by the square yard, first round the width of the room up to the next 6-foot increment (6, 12, 18, and so on), multiply that by the length of the roof, then divide the floor area's square footage by 9. Multiply the result by the cost per square yard to determine the total material cost. Don't forget to include any miscellaneous material needs, such as carpet padding and adhesives, and include a waste allowance of 5 to 15 percent.

Other Costs

Most of the other costs associated with the addition need to be figured in one at a time, depending on the individual needs and the cost of each item. Potential costs you need to be aware of include the following:

- Building permit fees and fees for variances or zone changes
- Disposal fees for old materials and other debris removed or accumulated during construction
- Concrete flatwork not associated with the foundation, such as sidewalks and driveways
- Gutters, flashings, and other sheet metal work
- Hardware (hinges, doorknobs, etc.)
- Cabinets and countertops
- Rental equipment

Another consideration is waste. As mentioned in a few of the previous calculations, a waste allowance must be figured in for some materials. Here are some guidelines in addition to those examples noted earlier in this chapter:

- Add 10 percent of the cost for foundation concrete, plaster, carpet, vinyl flooring, rough lumber, and electrical wire.

- Add 5 percent of the cost for concrete flatwork, plumbing pipe, conduit, and floor tile; add 10 to 30 percent for tongue-and-groove or other matched lumber, or for materials such as siding or paneling boards that are installed diagonally.

Profit and Overhead

If you intend to still be in business at this time next year, it's important to realize that you need to charge more than the cost of the materials and labor to construct the addition. If you do not figure in your profit and overhead (P&O), there's no way that your business will be able to survive.

Overhead is the everyday cost of doing business. It includes your telephone, the rent on your office, gasoline, stationery, insurance, and a long list of other things that seems to grow almost daily. If you are a one-person operation with an office at home, your overhead won't be as much as the contractor with an outside office and a secretary—in fact, it may seem as if you don't actually have any overhead at all. But you do, and ignoring it or neglecting to charge for it will ruin you in the long run.

Profit is the money your company makes—as opposed to the wages you pay yourself out of your per-hour fees. Without profit, your company will never be able to grow, you'll never be able to invest in new tools and equipment, and you'll never be able to hire office help or invest in a computer system. In short, you'll never expand beyond just making wages, and if that's all you're going to do, you might as well go work for someone else and save yourself the hassles that come with being self-employed.

Different contractors charge different amounts of profit and overhead, depending on the size of the company, their own personal goals, and even the competitiveness of the geographic area in which they work. A fairly standard rule of thumb is "10 and 10"—10 percent of the hard cost of the project for profit and 10 percent for overhead. This can vary, however, with some contractors charging as little as 12 percent total and others charging 30 percent or more.

As changes arise during the course of a project, don't forget that you need to add P&O onto any extra charges as well. If the client decides to add an extra window that will cost you $200 in labor and materials to install, you'll need to add P&O to that amount.

How you show the P&O in your estimate is up to you. Some contractors feel that it should be a separate line item right on the bid to avoid any confusion about what the client is being charged for. Others feel it should be incorporated into the bottom-line price for the project, the way P&O is built into the price of a pair of shoes or the cost of a meal in a restaurant. The method you choose is up to you. It may depend on the conventions of the market you're operating in. Either way, do not forget to include it!

Presenting and Selling Yourself and Your Ideas

Wearing a number of different hats is an important part of being a contractor. As you've seen in previous chapters, you need to be an estimator, a designer, and a draftsman. The upcoming chapters will talk about your need to be an effective businessperson, a sound employer, a capable supervisor, and a good craftsman.

But none of it means anything if you don't have work. So . . . adding one more hat to the wardrobe, you also need to be an effective salesperson. If you can't effectively present and sell yourself and your company to a prospective client, then your design and consultation time has been wasted, and your skills with a hammer and a piece of lumber will never be seen.

Selling is a difficult and often overlooked part of what a contractor has to do. Too many contractors feel that being a good craftsman is enough, that running the business and selling the jobs are secondary to that. Perhaps in a perfect world that's how it should be. It is not, however, the way things work in reality.

The Estimate Package

First of all, you need to adjust your thinking. You're no longer "sending out a bid," you are now "preparing and presenting an estimate package." These are not just empty words, either—this is a serious sales package that requires a lot of thought and effort. It won't guarantee you a job if your price is out of line or your work references are poor; however, done correctly, it will definitely improve the percentage of jobs you are able to estimate and land.

The Value of Professionalism: An Analogy

Too many contractors fail to see and understand the importance of a professional bid presentation, and then they wonder why their competitors are selling all the jobs.

Your clients are probably spending a minimum of somewhere around $30,000 to have this addition constructed (often a *whole* lot more than that), and in all likelihood most of that money is borrowed. They have a right to expect certain things from the person they hire to do the work.

If you don't see the value of spending much time on professionalism, the following analogy will help put it all in perspective.

You are in the market for a specific new car. The car you want costs $30,000, the same as your client's addition, and, like your client, you're going to have to finance it and make payments. You've been wanting this car for a long time. You're really excited about it, and you've narrowed your choice to two dealers: same car, same features, competitive pricing. How do you make your choice?

Dealer A has a clean lot. The cars are displayed in neat rows, and each is freshly washed. The saleswoman is neat and presentable, greeting you with an attitude that is friendly but not pushy, overbearing, or condescending. She is very knowledgeable about the car, listens to your concerns, and answers all your questions. At her fingertips is a complete selection of color choices, interior packages, and equipment options, including prices and lead time to get a car specifically meeting your needs, and she honestly presents the pros and cons of each option. She offers a list of previous customers you can call if desired. She negotiates the price with you in a straightforward manner, with no games. She clearly explains all of the lease and financing paperwork. She treats you with respect throughout the whole process and gives you as much of her time as you need to feel comfortable and make an informed decision.

Dealer B has a lot that is cluttered with dusty cars parked in haphazard fashion. The offices have litter in the corners and furniture that's a little frayed. The salesman is rumpled, unshaven, and could benefit from the application of a little deodorant. He greets you with an attitude that is transparently phony, sizing up your potential usefulness to him from the moment he sees you. He assures you it's the finest car on the market, far above the competition, yet he knows virtually nothing about it. All of your concerns and questions are laughed off with the same empty assurances. He tells you there are color, interior, and equipment options, but repeatedly steers you back to the specific models they have in stock on the lot. He informs you that his customer list is "confidential" and can't be given out. He acts shocked at any price you suggest for the car, then leaves you alone while negotiating with "the boss" in another room. He knows nothing about the financial side of things, and sends you to someone else to discuss it. Throughout the process, you are hustled and treated with disdain, and you walk off the lot feeling totally uncomfortable, as though you've just completely wasted an afternoon.

Once again—same car, same features, competitive pricing. Which dealer gets your $30,000 worth of business?

Preparing the Estimate Package

The estimate package has five basic elements, which you may wish to add to or alter (but not delete!) as needed for specific projects:

- A detailed written estimate
- Specification sheets as needed
- Referrals and references
- A cover letter
- A presentation packet

The Written Estimate

The first step in your presentation packet is the written estimate. The estimate needs to be clear, clean, detailed, and well organized.

First, list the specific details for the project, including the date of the estimate, the name(s) of the person or people to whom you're addressing the estimate, the project address, and a brief description of the project. The format may vary, but here is one example:

August 1, 1999

John and Jane Smith
123 Maple Street
Adamstown, OR 98765

ABC Construction proposes to furnish labor and materials to construct a master bedroom and bathroom addition of approximately 465 square feet to the Smith residence at the above address. Construction to be as per plans and specifications prepared by Jones and Jones Architects dated July 25, 1999, and are specified as follows:

You will notice through the paperwork sections of this book that the language recommended is very specific, and it may sometimes seem repetitious or even unnecessary. We are, to the detriment of everyone, living in a society where lawsuits abound over anything and everything, no matter how stupid, so the clearer you are, the better. For example, saying "approximately 465 square feet" will avoid the argument by some clients that the actual addition measures only 461 square feet and therefore they deserve a discount.

At one time, I used the standard phrase "furnish all necessary labor and materials to construct . . . ," but I now say simply, "furnish labor and materials." This change in wording was precipitated by a dishonest client who claimed that the former phrasing should make me responsible for repairing some hidden dryrot damage under the house!

You'll also notice references to *specific* plans and specifications in the estimate: "*Construction to be as per plans and specifications prepared by Jones and Jones Architects dated July 25, 1999, and are specified as follows.*" This accomplishes several things. First of all, you are clarifying exactly which set of plans you were using at the time you prepared the estimate. If there is an earlier or later set of plans that differ from the ones in your bid, this avoids any confusion. You are saying that your estimate is limited to these specific plans and specifications, and you are further saying that your estimate is limited to the things you have listed (i.e., "are specified as follows").

Next, break down the project into clear sections (permits, excavation and foundation, framing, etc.). Use the same progressive logic that you used in Chapter 5 to break down and prepare the estimate. Then, under each of the sections, write a description of what you intend to do. This description can be as short or as detailed as you feel is necessary to accurately explain what your estimate contains and, equally important, what it specifically excludes. For example,

> *Permits: Provide all necessary building permits, including structural, plumbing, electrical, HVAC, and fireplace. All necessary plans to be provided by others (*1). Building permit allowance to be $850. All permits and permissions required by the Architectural Review Committee for the Smith Acres Subdivision to be provided by owner.*

You can see that a description like this one leaves very little room for misunderstanding. You have stated the following:

- You will be getting the building permits. You have also specifically noted which building permits you will obtain rather than just saying "provide all permits," which can again lead to misunderstandings. If you do not know exactly what the building permits will cost, the use of an allowance—in this case $850—gives both you and your client a realistic number to work with and budget for.

- Someone else will be preparing the plans and will be providing them to you.

- There are elements of the overall project you don't wish to be responsible for, such as dealing with a homeowner's association. This wording clearly makes that someone else's responsibility.

Continue on through the entire estimate in this manner. List each item individually or group related items together, depending on the type and size of that item. For example, if the addition requires a lot of excavation work, you might want to list excavation as a separate category with its own description. If, on the other hand, that's a fairly minor item on this particular job, you can list it along with the foundation costs.

At the end of the section listings—either before or after the final price is stated—reserve a section for specific notes. Cite these with reference numbers throughout the estimate, as needed, and use the same numbering system in the "Notes" section.

In the preceding example, notice the reference "(*1)" following "All necessary plans to be provided by others." In your notes section, you might have the following listing:

Notes

*1: ABC Construction to be provided with a minimum of two (2) complete sets of blueprints for use in obtaining building permits, and an additional three (3) sets of plans for use by construction crews and subcontractors.

Again, this leaves no room for misunderstanding.

Next comes the cost. You may wish to list the cost for each individual section (e.g., "Permits, $850.00") or just work through all of the item descriptions and then put a total estimate at the bottom (e.g., "Total estimated cost as specified above, $36,295.00").

Finally, sign and date the estimate. The standard format is as follows:

Respectfully submitted,

(signature)

Don Green, President

Specification Sheets as Needed

Depending on the size and complexity of the project, individual specification sheets may be necessary to completely detail the project and avoid any misunderstandings about exactly what you are proposing to provide.

For example, if the addition you're bidding is using standard doors, your estimate breakdown might say, "6-panel interior doors, prehung, sizes as per plans," and that would be sufficient. But if the project involves a number of very specific doors, a specification sheet might be necessary. In that case, your estimate breakdown would read, "doors as per attached specification sheet labeled 'Door Schedule 1-1, July 20, 1999' "—again making a very specific reference to a very specific piece of paper.

On the door schedule sheet, you would break down the doors by name, number, description, color, room, or whatever is necessary:

—Entry Door: 3-0 solid oak carved door, left-hand swing, with 1-6 side-lights on each side. Door to be Acme Model 32-23 with Acme sidelights Model SL-2. Knob set to be Acme Model A-55 Country Classics, in antique brass.

Referrals and References

As part of your packet, you should include some additional information for the clients, whether it was requested or not. One of the most important and effective things you should make available in the packet are past-client references. These should be people you have worked for fairly recently, and you should request their permission before including them on the list. Ask if it's okay for prospective clients to call regarding your work, and perhaps to drive by to view the outside of their house.

You should have one to two pages of past-client references with name, address, phone number, and a short description of the job you did for them:

—Allen and Debbie Black, 345 Main Street, 555-9865. 700-square-foot second-floor addition and kitchen remodel.

Another way of showing your professionalism and openness is to have a separate page listing your company name and address, the names of the business owners and/or corporate officers, your contractor's license number, and other pertinent information:

ABC Construction
55 Apple Blossom Rd., Suite A
Adamstown, OR 98765
Phone: (503) 555-2288   Fax: (503) 555-2289   e-mail: abc@addition.com
Don Green, President   Susan White, Vice President
Contractor's License #449944, Expires 8-01*
Fully bonded and insured
*For information about the status and history of this license, contact the Oregon Contractors Board at (503) 555-8800, extension 211.

A Cover Letter

The final element of the packet is a cover letter. This should be a short, single-spaced, business-style letter:

- Present the estimate, explaining exactly what is included in the packet.

- Clarify or explain any pertinent information about the estimate and any other items not explained elsewhere.

- Give a *brief* sales pitch about your company.

- Thank the people for requesting an estimate from you and subtly encourage action on their part.

Putting the Package Together

Now that you understand the basic elements that should go into your estimate package, it's a matter of putting everything together. Again, the key word is *professional.*

If you were going to a lunch meeting with an important banker that you hadn't met before and with whom you were hoping to set up a six-figure line of credit for your company, you wouldn't think of showing up in dirty jeans and an old T-shirt (at least I hope you wouldn't!) and hope to make a good first impression. For the same reason, the materials you use to win over a new client need to be neat, clean, and completely presentable.

All written materials should be typed. Stop grumbling and put away your pencil—in this day of computers and electronic typewriters, it's simply what's expected of you. Your competitors are doing it (if they aren't, they won't be your competitors for very long), and if you don't, you won't present much competition either. Use a good-quality white bond paper and black ink, and correct all your spelling as well.

Assemble the presentation materials in a folder. Here again, you should be willing to spend a couple of dollars on the health and success of your business and have folders prepared with your company name and logo printed on the front. At the very least, pick up some blank folders at your local office supply store, and use one to arrange and organize all of the presentation materials.

If you want your prospective clients to assume that your work will be of the highest quality, show them your attention to detail with a truly professional presentation.

The Presentation

Another thing that a lot of contractors would rather not hear: if the job is important to you, make the presentation in person, not by mail.

- Make an appointment in advance. If there is more than one decision maker involved in the project (i.e., a husband and wife), choose a time when both of them can be present. This saves you a lot of presentation time and makes it easy to work toward a commitment on the project.

- Show up on time. If you absolutely have to be late, be sure to call, and also offer them the option of rescheduling.

- Be presentable. Even if you're coming to their house from a long day of working on another project—and people seem to understand this and are typically okay with it—at least take the time to wash up, comb your hair, and put on a clean shirt.

- Have all of the materials you need with you. This includes your presentation folder as well as any samples, brochures, pictures, or other material you would like to show them.

- Have several copies of the estimate. Present one to each of the owners, and have a copy for yourself so you don't have to borrow theirs or try and read upside down.

- Schedule enough time—yours and theirs—to make a complete presentation and to answer all their questions

Presenting Your Vision for the Project

Before going out for the appointment, take the time to review their file and all the particulars for their project. Determine the key elements of the project and be ready to discuss them. From your previous meetings, you probably have a pretty good idea of what's important to them about the addition, so make those areas your focal points.

Begin with an explanation of how you see the project unfolding. Describe how the addition would look, paying particular attention to how you would solve any problems that you or they have identified. For example, the clients may be concerned about how the roof lines will intersect or how the siding will match up. At this stage, it's important to demonstrate that you've given thoughtful attention to the structural aspects of the project and that you're fully competent to handle all the technical aspects of the job.

Next, inspire your clients with a little excitement. Let your own enthusiasm for the project show through. Discuss how great that new kitchen will be, how much light the new skylights will add to that drab dining room, and how enjoyable it will be to work on that dream model train layout in their huge, open hobby room. Let them see that you honestly care about what's important to them and that you're just as excited as they are about seeing the project become a reality.

Is the Customer Always Right?

In a word, no. If you feel that any of their ideas are not particularly good (unattractive, unsafe, or potentially have an adverse effect on the home's resale value), then you owe it to them to be honest about it. There are, however, right ways and wrong ways to do this:

- Never be condescending or sarcastic. Even if you feel that a suggestion is foolish or completely impossible, don't laugh it off—take it seriously, and explain why it won't work.

- Avoid the "seagull approach"—coming into the room, crapping all over everything, and leaving. If you don't like a suggestion, explain why you disagree and follow up with a positive suggestion about a better way to achieve what they want.

- Be aware of the fact that a lot of people don't understand the construction process. They don't know what is and isn't possible, and are often unaware of why something can't be done. Use this opportunity to educate your clients—they'll appreciate your time and effort, and you'll have a chance to demonstrate your own expertise.

Getting to the Bottom Line

One of the biggest questions that contractors have is when to get around to discussing the project's price. It's the one subject that's on everybody's mind, and despite all of the enthusiasm that everyone has for the project, if the homeowners can't afford, it's probably never going to get built.

You obviously can't avoid the issue, but try to spend some time going over the project before you discuss the price. Let them see what you've designed for them, and let them get a feel for the overall scope of the project. Build up their enthusiasm a little, and give them a sense of how this project can improve their lifestyle and achieve all of the things they've been hoping for.

Once you've spent some time going over the project, present them with your estimate folder. Explain briefly what it contains, and show them the client referral list. This is a great confidence builder, and it also helps them see that a lot of other people are remodeling, so maybe they should, too. From there, work your way down the estimate, explaining exactly what you'll be doing; then present them with the price.

If the client insists on seeing the bottom-line price right away, by all means show it to them. It's their project, and you certainly don't want to give them the impression that you're hiding something or that you're embarrassed by the price.

Dealing with That Unexpectedly High Price

The vast majority of people are totally unaware of how expensive construction is. It can even take contractors by surprise! For that reason, the price is almost certainly going to be higher than they expect. Beginning with the price will make it the focus of your clients' attention from that point on. It's more difficult to discuss your ideas with a client who is feeling disappointed over the fact that they can't afford what they want.

If the price is quite a shock and the clients' immediate reaction is that it's totally out of their price range, it may be. However, you've put a lot of time and effort into preparing this estimate, so don't give up right away—spend some time discussing things with them, and see if there's anything that can be done to make the project a reality.

It is important that you not try to sell clients on something they truly can't afford. Your integrity and reputation are at stake. However, you can discuss some options with them:

- Perhaps they can do some of the work themselves. Discuss those areas where this might be possible, and explain what would be involved, the time frames they would have to meet, and the potential savings.

- Discuss ways that the overall project might be altered. Perhaps they are looking at adding more space or more rooms than they really need. Quite often, clients really want to add specific room—a game room and a bathroom, for example—and they figure that as long as they're going through all that work, they might as well add a guest bedroom as well.

- Discuss specific items in the project that could be eliminated, changed, or perhaps left for another time. Maybe you've included decks and a spa in your estimate, and those could easily be added later. Perhaps they've specified wood windows and you can offer them vinyl as an alternative, or maybe laminate counters could be substituted for Corian in the kitchen.

Being the High Bidder

If you're a truly professional contractor, it's not at all unusual to find that you're not the low bidder on a project. Ideally, you should be in the middle to upper middle of the price range, but you may find yourself the high bidder as well.

First of all, don't apologize. Being a contractor with a solid reputation for excellence in workmanship and high-quality materials is something you never have to be sorry for. Instead, explain that you're not surprised to be one of the high bidders, and turn it into something positive.

Let them know that you are uncompromising in your standards for workmanship; that you hire only the best carpenters and subcontractors; that you stand behind your finished product far beyond the standard one-year warranty offered by most builders; that you don't low-ball your allowances or deliberately leave things out in an effort to keep the price low, only to come back to the client over and over again with requests for more money.

If you show a client honestly that you are worth what you charge, you'll often be surprised at the positive response you'll get.

Paperwork Without Panic

As a contractor, it's difficult to discover that paper is just as important to the success of your business as concrete, wood, and nails. From estimates to contracts, from change orders to lien notices, a complete and organized flow of paperwork is absolutely crucial to you and your clients, as well as to the health and well-being of your of your company.

In this chapter, you'll see several examples of the types of paperwork and forms that you're likely to need in the normal course of construction. In addition, many states have lien notices and other informational handouts that you are required by law to provide to your clients. If you're not already aware of what you need, be sure to check with the contractors' licensing agency in your state for specific details.

The Job File

All construction projects end up accumulating a lot of paperwork, and one of the first things you need to consider is what to do with it all. Here's where you have an opportunity to get yourself and your client organized and do a little company promotion as well.

For your own paperwork, a single, standard file folder won't work. There is simply too much paperwork to stuff into a folder and hope to maintain any semblance of order. You'll end up spending as much time looking for papers as you will working on the addition.

Instead, a multisection file folder works well. These are available with prongs for holding standard, two-hole, top-punched papers and are easy to separate into sections. Make sections for estimates and changes orders, contracts, client correspondence, subcontractor bids, permits and official papers, and other sections as needed.

Remember that you are required to provide at least a one-year warranty on construction jobs in most states, and most of the records you need to hang onto for the IRS and other purposes must typically be available for seven years. Folders such as these help keep all that paper in one organized area, and they're available in colors as well—consider using a particular color for each year, making it quick and easy to locate client files from previous years.

For a nice, professional marketing touch, provide your clients with a three-ring binder for the job. You can purchase these quite inexpensively from office supply stores or most discount outlets. Look for the type with a clear plastic sleeve on the front. Make a personalized cover sheet on your computer, slip it into the sleeve, and you'll make a very classy presentation. If you decide to do this, purchase a three-hole punch for your office and prepunch all the paperwork you provide to your clients to simplify their use of the binder. This is an easy and inexpensive way to gain client appreciation and set yourself apart from other builders. It's also a permanent advertising item, with your name, address, and phone number prominently displayed.

Contracts

Besides the estimate and specification sheets covered in the last chapter, the first and perhaps most important piece of paperwork for the addition will be the contract (Figure 7.1). The contract spells out all the legal and financial terms of your agreement with your client, and it must be accurate and complete.

Many contractors use a simple, plain-English contract that can be purchased from many local or mail-order printing outlets and imprinted with your name and license number. The problem with these is that they are often too simple for today's litigious world, and

TIMBERLAND BUILDERS
1234 99th St.
Kellville, WA 95959
Contractor's License. No. 555-678

PROPOSAL AND CONTRACT

TO:_____ AT: _____
(address & zip)

Dear: _____

TIMBERLAND BUILDERS proposes to furnish all materials and perform all labor necessary to complete the following:

Room addition, approximately 14-6 x 19-6, as per attached specifications. _____
_____
_____

(All other materials and labor not specified above shall be further set forth in attachments to this contract).

 All of the above work (and any work set forth in attachments, if applicable), shall be completed in a workmanlike manner according to standard practices for the total sum of: $17,800.00 (Seventeen thousand eight hundred & 00/100   Dollars)

Payment shall be made according to the following schedule:
Amount: Due:

$ 1,700.00   Upon signing contract____
$ 3,000.00   Upon completion of foundation____
$ 9,000.00   Upon completion of framing inspection
$ 3,000.00   Upon completion of drywall inspection_
$ 1,100.00   Upon completion of final inspection___

 The approximate date when the work herein described shall commence shall be May 17, 19xx, and the approximate date the work shall be substantially completed shall be August 17, 19xx. The entire amount of the contract price shall be paid no later than 10 days after completion.

 Any alteration or deviation from the specifications set forth in this proposal and contract involving extra cost of material or labor will only be executed upon written orders for same, and will become an extra charge over and above the sums set forth in this agreement. All agreements must be in writing.

Dated: May 1, 19xx   Respectfully submitted,

                                        _____
                                        Samual Hawley, Owner
                                        TIMBERLAND BUILDERS

FIGURE 7.1

A typical construction contract. Note the draw schedule.

they don't spell out your agreement and responsibilities in sufficient detail. If you intend to use this type of contract, be sure to have it reviewed by your attorney to confirm that it's legal and applicable in your state.

A better alternative is to have a contract designed for you by your attorney. Granted, this is considerably more expensive than simply buying a preprinted form, but it assures you that your legal rights are protected. Should you ever need to go after a client for nonpayment, a strong, clear contract will make it easier to win and enforce a financial judgment.

The general rule of thumb in preparing a contract is to assume nothing! Include as many details as possible, no matter how small. Remember that this contract binds you as well as your client, and as such it should clearly state each and every detail of your final agreement.

Your contract should be thorough and specific. Things will almost certainly change during the actual course of construction (see the section on Change Orders that follows), but at the beginning you want to lay out as much as possible.

No matter what type of contract you are using and no matter what the size of the job, there are a number of basic elements that you need to spell out in writing. Please note that this is generic information only. *It is not intended to be construed as legal advice.* You need to discuss all details pertaining to any legal documents with a competent, licensed attorney.

Contractor Information

At the top of the contract, provide all pertinent information about your company: your name and address, phone number, and license number. On blank forms from the office supply store, you'll need to fill this information in by hand. If you're using a custom form, all of this information will be printed on the contract.

Owner Information

Next comes a blank area for information about your clients. Include here the names of all people who are a party to the contract. If you are dealing with a husband and wife, both names need to be on the contract. In the case of an unmarried couple, include both names if both are legally responsible for the house and the remodeling work being done.

You will occasionally run into a situation where a parent, guardian, or other responsible party has co-signed a loan to enable another person to acquire financing. In this case, list all the co-signing parties. You may also run into a situation where you are being asked to do work for a person who is under the legal age for signing a contract (18 or 21, depending on the state). A contract signed by a minor may be unenforceable, so you need to move very carefully in this situation.

The address of the job site must be clearly listed on the contract, including city and state. If the owners or responsible parties live at an address other than where the work is being performed, you need to list that address as well.

Details of the Work

The next item in your contract is a clear and complete description of the work. This includes a list of what you plan to do, along with the specific sizes, types, and grades of materials and the brands and model numbers of appliances and fixtures. The easiest way to do this is simply to reference your original estimate, which is another reason for being detailed in your estimate layout in the first place.

Also reference the agreed-upon plans that will be followed during the course of construction. Remember, a person who's been working on the plans for an addition for a long time could have several different sets of drawings, so make sure you reference exactly which plan you'll be using.

For example, your contract might read:

Construct a 940-square-foot addition to the south and east sides of the house at 334 Jefferson St., Barkerville, CA, to include a master bedroom, master bathroom, and guest bedroom. Construction to be as per plans and specifications provided by Dream House Designs dated 6-22-01 and revised 7-9-01, and as per the estimate provided by Carter Construction dated 7-28-01.

If the owners are doing any of the work themselves, or if they intend to hire other people to work on the project who are not under your control and supervision, spell this out very clearly. Include the following information in your contract:

■ Define *exactly* what work the others are doing. Be very specific here. For example, if they are going to paint the interior of the addition, saying "paint interior" is not sufficient. You need to make note of who is providing the paint; who will do the caulking, sanding, spackling, and other prep work; who will do the masking and cleanup; who provides any scaffolding and ladders; and so on. This entails extra work, but you really need to take steps to protect yourself and avoid as many arguments and misunderstandings as you possibly can.

- Lay out the time frame for the other people to complete their portion of the work, and clearly delineate what happens if they don't meet this schedule. A common situation occurs with homeowners who are doing some part of the addition themselves—the painting, for example. They both work, they think they can finish the job in a weekend, but it ends up taking three weekends. In the meantime, you're at a standstill. Be certain your agreement makes provisions for any payments that are due to you during this period so that your cash flow is not interrupted. Also make sure that your completion date will be extended accordingly.

- How are owner-supplied materials handled? This includes warranties on the product itself, as well as on any parts of the addition that could potentially be affected. For example, what if the homeowner supplies a shower valve that fails after it's been in the wall for two months, soaking the drywall and the bathroom floor? Who is responsible, and how will the damage be taken care of?

- If the homeowner is hiring a subcontractor personally, it's up to you to be certain that the person is legally licensed, bonded, and insured as per the requirements of your state. Remember that as the general contractor, you are fully responsible for all work done on that site and for all of the people doing it—you could potentially be fined for having unlicensed subcontractors on your job, even if you didn't hire them, so be sure you know your specific rights and responsibilities.

Financial Details

In this section of the contract, you need to clearly list all financial terms for the entire project. This basically includes two things: the total cost of the job and the payment schedule.

The cost of the job is pretty obvious. This should include the entire cost of the original estimate, plus any additional items that have been added or deleted in the meantime. Again, there will probably be changes along the way that will affect the final price for the entire project, but the total amount on the signed contract should be as accurate as possible.

A payment schedule is a breakdown of due dates and amounts for each payment. For a very small job, the entire amount of the contract may be due upon completion, while for a large job, you may need as many as five or six progress payments. When setting up a draw schedule, keep the following questions in mind:

■ When will your subcontractors and suppliers be billing you? You want to time your draws in advance of when your bills are due so you can pay everything on time and also take advantage of supplier discounts for early payment.

■ How much is going to be due at any given time? If you take a draw at the completion of the demolition stage, for example, you may not owe very much at that point—probably just some disposal fees and a little bit of labor. On the other hand, if you have a draw at completion of framing, you'll have large lumber bills to pay, perhaps a bill for roof trusses, plus a fair amount of labor. As you can see, you'd want your demolition draw to be relatively small and your framing draw to be relatively large.

■ What triggers the draw? Try to have your draws tied to a clearly defined event. For example, a draw that is due upon frame inspection is very clear—both you and your client can see that the inspector has been out and the permit card has been signed. If you tie a draw to completion of drywall, you need to clarify if that means completion of hanging the drywall or all the way through to texturing. As always, the clearer your understanding is, the less room there will be for argument.

For a room addition with several stages and a variety of subcontractors, a typical draw schedule might be as follows.

Deposit: This is a relatively small amount of money that I think is important. It commits the clients financially to the project and allows you to purchase the building permits and make other initial arrangements for the job, using their money rather than your own. Deposits may be limited by the state in which you're operating, and you need to know this up front, but a typical amount would be 5 to 10 percent of the total cost of the job.

Upon completion of foundation: This is a good time to take a draw. The inspectors will look at the excavation and approve the forms, and once the concrete is poured, it's very clear to everyone that the foundation is complete. This is typically about 10 percent of the job.

Upon completion of frame inspection: This is tied to all of the framing being completed and inspected, which also involves an inspection of the rough wiring and rough plumbing. You have a lot wrapped up in the project at this point, so this is your largest single draw, usually 40 to 50 percent of the total project cost.

Upon completion of drywall: You need to pay your drywall subs or your suppliers at this point, so take another 10 to 15 percent. Remember to be specific about what constitutes "completion."

Upon completion of cabinets (*trim*): This draw is optional, depending on how much cabinetry is being done. If you remodel an entire kitchen as part of the package, you'll need this money to pay off all your suppliers. An alternative would be to take a draw once all the trim is installed, but this is sometimes a little difficult to accurately define—I've known homeowners who will hold up this draw because a piece of baseboard was missed in a closet. Take 5 to 15 percent at this point, depending on your projected expenses.

Upon completion of final inspection: Final inspection is a good, positive ending point for a job because it's clearly defined by the inspector signing off on the entire project. This amount will obviously be any payment left owing from the combination of the previous draws, but don't make it too big. Many contractors like to collect a large final payment so they have some serious money coming in as the job winds down, but if anything goes wrong and your clients decide to withhold final payment, having a large unpaid amount can cause you some serious financial hardship.

Start and Stop Dates

Every contract contains an area for noting the date the job will start and the date it will be complete. Be specific. Define what each date means. For example, in your mind the project will start when you go down to apply for the building permits, but in the client's mind that date on the contract means that someone will be at the house with lumber and a hammer.

Completion is a little tougher, since it's only an educated guess on your part. Figure out how long you think the job will take, then add anywhere from a week to a month to that number. It's much better to set the date out a ways and impress your client by finishing up early than it is to set a tight schedule and have your clients be upset because you can't finish on time. If you live in an area known for inclement weather, you should also incorporate some type of weather-delay clause.

Unless you really want and need the project, you should not agree to any type of penalty clause for being unable to finish on time. There are simply too many things that can—and will—go wrong on any sizable construction project, and you don't want to be subject to financial penalties if things take longer than you anticipated.

Signatures

Finally, there will be a place for all of the various signatures (Figure 7.2). On your side of things, the contract can be signed only by an authorized representative of your company. On the client's side, be sure that anyone financially involved with the project signs the contract, unless the contract contains a clause that authorizes one signature for everyone involved—the legal phrase is "jointly and severally." Consult with your attorney for the proper wording.

Give a copy of the contract to your client and keep one for your files. Two-part carbonless forms are the best way to ensure that each party gets an exact duplicate immediately upon signing.

State-Mandated Paperwork

Many states require that contractors provide specific paperwork to homeowners at the time of signing the contract. This varies from state to state, but usually includes information about how the construction lien laws work and how they affect homeowners in the event that they pay their contractor but the contractor fails to pay subs or suppliers.

Other state paperwork may include a copy of the contractor's licensing requirements, information about "cooling-off periods" (a period of time after signing a contract, usually 24 to 36 hours, in which

ACCEPTANCE

TIMBERLAND BUILDERS is hereby authorized and directed to furnish all materials and labor required to complete the work as set forth in the above Proposal (and in Attachments, if applicable), for which the undersigned agree to pay the amount mentioned in said Proposal and according to the terms thereof.

The undersigned further agrees that in the event the undersigned defaults or fails to make payment(s) as herein agreed, the undersigned will pay all reasonable attorney's fees and costs and any other collection costs necessitated by said default to enforce this contract. Default or non-payment is defined as failure to make payments to TIMBERLAND BUILDERS or their order within 30 days of the due date. Further, the undersigned agrees that for any balance due under this agreement outstanding for a period of more than 30 days after due date, an interest charge of 1% per month of the balance due shall be charged and added to any and all outstanding amounts.

The undersigned further represents and acknowledges they have fully read and understand the terms and conditions of this Proposal and Contract and FULLY ACCEPT EACH AND EVERY TERM AND CONDITION herein. No other promises or acts have been contracted for other than as set forth in this Proposal end Contract.

Signed: _____   Dated: _____

Signed: _____   Dated: _____

NOTICE TO ABOVE

TIMBERLAND BUILDERS, Sacramento, CA, has furnished or has agreed to furnish the materials and services herein described. YOU ARE FURTHER NOTIFIED that if payments are not paid in full for labor and materials furnished or to be furnished, the improved property may be subject to Mechanics Liens. (CCP U1193 or Govt. Code. 14210)

FIGURE 7.2

The acceptance portion of the contract. Both the contract and the acceptance need to be reviewed by an attorney before you begin using them.

the homeowners can change their minds and cancel the contract without penalty), and a copy of the federal Truth in Lending law.

You are responsible for knowing what paperwork to provide and having it available at the time the contract is signed. Failure to do so can result in fines, legal action against your license, and may even nullify the contract. As an added protection for you, your contract should have an area at the bottom for the homeowner to initial acknowledging receipt of the proper state paperwork.

Bonds

In almost all states, a contractor must post a bond with the state contractor's board, usually for $5,000 to $10,000. In the event the contractor defaults on a contract, the state, after a hearing, might award the bond to the client for financial damages. In order to be bonded, a contractor must show a certain amount of net worth and a history of financial responsibility—a good thing to point out to your clients when you emphasize why they should be using only a licensed contractor.

Although this bond might be awarded by the state, it does not assure the homeowner that the job will be completed. Occasionally, a client will want some additional protection and will request that you provide a completion or performance bond for the amount of your job. This type of bond ensures that if you as the contractor cannot finish the job for any reason, money will be available from the bonding company for the homeowner to complete the job properly.

Performance bonds are expensive, anywhere from 2 to 5 percent of the value of the job. If your clients request this type of bond, it should be their responsibility to pay for it. A better alternative is to explain to them that careful control of the payments they make—ensured by the draw schedule in their contract—is enough protection when dealing with a reputable contractor.

Change Orders

As construction progresses, changes are a virtual certainty. This is something you need to get used to and just take in stride. The two things to remember about changes are to discuss them with your client as early as possible, thus avoiding costly delays in the schedule, and to get them in writing.

Change orders need to be very clear and very specific, and they need to contain the following information:

- *The nature of the change:* Clearly spell out what change is being made and how it affects the original estimate and specifications. It may be a minor thing, such as "substitute 2¼-inch Colonial-style baseboard for 2¼-inch sanitary baseboard," or more involved: "add two 6-0 French doors in master bedroom; substitute whirlpool tub for standard tub; and change fiberglass stall shower to ceramic tile."

- *Specific model numbers, sizes, and so forth:* In the preceding example, you want to specify that it's an "Acme 6-foot whirlpool bathtub with 10 jets, model A-610, in passion gray."

- *The amount that the change will add or subtract:* Whether the cost goes up or down, it needs to be specifically spelled out.

- *Changes in the draw schedule, if any:* If the amount of the change order is substantial, you may need to change the amount of the affected draw, or even add in an additional draw. Also, specify the event that will trigger the draw being due and payable.

- *Changes in the completion date:* Large changes will take additional time, and that means the job will now take longer to complete. Be sure to adjust the original completion date accordingly so there is no confusion or misunderstanding.

- *The adjusted amount of the contract:* It's best to tie the change order to the original contract to avoid confusion. The wording might be something like, "alter and amend original contract dated 2-9-99 as follows," then spell out the changes. You should also list the original contract amount and the amended amount: "Original contract amount $32,590.00; new contract amount $34,115.00."

- *Signatures and copies:* The change order needs to be signed by a representative of your company and by the person or people who signed the original contract. Once again, use a two-part form to simplify things, and give one copy to the client and keep the other in your job file.

Construction Liens

In cases of nonpayment by the client, the laws of most states allow anyone who furnishes labor or materials to file a *construction lien,*

NOTICE OF THE RIGHT TO LIEN
WARNING: READ THIS NOTICE. PROTECT YOURSELF FROM PAYING
ANY CONTRACTOR OR SUPPLIER FOR THE SAME SERVICE.

Date of Mailing: _____

TO: _____

_____

THIS IS TO INFORM YOU THAT: _____

_____

has begun to provide (description of materials): _____

_____

_____

_____

_____

ordered by: _____

_____

for improvements to property you own. Said property is located at:

_____

_____

   A lien may be claimed for all materials, labor and services furnished after a date that is eight days not including Saturdays, Sundays and other holidays as defined in ORS 187.010 before this notice was mailed to you.

   Even if you or your mortgage lender have made full payment to the contractor who ordered these materials or services, your property may still be subject to a lien unless the supplier providing this notice is paid.

   THIS IS NOT A LIEN. It is a notice sent to you for your protection in compliance with the construction lien laws of the State of Oregon.

This notice has been sent to you by:
Name: _____
Address: _____
Telephone: _____

**IF YOU HAVE ANY QUESTIONS ABOUT THIS NOTICE, FEEL FREE TO
CALL US.**

FIGURE 7.3

A preliminary lien notice from a material supplier.

NOTICE TO MORTGAGEE OR BENEFICIARY UNDER TRUST DEED OF DELIVERY OF MATERIAL AND SUPPLIES

TO: _____

This is to advise you, the owner of record of a mortgage or a beneficiary in a trust deed, on either the said land or improvements thereon, that the undersigned is delivering materials and supplies upon the order of:

_____

_____

for use in the construction of an improvement located upon the following described site in _____ County, Oregon:

_____

_____

_____

also known as _____, Oregon.

(street address)

You are further notified that a lien may be claimed for all such materials and supplies so delivered, after a date that is 8 days, not including Saturdays, Sundays and other holidays, as defined in ORS 187.010 before this notice is delivered to you in person or mailed to you by registered or certified mail, and that payment by the owner or lender to the contractor does not remove the right of the undersigned furnishing such materials or supplies to claim a lien against the above described property unless the undersigned is in fact paid. No further notice to you of this or any subsequent delivery is necessary.

_____
NAME

_____
ADDRESS

Delivered by registered or certified certified mail at:

_____

_____ ,Oregon

Dated: _____, 19__

When delivered in person, receipt of above notice is acknowledged by: _____

_____

Dated: _____, 19__

FIGURE 7.4

Another type of preliminary lien notice.

also called a *mechanic's lien,* against the home where the work occurred. In extreme cases, such a lien could conceivably result in the legal forced sale of a person's home to satisfy these debts.

Soon after the job gets under way, some of your suppliers or sub-contractors may send your client preliminary lien notices (Figures 7.3 and 7.4), which is often required by law in order for them to keep their lien rights in place. This is simply done to inform the homeowner that the supplier or subcontractor is providing labor and/or materials to the job and may be entitled to slap a lien on the property for nonpayment. As the general contractor, most states do not require you to file a preliminary lien notice, because you hold the original contract with the homeowner.

Preliminary lien notices are frightening to most homeowners. They don't understand what they are, and they incorrectly assume that a lien has actually been filed against them. Take a moment to explain the process and the preliminary lien notice. Then have your clients add the paperwork to their job file for future reference.

Zoning, Variances, and Permits

Room additions, like all types of construction, need to comply with local land-use laws. They are also subject to inspection by the building department to ensure that all phases of the construction are done in complete compliance with the current building codes.

Part of your responsibility as a contractor is to know and understand at least something about the land-use laws in the areas where you intend to work—what they are, how they affect the buildings you work on, if there's any flexibility in the way they're applied.

Zoning

Every community is broken up into a variety of areas known as *zones*, and each zone has a specific purpose and a specific set of rules, guidelines, and restrictions. Most communities define several basic zoning categories, each containing a number of subzones. In very broad generalities, zoning categories include the following:

- *Residential:* These are the zones where people live, either in single-family or multifamily residences. These zones include houses, duplexes, triplexes, townhouses, condominiums, apartment buildings, and mobile home parks. Schools, because of their association with residential areas, are typically also located in residential zones.

- *Commercial:* Commercial zones are made up of retail stores, office buildings, medical offices, restaurants, movie theaters, auto dealerships, and a wide variety of other uses related to the supply of goods and services to retail consumers.

- *Industrial:* Within the industrial zoning falls all types of manufacturing, warehouses, and wholesale distributorships.

- *Agricultural:* This zoning is for farms, ranches, woodlots, forest areas, and other uses not typically associated with housing or commercial uses, although residences and some related commercial activity are often allowed in the agricultural zones.

- *Mixed use:* Mixed-use zones are combinations of two or more zones in one area. An example would be a residential area that also has a couple of restaurants, some stores, a doctor's office, and maybe a few light manufacturing facilities.

The purpose of zoning laws is to group like types of activities in the same area. A store, office building, or pig farm, for example, cannot typically be built in an area zoned only for residential use, because the noise, traffic, and odors would be disruptive to the neighborhood in general.

Within each zone are subzones, created for the same reasons. A multifamily dwelling such as an apartment building, even though considered a residential building, would usually be found only in an area zoned for residential multifamily use, not in a residential single-family zone.

It's rare that the addition you are planning would be subject to zoning restrictions, but it does happen sometimes, so it pays to check. The addition of a shop, for example, might violate a residential zoning area if you intend to service paying customers or park commercial equipment. The addition of a single apartment unit with cooking facilities above a garage would be another example, even if it's to be used only as a guesthouse. Because it has the potential for being rented out as a self-contained dwelling, it might not be an acceptable addition in a neighborhood that's zoned for single-family residences only.

As a precaution, determine the zoning category of the neighborhood in which the addition is to be built. If you have any questions about whether the planned addition might violate that zoning ordinance, take the plans and a legal description of the property to the planning department to confirm that you will be in compliance with the specific zoning requirements for that area.

Setbacks

In order to regulate and control where structures are situated on a piece of property, most municipalities have setback ordinances in place, and this is one of the most important things you need to be aware of when dealing with room-addition construction.

A setback is simply the minimum allowable distance between a structure and the property line (i.e., the minimum distance it must be "set back"). Every community will have a variety of setback requirements, depending on the zone and the intended use of the building. A commercial or industrial building, for example, may have zero setback, allowing it to be built right up to the property line, while a single-family residence will be required to be built some distance from the property lines in order to preserve the look of the neighborhood and the privacy of the surrounding houses.

This is one of the very first things you need to check when planning and designing a room addition. Suppose the neighborhood you're working in has a rear setback (the distance from the back of the house to the rear property line) of 15 feet. If you measure the existing house and find that it is currently 32 feet from the property line, you know that any addition you design can extend a maximum of 17 feet off the rear of the house.

It is sometimes possible to exceed these setback requirements through the use of a variance (see page 118), but this is a time-consuming and often relatively expensive process with no guarantee of success. Wherever possible, plan your addition to fit within the allowable setbacks.

Covenants, Conditions, and Restrictions

Within a subdivision there are often specific rules concerning what can and can't be done with a piece of property. Called *covenants, con-*

ditions, and restrictions (CC&Rs), they can cover a wide variety of things that you may not be aware of.

For example, even if the house you're working on falls into a single-family residential zone that calls for 15 foot setbacks from the house to the rear property line, the CC&Rs for the *neighborhood* may be even more restrictive (they can't be less restrictive), calling for a minimum 20-foot setback. This lengthens the minimum amount of space between the back of the house and the property line by 5 feet, and may make it impossible for the planned addition to be constructed. In the example given in the preceding section, your 17-foot room addition would now be reduced to 12 feet.

CC&Rs may be virtually nonexistent in some communities and extremely restrictive in others. For example, CC&Rs may dictate the type of roofing materials allowed; the size and type of fences; the design of decks and deck railings; the placement of spas, sheds, and other outdoor structures; the types of siding and windows that can be used; and even the color of the exterior paint.

The CC&Rs are administered by elected but unpaid members of the community called a homeowners' association. These groups have bylaws and rules of conduct, and typically hold regularly scheduled meetings within the community. Again, how much power is exercised by these associations varies from a little to a lot, and in some areas you may find yourself having a tougher time dealing with the association than you do with the city or county officials.

One of the first things to discuss with your clients is whether there are CC&Rs in effect for their subdivision. If there are, get a copy of them to study. The owners should have received a copy when they purchased their house, or else you can check with any title company and get a copy for a nominal fee.

Many homeowners' associations have an architectural review committee that looks at all plans for new construction and major remodeling within the subdivision. If so, you will need to know their design rules and the procedures for filing an application for review. It may even be necessary to register your company with them if you have never done work in that community before.

Quite often, a person who is not a homeowner within the community cannot deal directly with the homeowners' association. This is something you'll need to ascertain from reading the bylaws, and you may find it necessary to have the homeowners themselves undertake all dealings and approvals having to do with the community's association board. There are typically fees involved for having the association review plans, so be sure to discuss this with your clients and determine who will be responsible for those payments.

Special Land-Use Applications

You will occasionally encounter the need to apply for specific permissions from the city or county planning department. This occurs when the project you are planning does not meet the specific criteria for a given zone and you are seeking permission to deviate from those requirements.

Different communities have different rules, application procedures, hearings requirements, and procedural standards that you need to be aware of, so what follows is only a generic look at some of the more standard land-use situations you may encounter.

Understand that land-use proceedings can often be time-consuming and expensive, and if the project is complicated and the land-use exceptions you're seeking are fairly involved, you'll probably need the services of an attorney who specializes in land-use law. You need to have a very clear understanding with your clients regarding who will be responsible for undertaking the land-use applications. If you do it for them, you'll need to be compensated for your time as well as the cost of the fees.

Conditional-Use Permits

In land-use ordinances, there are usually three basic provisions for what you can and cannot do in a given area.

- *Permitted outright:* This means that the use is permitted within that zone with no further permissions being required. An example would be a single-family home in a residential zone.

- *Not permitted:* Some things simply cannot be done within certain zones, such as building a warehouse in the middle of a subdivision. There is no point in even making application in these instances, because the use is not allowed under any circumstances.

- *Permitted by conditional use:* This is a middle area between the other two, giving the planning department a certain amount of latitude in allowing certain marginal uses within an area. For example, a duplex may be allowed in certain parts of a single-family residential zone if it can be shown that the duplex will not have an adverse effect on the rest of the neighborhood.

You may occasionally encounter the need to apply for a conditional-use permit. This may occur when adding an apartment unit to a single-family home or when building an addition to accommodate a certain commercial use in a building that currently has a different use.

The conditional-use process is typically not too cumbersome. Make application to the planning department, and you will be given a list of things to submit and specific criteria that must be met. There is a fee for the review, but if the application is not too involved or controversial, there is usually no public notice or hearing process involved.

Variances

As discussed previously, certain ordinances and zoning rules apply to every structure within a community. These restrictions are for the good of everyone, helping to guarantee that each new building becomes an asset to the neighborhood, not an eyesore. At times, however, the construction of an addition might require that one or more of these restrictions be exceeded. In those cases it will be necessary to request a variance, which is basically a request for legal permission allowing your building to vary from the accepted standards.

Setback Variances

A variance from setback restrictions is probably the most common type that you'll be dealing with (Figure 8.1). Some older homes were built when no setback rules were in effect for their neighborhood, and when judged by today's rules, these homes might be too close to the neighboring property line. If you intend to construct an addition that follows the existing walls of such a house, your addition will violate the setback restrictions. In this type of situation, it's necessary to

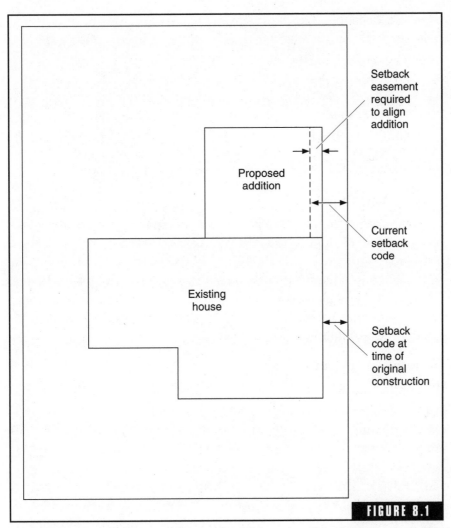

Setback
easement
required
to align
addition

Proposed
addition

Current
setback
code

Existing
house

Setback
code at
time of
original
construction

FIGURE 8.1

A setback variance would be needed on this addition to avoid having to jog the wall to meet a more restrictive setback than the old one.

request an exception from these restrictions to avoid having to jog the addition in from the existing house.

Height Variances

Most neighborhoods restrict the height of residences to two or three stories. If you intend to construct an addition that requires raising the roof to a new height exceeding the local height limits, you'll need to request a variance. If you are converting an existing attic into living space and the height of the existing roof will not be affected, these restrictions usually will not apply. However, it pays to double-check with the planning department before proceeding.

Height restrictions are being watched much more closely these days, primarily due to the advent of solar access laws. With the growing popularity of active and passive solar systems in residential construction, these laws are intended to guarantee that your neighbor's access to sunlight is not blocked by the height or positioning of your building.

Zoning Variance

In some cases, such as the example of the apartment addition cited previously, a zoning variance might be necessary. These variances occasionally are granted if the intended use of the addition does not seriously violate the neighborhood standards set forth by a particular zoning. Zoning variances usually require a full hearing of the city or county planning commission, and they are more difficult and time-consuming to obtain than simple setback variances.

Variance Applications

An application for a variance needs to be made at the offices of the planning department in the city or county where the house is located. Variances are usually time-consuming affairs, requiring from two weeks to a month or more to complete, and the fees associated with them can be substantial.

You'll need to complete the forms provided to you by the planning department. You will need to supply most or all of the following:

- A legal description of the property.
- A description of the addition, including a plot plan showing the location of the house and the proposed addition.
- A set of plans.
- A "burden of proof statement" that presents your arguments regarding why the variance should be granted.
- An application fee, which can be in the hundreds or even the thousands of dollars. Be aware that most or all of the fee is non-refundable if the variance is denied.

The planning department will review the application with you to be certain that it's complete and that you are applying for the proper thing. They will then go over the entire application and plans to determine which laws and ordinances apply to this particular situation and whether you are in compliance with them. Depending on the type and complexity of the application, other city and county departments (police, fire, public works, environmental quality, etc.) may be contacted or their input solicited.

For a variance application, notification of adjacent property owners who might be affected by the proposed variance is typically necessary, allowing your neighbors an opportunity to review the scope of the intended project and to respond within a certain time frame with their specific approvals or objections to what you have planned. You can usually avoid a considerable amount of conflict if you or your clients take a moment to visit the affected neighbors and discuss the project with them, including which variance you're applying for and why you feel it's necessary.

Remember that requesting a variance is no guarantee that it will be granted. It depends on the strictness of the ordinances in the area, the type of addition being constructed, and the cooperation of the adjacent property owners. The better the case is prepared and presented, and the more convincing you are about the need for a variance and why it cannot be avoided, the better your chances of success.

Building Permits

Any project requiring alterations to the structure, electrical wiring, or plumbing system of a home will almost certainly require a building permit. As with the zoning, height, and setback restrictions, building permits serve an important and necessary function in promoting safety in construction and avoiding potential life-threatening hazards such as faulty wiring and poor framing. Although they admittedly can be a nuisance, they are not something that can or should be avoided or circumvented.

The building permit process is the last step before actual construction begins. By this point your clients should have completed their plans, arranged their financing, applied for any necessary variances, and signed all necessary contracts.

You will need to visit the offices of the city or county building department having jurisdiction over the area in which the house is located. As with the other agencies you'll have to deal with, you will be required to fill out an application describing the addition and estimating its value. You will need the legal description of the property and at least two complete sets of plans.

A deposit will be required at the time you submit the application and plans for review, with the balance of the permit fees due at the time you pick them up. The final fees will be based on the size and estimated value of the addition.

Your plans will be checked to be sure they are in keeping with current building codes and other applicable standards. Changes might be required, and they will be listed on the plans for reference by both you and the building inspector.

Approved plans will be stamped as official copies. One set will be returned to you along with a permit card, and the other will remain on file at the building department. Depending on the complexity of the plans and the backlog at the building department, the entire process might take anywhere from a couple of days to a month or more, so plan your start dates accordingly.

Post the permit card and the stamped set of plans on the job site where they are visible and accessible to the inspector. Provide a plastic covering or other weather protection to keep the paperwork safe and dry. Failure to have the approved plans on site and accessible may prevent the inspection from taking place. You may also be required to pay a reinspection fee for the inspector to return. Also, should you lose the plans or permit card, a fee will be required to obtain replacements.

During the course of construction, it is your responsibility as the general contractor to call the building department and request inspections at the appropriate times. An inspector will visit the job and check the work, usually within 24 hours, and you must receive the inspector's approval before you move on to the next stage. Any violations will be noted on a corrections card, and you will be required to correct them and have them reinspected before you can proceed with the work.

The specific types of inspections required will vary with the type of addition and the requirements of your particular community. The most common ones follow.

Excavation, Form, and Setback Inspections

Excavation, form, and setback inspections are the first set of inspections, and the inspector will be double-checking for setback and other possible zoning violations. Footing and stem wall forms will be checked, as will any plumbing or electrical work that will be underground or contained within the concrete. These inspections need to be completed before any concrete is poured.

Underfloor Inspections

Before the subfloor is installed, some inspectors require a site visit to confirm that the floor framing is properly constructed. Plumbing, wiring, and heating ducts that will be covered by the floor are also checked at this time. You cannot cover the floor until this inspection is completed.

Rough Inspections

During the rough inspection, the inspector checks a number of things. Underfloor framing, wiring, plumbing, and mechanical systems will be inspected if they were not already checked during the underfloor inspection. You will need to have the subfloor installed, all of the walls completed (including the siding), the ceiling and roof framing in place, and the roof sheathing and roofing installed. Woodstoves and fireplaces need to be roughed in, as does the heating and cooling system.

At this time, the inspector will also typically be looking at the rough plumbing and electrical wiring and the vents for the exhaust fans. Do not install any insulation or otherwise cover the insides of the walls until this inspection has been completed successfully.

Insulation and Drywall Inspections

Requirements for the insulation and drywall inspections vary from place to place, and they may not be necessary in your area. If an insulation inspection is required, the inspector will verify that the insulation levels in walls, ceiling, and floor meet the current codes and that the material is securely and correctly installed. Dams used to prevent the insulation from contacting heat-producing fixtures such as exhaust fans, flues, and ceiling heat lamps also will be checked, as will the location, orientation, and integrity of any vapor barriers. Have this inspection done before you apply the drywall.

If a drywall inspection is required, the inspector will verify that the panels are securely fastened and that fireproof and/or waterproof drywall was used where required. The lath base for a plaster finish also will be inspected. Do not tape the drywall or apply the plaster until the insulation and drywall inspections are done.

Gas Piping Inspections

If you are installing natural gas or propane appliances, including fireplaces, there may be a gas piping inspection. You will be required to conduct a pressure test on the gas lines and show that all the lines are tight and correctly secured. A special tag is usually issued to indicate that this inspection has been passed, and that tag is necessary before the gas company will connect the appliances and activate your gas service.

Final Inspection

Before the addition can be legally occupied, the inspector will make the final inspections. Building, electrical, plumbing, and mechanical systems will all be checked. Items inspected will include proper electrical grounding, proper operation of heating and cooling equipment, compliance with fire regulations around woodstoves and fireplaces, plumbing systems and electrical appliances, and the overall quality of the structure. After this inspection is successfully completed, retain the permit card for your records.

If you have any questions about what inspections are required or what they entail, check with your building department before requesting a site visit. You can also check with the reference department of your local library for copies of the Uniform Building Code (UBC), the National Electrical Code (NEC), the Uniform Plumbing Code (UPC), the Congress of American Building Officials (CABO) code, or any other codes that are in effect in your area. Your local building department can tell you which code books are used for your particular jurisdiction.

It is a good idea to have copies of these books in your own personal library for ongoing reference. They contain a wealth of information about standard construction practices, and you'll know beforehand exactly what your inspector will be looking for.

Planning for Future Business

If you've been around construction for any length of time, you understand the concept of feast and famine. One day you have more work
than you can ever hope to handle, and the next day you're wondering
where the next job will come from. It's all part of the process of being
a contractor, but you can do a lot to increase the feast and decrease the
famine by taking some steps to plan for future business.

Ending on a High Note

Planning for the future begins with your current job. It comes from
treating your current clients right and by being genuinely concerned
about the quality of the job you're doing for them. Word-of-mouth
referrals are the lifeblood of our industry, and you get them by being
professional in your attitude about how you run your company.

As your current job winds down, it's important to keep your relationship with your clients positive. You need their final payment,
obviously, but more than that you need their respect and appreciation
for the quality of your workmanship and the honesty with which
you've treated them.

The Final Walk-Through

At the end of the job, you'll want to arrange a final walk-through with
the clients. Here again, as with your initial presentation when you were

selling the project, you'll want to have all interested parties do the walk-through at the same time. There's nothing more frustrating than taking the time to tour the job and list any corrections only to hear, "Well, it looks good to me, but you'll have to talk to my wife also."

Do the tour methodically, walking through one room at a time. Carry a clipboard, and make a note of each thing that is pointed out to you, no matter how minor. Even a small mar in the paint or a nailhead that wasn't set should be jotted down and taken care of.

If you are asked to correct something that is not your fault or that you don't feel is wrong, you need to carefully consider how to handle it. If there's a cracked molding in an area where you didn't work, you may want to point out that you didn't do anything in that area but you'd be glad to take care of it at no charge to them. On the other hand, if they're trying to pass along larger problems that were not your fault, you'll need to be polite but firm, explaining that those problems were preexisting and that repairing them would entail a charge.

Once you have the punch list completed, correct the items as quickly as possible. The longer these items wait, the more it looks like you don't wish to take care of them and the more little things the client will find to complain about. Get one of your crew over to the house that day or the following day, and get everything on the list resolved.

One idea for simplifying the punch list and making a positive impression on the homeowner is to have a punch list form made up on three-part carbonless paper. List the name of the room and the date of the walk-through at the top of the form. As you go, list each item on the form, then tear off a copy and give it to the homeowner on the spot. Give the other two copies to the crew members performing the corrections so they can check off each item as it's completed.

When the entire list is checked off, have the clients sign off at the bottom that everything is complete. They can compare the checked-off list with the original list (which is obviously the same) and confirm that everything they pointed out is now satisfactory. Give them a copy of the signed, checked-off form for their files, and keep the third copy in your own files for future reference.

Callbacks

In any construction project, it's likely that something requiring correction will surface later. A molding will warp, a faucet will start to leak, maybe a shingle or two will come loose. These latent defects, known collectively as *callback items,* need to be taken care of by the contractor as part of your original agreement with the homeowner. How well and how quickly you take care of them speaks volumes about you and your company.

Callback items, like punch-list items, need to be taken care of immediately and with a minimum of hassle for the homeowner. As soon as you are made aware of the problem, discuss it with the homeowner and perhaps swing by the house to examine it yourself. Then, assuming it's not an item that needs to be ordered, arrange to have one of your crew repair or replace the problem within two days at the most.

If the problem comes from work or materials supplied by a subcontractor, this is your responsibility as well. Arrange for the sub to meet you on the job site, and take care of the problem as quickly as possible. If you have quality subcontractors that work with you regularly, this shouldn't be a problem—they should be as concerned as you are about taking care of the client, or else they stand to lose business.

If, however, the subcontractor is unwilling to make the necessary repairs, the problem will fall back on you. You will need to either fix it yourself, if you're licensed and qualified to do that, or get another company to take care of it—at your expense—and make it clear to the original subcontractor that he or she has lost all of your future business. If the repair is expensive, you can also consider taking action against the original subcontractor's bond or pursuing the matter in civil court. You cannot, however, leave the client hanging just because your sub is unprofessional.

In virtually every state, there is a 12-month warranty on the labor and materials you provide for a construction project. But if you really care about your reputation and the future of your business, that 12-month time frame shouldn't be viewed as a magic date that lets you off the hook for any further callbacks. Within reason, you should be willing to go back out and repair items that break or wear out prematurely, either for free or at a nominal charge that covers your costs.

Documenting Your Work

If a picture is worth a thousand words, then nowhere is this more true than in remodeling, where clients often have a difficult time visualizing construction projects, and where a room addition or a bright new kitchen can make a dramatic impression.

One investment that will pay great dividends in the future is a good-quality 35mm camera or a video camera. Purchase both if you can afford it. Get in the habit of photographing your projects from the moment they begin. As a job progresses, take color pictures or videotapes of the following areas:

- *The job site prior to starting.* Photograph or tape every room that will be affected by the new addition, and also take several shots of the exterior from a variety of angles, including the walls, roof, windows, and other areas where you know you'll be making tie-ins.

- *Structural solutions.* Photograph how the foundations tie together and how the new walls intersect with the old ones. Get pictures of how you removed a wall and what was done to support the new framing. You'll also want pictures showing how you framed the roof intersections, and don't forget your siding tie-ins. Frame your shots with future clients in mind, and minimize pictures of clutter and demolition.

- *In-progress pictures showing other interesting facets of the construction.* Include setting tile or cabinets, special trim features, different door and window surrounds, and other areas that will help you illustrate a point in the future.

- *Unique features.* Always take pictures of any remodeling you do that is particularly unique and impressive. A custom-built bathtub or shower, for example, or a deck anchored to a rock outcropping. Special-purpose cabinets, interesting trim materials or patterns, custom windows—anything that's out of the ordinary. Even if it's something you'll probably never do again, it serves to illustrate your craftsmanship and your ability to be innovative and creative in the face of difficult requests.

- *"After" photographs.* Be sure to get a selection of photos or tapes after the job is completed. When taking these, review your original "before" photos, and try to shoot the pictures from the same vantage points. It's very impressive to compare the original house to its perfectly blended new addition by viewing side-by-side photos taken from exactly the same spot. Don't forget the interior views as well.

Now that you have the pictures, don't just toss them into a box somewhere. Take the time to organize some of the better photos into an album. You can arrange the before-and-after photos by job, and you can also arrange a section or a separate album showing all your structural solutions. Take the albums with you when you call on a new client—before and after shots are a great inspiration for someone considering remodeling, and the structural solutions can really help you explain difficult concepts such as wall removal and roof intersections.

If you have taken videotapes of several jobs, you should arrange to have them professionally edited onto one tape in standard VCR format. Keep the tape short—no more than 5 to 7 minutes—and have copies made for new clients. You can view it with them at their house or your office, or leave it with them so they can view it at their leisure.

Soliciting Referrals

As mentioned several times previously—this a concept that can't be overstressed—word-of-mouth referrals are *the* best source of new business. You can spend a fortune on newspaper ads, brochures, Yellow Pages ads and other forms of marketing, but you'll almost certainly end up getting more work from positive referrals then from anywhere else.

As the job comes to a close, don't forget to ask your clients if you can use them as references. Ask if you may place their names on your former-client list and if they're willing to receive phone calls from new clients. Also, if they have specific positive things to say about the project ("I never thought anyone could add on to this old house and make it blend in so well," "I can't believe how efficient this new kitchen layout is," "None of the neighbors can tell where the old house stopped and the addition begins"), write them down and ask if it's okay to quote them in future advertising.

Create a client referral list and make it a point to keep it updated. List the clients' name and address (and their phone number if you've received permission to give it out), along with a brief description of the work you did. You should always have this list available to hand out to anyone who is considering using your services.

Client Evaluation Forms

At the end of each job, ask your clients to complete a simple evaluation form. You can hand it to them at the completion of the final walk-through and punch list, at the time you collect your final payment, or in the envelope accompanying your final billing.

Custom-tailor the form to solicit the type of information you need to help your company learn and grow. You should ask about the bid process and whether they were given the answers and information they were looking for. Were they happy with the time frame for the estimate and the overall project? Did they like the subs you had on the job? Were they pleased with your crew and your office staff? What about the quality of the workmanship and the quality of the materials?

Make the questions easy to answer, and use a rating system that's easy for you to refer to and compare (rating 1 through 5, poor through excellent, etc.) and also give them a few lines for comments. Follow up on any problems they point out, and use the information as a learning tool for you and everyone in your company. And, of course, make copies of the best ones for inclusion in your estimating package!

Conducting an Open House

One of the first things that many clients want to do is to have a party to show off their shiny new addition, and this can be a wonderful opportunity for you to do some marketing. This can take a number of forms, from a summer barbecue on their new deck to a holiday cocktail party to a two-hour open house after work.

If they mention that they are planning a party and they want you to attend, consider asking how you can help out. Offer to donate some money toward the refreshments or to have your crew come over and help get things ready or clean up afterward. If they're receptive, ask if they mind if you have a small, tasteful display set up on a table in one corner. Have a couple of the before-and-after pictures blown up and framed to use as a focal point—you can give them to the clients afterward if you like—and have some of your business cards and brochures available.

Be sure to attend the party in person. You don't have to stay long, and you shouldn't treat it as an opportunity to solicit everyone in the room. On the other hand, it's a great opportunity to meet new people—

and potential clients—and to take a moment to bask in the compliments that inevitably accompany a job well done.

Thank-You Cards and Gifts

When the job is completely finished and you've received your final payment, a nice, easy way to wrap things up is to send a thank-you card. You can buy these individually at a card store, or you can buy a box of them printed with your company name and logo. The card should be simple and professional, thanking the clients for the opportunity to work with them—don't use it as an opportunity to make a sales pitch. Even if the card is imprinted with your company name, be sure you sign it and add a couple of personal words.

Thank-you cards should also be sent to people who give you referrals. If a past client, supplier, or subcontractor refers a new client to you, don't ignore it. A thank-you card with a few personal words at the bottom really means a lot to clients who went out of their way to do something nice for you. Acknowledge it, and it's much more likely to happen again in the future.

Small gifts are another way to express your appreciation and to help generate future business. At the completion of a job, you might want to send a potted plant to your clients as an "addition-warming" present. Plants are better than flowers because they last longer—whenever the client waters the plant, he or she will remember where it came from.

For subcontractors and suppliers who go out of their way to be helpful, either by sending you a good referral or by helping you solve a problem or deal with a troublesome client, a small gift would also be very appropriate. Consider a gift certificate to a local restaurant or a favorite store, or deliver some of their favorite wine, beer, pastries, or other treats. The main idea here is not how much you spend—gifts of this sort shouldn't be too expensive or the recipient will feel awkward and even obligated—it's the fact that you took the time to acknowledge what they did for you.

Name Recognition

You probably know someone in your town whose name is almost always associated with a particular product or service—"Yeah, you need your car fixed, see Tom at T&R Auto." That type of name recognition is absolutely invaluable to the success of a company, but it takes time and effort to develop. Depending on your personality and your likes and dislikes, there are a number of relatively easy (and mostly free or inexpensive) things you can do to promote your business, keep your name in the public eye, and be recognized by others as an expert in your field.

Community Organizations and Events

Joining a community organization such as Rotary is a great way to meet new people and further your business. There are regular lunches you can attend and a variety of special events in which you can participate. The Chamber of Commerce is an excellent organization to join—it's great for both promoting your business and letting your clients know that you choose to be associated with other professional businesspeople.

Whatever your particular preferences and talents outside of the building trades, you're sure to find a niche where you can volunteer some time, have some fun, and get your name out into the community in a "soft," nonadvertised manner:

- Volunteer with your local community theater to build sets. It's fun, people will admire your handiwork, and you'll get your company name in the program.

- Play in a local golf tournament. You'll meet people and get your name out there, and what's better than playing golf while still being able to say you're working. There are also tennis tournaments and other competitive events you might find interesting.

- Sponsor a team. If you enjoy playing softball, get a team together from your employees, subs, and suppliers. It's a nice treat for them, and you'll have a group of people out there once or twice a week with your company name on their shirts. The same holds true for a bowling team, cycling team, ice hockey team, rowing team, ski team, or any other sport you find interesting in your community. You can also sponsor a Little League team.

Press Releases

An often-overlooked promotional idea that's free for the asking is to send press releases to your local newspaper, the Chamber of Commerce (if you're a member), and business or trade papers in your area. These can be on just about anything noteworthy that's happening in your company, from seminars you attended to new equipment or skills you've just acquired.

A press release should follow the specific format required for the publication you're sending it to, and you can get that by simply requesting it. The generic form is as follows:

T&T Builders
For information contact: Tina Smith, 555-4958

For Immediate Release:
Tim Thompson of T&T Builders in Adamsville recently attended a three-day comprehensive seminar on new roofing techniques for contractors. The seminar was sponsored by the National Bureau of Roofing Suppliers, and covered a wide range of the most current roofing products and installation procedures. T&T Builders is a full-service remodeling company specializing in room additions.

Writing, Lecturing, and Teaching

If you enjoy the written word or aren't frightened to death of appearing in front of a group, there are dozens of opportunities all around for promoting your company.

WRITING

- *Article Writing* You might consider writing an article for the local newspaper, trade journals, supplier newsletters, or any of a wide range of other publications that are always looking for material. Select a specific topic that you're comfortable with, and keep it focused (for example, "Roof Intersections for Room Additions" rather than an article on room additions in general).

  Before preparing the article, write or call the publication you're interested in and request its writer's guidelines. This will give you all the information you need about length, style, layout, and intended audience. Follow the guidelines, and submit the article in a time frame that meets the publication's specific deadlines.

- *Newsletters* If you like to write, consider a company newsletter. You can send it to past clients and others in the community that you think might be interested—real estate companies, for example. Keep your newsletter fairly short, interesting, and diverse, with a wide range of topics. Focus on construction, but include a few humorous pieces as well—a joke, perhaps, or a reprint of a humorous article or story (get permission first).

Newsletters published more than four times a year probably won't be read, so conserve your resources for maximum effect. Be sure to note new advancements in the industry and new occurrences at your company. You can also include photos of your latest additions.

SPEAKING ENGAGEMENTS

Many local community organizations are constantly looking for people to speak at their functions. This is usually only a 10- to 15-minute presentation, and it can be on just about any topic. Stick to subjects you know, and try to have some handouts or visual aids—slides, overheads, a short video—to liven up the presentation.

You can usually get the names of organizations looking for speakers through the local Chamber or thorough community groups. Some larger towns and cities have speakers bureaus listed in the Yellow Pages, and you can also ask around among your suppliers.

TEACHING

One fun and interesting way to promote your business is to teach a class. Many communities have adult or continuing education classes that cover a wide range of topics, including woodworking, remodeling, home maintenance, interior decorating, drafting, design, and a host of others.

Teaching of this sort does not require a college degree or teaching credentials, and the sponsoring organization (your local community college, for example) will take care of all the advertising, class schedules, meeting rooms, and so forth—you just have to show up and teach. And you'll even get paid for your efforts.

Have a clear idea of what you'd like to teach and how long the class should be, what types of materials you want to make available, and how many students you want to deal with at one time.

Payment Issues and Conflict Resolution

N o matter how well you try to run your business and conduct your jobs, it's pretty much inevitable that you'll eventually have problems with one of your clients. These can range from minor misunderstandings to larger disputes over materials or workmanship all the way up to court action for nonpayment.

It is a sign of our times that problem situations involving contractors are becoming more likely to occur with each passing year. Many reputable, long-term contractors (and people in other facets of the building trades, as well) have commented that they've spent more time huddling with lawyers and chasing after money in the last two or three years than they have in the 15 or 20 years previously. As one accountant told me, "It's no longer a matter of *if* you'll get sued, it's a matter of *when.*" For many people, this is all too true.

People have become accustomed to the mind-set that the only solution to a problem is litigation, and no matter how stupid the reason and how frivolous the lawsuit, they'll find a lawyer willing to take the case. Until we have some sort of tort reform in the United States, and until we limit the number of new lawyers that can be admitted to the bar each year, this problem is only going to get worse. Accept it and prepare for it.

The best that you, as a contractor, can do to protect yourself is to be professional and honest in your dealing with people, and don't take anything for granted. The lawyers have made it a reality that the handshake deal and the verbal agreement are things of the past, so get anything and everything in writing, and in as much detail as you can. Have your clients sign a contract that you've had checked by a lawyer, and have all your changes put in writing and signed as well (see Chapter 7).

Payment Requests

If you've been thorough in your preparations for your job (and you have to be), you will have a signed contract with a payment schedule. As noted in Chapter 7, that payment schedule must be clearly spelled out, including the amount due and the specific event (frame inspection, final inspection, etc.) that triggers the payment.

A few days in advance of the payment due date, send a statement to your client. The statement should indicate the exact amount of the next draw payment that's due, plus the amount of any extras that have been added during this billing cycle. You should also show any credits accrued to the client, as well as a running total of the amount paid to date.

Banks and Mortgage Companies

If your client has financed the addition through a bank, credit union, mortgage company, or any of a variety of other lending institutions, it may be necessary to make draw requests to the bank as well as to the client. At the time you sign the contract, this should be discussed and clarified.

Every lender is different in how it disperses its loan proceeds. Some may require only a phone call from the client to transfer the money immediately into the client's account. Others may require that a request form be completed, specifically listing what work has been completed and what the draw money is to be used for. Still others will require an inspector—either an employee of the lending institution or an outside inspector—to check and verify completion of that portion of the job for which the money is being requested.

It is technically the client's responsibility to handle all of these arrangements, to complete whatever forms are necessary, and to arrange for any inspections. It is, however, in your own best interest to help out in any way you can. Make calls, write letters, hand-deliver paperwork, meet the inspector—do what you can to speed things along.

You might be surprised to find out how long some of these payment draws can take. It's not unusual, for example, to wait a week or more for an inspector to come out for a 5-minute walk-through to verify what you already told the bank on the phone and in writing. Other lending institutions may have their main offices halfway across the country, so you sit in Oregon or wherever and wait for a check to be issued at some faceless accounting office in Chicago or Texas and make its way to you by what always seems to be the slowest possible route.

Again, clarify with your clients any potential problems so you can be prepared for them. If you know there will be delays in inspections or checks being issued, start the draw payment schedule as soon as you possibly can.

Late Payments

Your contract and your own company policy should dictate how you handle late payments. For a small company, the best solution is always to just ask your client about the payment. The most common problem you'll encounter is that construction companies don't typically bill on regular cycles—they bill when the work reaches predetermined levels of completion. This sometimes leads people to simply set the bill aside and neglect to pay it. A simple phone call reminding them that the payment is overdue is often enough to handle the situation. You may also need to write a letter stating that the payment is past due and requesting your draw.

If a payment continues to be in arrears even after your phone call, you need to find out why. I've heard a variety of reasons from a variety of different types of clients, but here are the three most common:

1. *The suspicious client:* "I'm not going to pay that next draw until you fix that broken piece of molding in the closet. If I pay you, I know you'll never fix it." It's a shame that some people go through life being so mistrustful of everyone that you are left waiting for a $10,000 draw until you replace a $2 piece of molding. The best thing to do with clients like this is tell them you'll be out right away to fix the molding, and ask them to please have a check ready when you finish.

2. *The anal-retentive client:* "I'm planning to pay you, I just haven't finished going over all of the bills and receipts. I've added everything up, and there's a 65-cent discrepancy that I need to locate." In this case, I usually tell the client to send me the draw minus the 65 cents, and we'll sit down and get that straightened out before the next draw is due. But be forewarned—with this type of client you'll have to find that 65 cents sometime.

3. *The dishonest client:* After repeated assurances that the check is in the mail, these clients finally admit that they don't have the money. They may claim they're waiting for a CD to mature or for loan proceeds to be transferred into a different account, or they may simply look you in the eye and say, "Sorry, we spent the money on something else." Whatever the reason, when clients admit that there is no money to pay you, *stop work immediately.* Do not dig your financial hole any deeper. Instead, explain that as soon as they catch up on their past-due account, you'll get going again. If payment still is not forthcoming, legal actions may be necessary (see following).

Late-Payment Charges

This matter of company policy is something you should decide on *before* you draw up your contract. Different states have different rules on whether you can charge interest or late-payment charges if you have not previously specified it in your contract, so the best course of action is to have your attorney prepare the contract form with the proper language to alert your clients of financial penalties that may apply if they fail to make specified payments within a set time period.

Once you have established your right to assess a finance charge, whether you actually do so is up to you. If, for example, you learn from your clients that they are waiting for their bank to release the loan funds, and if that client has been honest with you in the past, you'd probably want to waive the finance charges. On the other hand, with someone like the dishonest client mentioned earlier, you'll want to garner every dime that you're legally entitled to.

Collection Agencies

If you are unable to collect your money on your own, you may need to resort to a collection agency. Collection agencies typically charge either a flat fee or, more commonly, a percentage of what they collect. This percentage is usually pretty steep—30 to 40 percent or even more—so going this route should be a last resort. On the other hand, if you've tried everything else, getting 60 to 70 percent of what's owed you is certainly better than nothing.

Each state has very specific laws concerning the conduct of collection agencies, and while you certainly want to collect your money, you don't want your company associated with an agency that is not legal, ethical, and honest. Ask around for some recommendations from contractors or others who've had to use a collection agency. If you need to resort to the Yellow Pages, be sure to ask for client references, and follow up on a few of them before hiring anyone.

Once your client's account has been turned over to a collection agency, remember that you can have no further dealings with it. Even if the client calls and offers to pay you in full or wants to set up a payment schedule, you will need to refer them to the collection agency.

Small-Claims Court

Another avenue for collecting what's owed to you is to file in small-claims court. The fee is nominal, and you can request that the sheriff or other official serve the papers.

At the court hearing, the burden of proof will be on you to show why these people owe you money, so be prepared to present a clear, concise, and well-researched case. You need to have all of your dates and figures in order and be able to document as many previous conversations with your clients as possible. You will also be asked to document exactly how you arrived at the figure you are suing for.

If you win—or if the other party doesn't show up in court—you will receive a judgment against your clients. You will then need to take action to collect the judgment, which may be as simple as requesting and receiving a certified check from them, or it may involve further legal action (see following).

When Problems Occur

When problems occur during or after the job, sit down with your clients as soon as possible and attempt to resolve them. Most problems are the result of simple misunderstandings, and talking them out is usually all it takes. Have all parties present if possible. This should include both homeowners and, if applicable, a subcontractor or material supplier.

- Ask for a clear explanation of exactly what your clients don't like. Don't allow vague answers ("It just doesn't look right"). Ask for specifics.

- Ask them specifically what they feel should be done to rectify the situation. Do they want something to be replaced, repaired, cleaned, or repainted, or are they looking for some sort of financial compensation?

- If you're at fault, fix the problem immediately. Don't make excuses about how or why something turned out the way it did. Don't look for employees or other people to blame—just fix it promptly and pleasantly and put it behind you.

- If there is some disagreement over who's at fault, seek a compromise. Suggest that you will take care of the labor if they will pay for the materials, or maybe you could share the repair costs equally.

- Put practicality over principles if you need to. If the client is asking you to fix something you really don't feel is your fault, and they're holding up thousands of dollars that will be difficult and expensive to collect, swallowing hard and just fixing the thing may be the most practical thing to do.

Third-Party Arbitration

If the problem still can't be worked out, third-party arbitration (the use of a disinterested third party to hear both sides and work out an agreement) may offer a good solution. Arbitration, however, like any legal action, takes time, so make every effort to resolve the problem yourselves before seeking any outside help.

Most state contractors' boards have an arbitration department that is there for just this type of situation. There are also independent arbitration companies, and some attorneys and even judges offer these services. Also, a growing number of communities are offering community dispute-resolution programs to assist with this type of arbitration.

The first thing you need to do is to select a mutually agreeable third party. You may need to offer your clients several names that are agreeable to you and ask them to select one. You then need to agree on a time and place for the arbitration (possibly the job site if there are workmanship issues to be inspected and discussed) and the type of arbitration that will be conducted.

There are two basic types of arbitration: binding and nonbinding. With *binding arbitration,* both parties agree that the decision of the arbitrator is binding. If the arbitrator tells you to fix something or tells the homeowner to pay you a certain amount, that's the end of it.

With *nonbinding arbitration,* the arbitrator is there simply to render an opinion, but no party is bound to act upon it. Nonbinding arbitration is, in my opinion, a waste of time—if either party doesn't like what the arbitrator suggests, he or she can walk away and nothing will have been resolved.

Liens and Lawsuits

The absolute last resort for resolving a dispute and collecting money is a lawsuit. We're all aware of how expensive lawyers are and how ridiculously time-consuming and drawn out any legal action is, so be sure you have exhausted every other avenue open to you before resorting to a lawsuit.

If you've determined that a lawsuit is the only alternative, the first thing to do is file a construction or mechanic's lien against the property where the work was performed. This is a fairly involved process to do correctly, and, unfortunately, you'll probably need to hire a lawyer to do it. You can do it yourself, but if you make any mistakes along the way, you could invalidate your entire claim, so it's best to leave this to an attorney.

The lien has several elements to it, as follows.

- *An exact accounting of what you claim is due you.* This figure will reflect the amount of the original contract, the amount of any change orders, and the amount of any payments that have been made against the account. To the final amount owed you for the work will be added interest payments, court costs, attorney fees (if your contract provided for them), and any other reasonable costs associated with the construction project and your efforts to collect the account.

- *Notification of all parties with an interest in the house.* This list includes the homeowners, their mortgage company, any lenders holding a second deed of trust on the home, even family members who have loaned money and taken an interest in the house as collateral.

- *Specific time frames.* You need to file the lien within a specified time frame as allocated by law, usually within 75 days of the last *substantial* work you did on the house. Note the word *substantial*—you typically can't go out and fix a piece of trim or paint a window just to extend your lien rights.

Once the lien has been filed, you can simply leave it at that if desired. The lien is against the piece of property, so the owner will be unable to sell or otherwise legally transfer the property without first having to deal with the lien. If the house is about to be sold, this gives you some very powerful leverage. If, on the other hand, the owners plan to stay put for the foreseeable future, it really doesn't help you out in your efforts to get paid.

Foreclosure

For that reason, the next step after filing the lien is to take legal action to foreclose against the property. The same would hold true if you have received a small-claims court judgment and are unable to collect in any other way.

Foreclosure requires a court hearing, which may be in front of a judge or in full court with a jury present. Your attorney will present your side of things, outlining the construction project, what has been paid to date, what is still owed, and why you are seeking foreclosure. The other party will do the opposite, describing what you have done wrong with the project and outlining reasons you should not be paid. In some instances, the other party may file a countersuit, seeking damages from you.

If you win, a judgment will be issued against the house, forcing the owners to vacate it within a certain period of time. You will have a couple of different options at that point, including satisfying any outstanding debts against the property and taking it over or forcing the sale of the property to collect the proceeds. Remember that the first mortgage holder and possibly other lien holders may have the right to be paid ahead of you, and, after all your work, time, and expense, it may turn out that there is not enough left over to satisfy your judgment.

Foreclosure is obviously a very serious and complicated process. It should be strictly a last resort, and should definitely be left in the hands of a competent attorney.

The Building Side

Demolition and Transitions

One of the most unique aspects of building a room addition is the need to remove a portion of the existing home in order to tie the old and new sections together, all the while making the new section look like it has always been there.

The amount of demolition work and the number of transition areas will vary widely among room additions. Some might require only the removal of a little siding, while others might necessitate removing walls, plumbing, and electrical wiring. All the demolition may occur at the start of the job, or there may be ongoing demolition in different areas as the addition progresses. For that reason, this chapter is the first to discuss the actual construction. It offers an introduction to some of the problems that may come up, so you'll be better equipped to deal with them.

Demolition Safety

No matter how small or insignificant a task might seem, the first and most crucially important rule of demolition is to do it safely. Too many people have been seriously injured by not paying attention to basic safety issues, losing limbs, eyesight, hearing, even lives. Besides human injury or loss of life, a serious accident involving one of your employees can result in lawsuits and/or major fines from the Occupational Safety and Health Administration (OSHA), possibly putting your company out of business.

Be Prepared

First of all, never take any demolition project for granted, no matter how minor it seems. Think through your actions ahead of time, and be ready with the proper clothing, tools, and equipment for the job at hand. Always remain aware of your personal safety and the safety of the others around you, as well as the need to prevent your actions from undermining the structural integrity of the building:

- Always know exactly what it is you're about to remove. Before you move or remove anything, always check to see what's behind it, below it, and what it might support.

- Never assume that a structural member you're about to remove doesn't support anything.

- When removing framing that is near electrical wiring, shut off the electricity, even if you're not actually removing the wiring. Do the same for any plumbing or gas lines. A single nick with a saw blade or a drill bit can have disastrous results.

- When removing electrical wiring, turn off the circuit breaker or remove the fuse controlling the circuit you're working on, then post a note on the electrical panel warning others not to turn it back on.

- Never attempt to work on a gas or water line without first making certain it has been shut off. Also, do not assume that a shut-off valve works—after closing the valve, test the line to be absolutely certain it's off.

Tools and Clothing

A worker wearing a pair of shorts and equipped with only a hammer and a big screwdriver is hardly well equipped for demolition work, but you'd be surprised how often you see this on job sites every day. Once again, you open yourself and your crew members to serious injury, and you put your company at risk for crippling financial penalties.

- Use only the proper tool that is designed for a particular task—don't improvise. If you are prying up a board, use a heavy pry bar, not a big screwdriver. On the other hand, use a screwdriver to remove a screw, don't yank it out with a pry bar.

■ If you don't have the proper tool for the job, don't proceed until you are able to buy or rent one. If you need a jack to lift a heavy beam, get one—don't try to rig up a couple of 2 × 4s as a lever. If scaffolding is required to work safely at a given height, get some and take the time to set it up correctly—balancing a 2 × 12 on a couple of ladders is an invitation for disaster!

■ Wear the appropriate clothing. Demolition work requires long pants, a heavy shirt, and solid shoes—allowing your crew to work in shorts and tennis shoes can net you a serious fine. Wear gloves, and always wear eye protection. If anyone is working above you, or if there is any potential for falling objects, make hard hats mandatory.

Homeowner Protection

When you are working in someone's home, you have a legal and moral obligation to protect both the home and its occupants. This requires that you be aware of the work you are doing at all times and that you leave the site in a safe condition every evening—the last thing you want is for someone to be injured on your site as a result of your negligence.

Beyond the devastating personal effects of an injury, there are the financial effects as well. Construction is a dangerous business, and fair or not, you will almost certainly be held liable for anyone who comes on the job site and injures him- or herself with your equipment. One thing you can count on these days is the willingness of people to sue you over anything and everything, and there is always a lawyer hovering in the wings, ready to take the case and sue you out of existence.

Be safe, and keep the security of your job site in mind at all times:

■ Secure all tools at lunchtime, at the end of the day, and during extended absence from the job site (e.g., when you go to pick up materials). Cords need to be unplugged and sharp tools placed in a safe and secure enclosure. Remember that children are fascinated with construction sites, and this curiosity can lead to serious injury.

- Motorized equipment (tractors, backhoes, hoists, etc.) needs to be securely locked and the keys placed in a safe, locked area.

- Take down ladders at the end of the day. Whenever possible, secure and protect scaffolding to prevent unauthorized use.

- Cover holes and other danger spots. This includes covering holes in the floor and placing temporary barricades over window and door openings.

- If you cannot cover or otherwise close off an area—such as an open trench that is still in use—ring the area with caution tape and place lighted barricades at regular intervals as a warning.

Material Safety Data Sheets

No discussion of job-site safety would be complete without mentioning the importance of Material Safety Data Sheets (MSDS) (Figure 11.1). People in the building trades are constantly exposed to fumes and incidental chemical contacts that have harmful—even deadly—potential. That's why OSHA (and common sense) dictates that you and all of your employees have access to MSDSs, a mandatory system of safety and medical information provided by manufacturers about the products they sell. If a product or natural compound is available for public use, an MSDS exists for it.

Granted, this can get a little ridiculous (there's an MSDS for sand and even one for water), but for the most part an MSDS provides you with vitally important information. MSDSs are available wherever you buy your products, whether from a wholesaler or directly from the manufacturer—just ask.

The MSDS is broken into 10 standard categories using consistent codes, abbreviations, and terminology. The following example for sodium hydroxide (the chemical name for common lye) gives you an idea of how the categories are arranged and the information they contain.

1. Product Identification

The first category gives the generic product name, in this case sodium hydroxide, and, if the MSDS is for a specific brand (Acme Lye, for example) it also lists the brand name. Also here is the product's

```
------------------------------------------------------------------------
MSDS for   SODIUM HYDROXIDE                          Page  1
------------------------------------------------------------------------

------------------------------------------------------------------------
   1 - PRODUCT IDENTIFICATION
------------------------------------------------------------------------

PRODUCT NAME:    SODIUM HYDROXIDE
FORMULA:         NAOH
FORMULA WT:       40.00
CAS NO.:         01310-73-2
NIOSH/RTECS NO.: WB4900000
COMMON SYNONYMS: CAUSTIC SODA;  SODIUM HYDRATE;  LYE
PRODUCT CODES:   3730,3722,5312,5104,3729,3734,3726,5045,3728,3723,5022,3736
  EFFECTIVE: 08/28/86
  REVISION #02

                       PRECAUTIONARY LABELLING
BAKER SAF-T-DATA(TM) SYSTEM

                    HEALTH        - 3  SEVERE (POISON)
                    FLAMMABILITY  - 0  NONE
                    REACTIVITY    - 2  MODERATE
                    CONTACT       - 4  EXTREME (CORROSIVE)
HAZARD RATINGS ARE 0 TO 4 (0 = NO HAZARD; 4 = EXTREME HAZARD).

LABORATORY PROTECTIVE EQUIPMENT

GOGGLES; LAB COAT; VENT HOOD; PROPER GLOVES

PRECAUTIONARY LABEL STATEMENTS

                       POISON DANGER
                    CAUSES SEVERE BURNS
                  MAY BE FATAL IF SWALLOWED
DO NOT GET IN EYES, ON SKIN, ON CLOTHING.  AVOID SPATTERING BY SLOWLY
ADDING TO SOLUTION.
AVOID BREATHING DUST.  KEEP IN TIGHTLY CLOSED CONTAINER.  USE WITH ADEQUATE
VENTILATION.  WASH THOROUGHLY AFTER HANDLING.

SAF-T-DATA(TM) STORAGE COLOR CODE:    WHITE STRIPE (STORE SEPARATELY)

------------------------------------------------------------------------
   2 - HAZARDOUS COMPONENTS
------------------------------------------------------------------------

                  COMPONENT                    %    CAS NO.

SODIUM HYDROXIDE                             90-100  1310-73-2

------------------------------------------------------------------------
   3 - PHYSICAL DATA
------------------------------------------------------------------------

BOILING POINT:    1390 C ( 2534 F)    VAPOR PRESSURE(MM HG): 0

MELTING POINT:     318 C (  604 F)    VAPOR DENSITY(AIR=1):  N/A


------------------------------------------------------------------------
MSDS for   SODIUM HYDROXIDE                          Page  2
------------------------------------------------------------------------
SPECIFIC GRAVITY: 2.13                EVAPORATION RATE:     N/A
   (H2O=1)                              (BUTYL ACETATE=1)
```

FIGURE 11.1

An example of a Material Safety Data Sheet (MSDS).

```
    SOLUBILITY(H2O):     APPRECIABLE (MORE THAN 10 %)  % VOLATILES BY VOLUME: 0

    APPEARANCE & ODOR:  WHITE, ODORLESS SOLID.

    -------------------------------------------------------------------------
       4 - FIRE AND EXPLOSION HAZARD DATA
    -------------------------------------------------------------------------

    FLASH POINT (CLOSED CUP   N/A              NFPA 704M RATING:  3-0-1

    FLAMMABLE LIMITS:  UPPER - N/A  %        LOWER - N/A  %

    FIRE EXTINGUISHING MEDIA
      USE EXTINGUISHING MEDIA APPROPRIATE FOR SURROUNDING FIRE.

    SPECIAL FIRE-FIGHTING PROCEDURES
      FLOOD WITH WATER, DO NOT SPLATTER OR SPLASH THIS MATERIAL.

    UNUSUAL FIRE & EXPLOSION HAZARDS
      CONTACT WITH MOISTURE OR WATER MAY GENERATE SUFFICIENT HEAT TO
      IGNITE COMBUSTIBLE MATERIALS.
      REACTS WITH MOST METALS TO PRODUCE HYDROGEN GAS, WHICH CAN FORM AN
      EXPLOSIVE MIXTURE WITH AIR.

    -------------------------------------------------------------------------
       5 - HEALTH HAZARD DATA
    -------------------------------------------------------------------------

    TLV LISTED DENOTES CEILING LIMIT.

    THRESHOLD LIMIT VALUE (TLV/TWA):    2   MG/M3 (       PPM)

    PERMISSIBLE EXPOSURE LIMIT (PEL):   2   MG/M3 (       PPM)

    TOXICITY:   LD50 (IPR-MOUSE)(MG/KG)        - 40

    CARCINOGENICITY:  NTP: NO     IARC: NO     Z LIST: NO     OSHA REG: NO

    EFFECTS OF OVEREXPOSURE
      EXCESSIVE INHALATION OF DUST IS IRRITATING AND MAY BE SEVERELY DAMAGING
      TO RESPIRATORY PASSAGES AND/OR LUNGS.
      CONTACT WITH SKIN OR EYES MAY CAUSE SEVERE IRRITATION OR BURNS.
      INGESTION IS HARMFUL AND MAY BE FATAL.
      INGESTION MAY CAUSE SEVERE BURNING OF MOUTH AND STOMACH.
      INGESTION MAY CAUSE NAUSEA AND VOMITING.

    TARGET ORGANS
      EYES, SKIN, RESPIRATORY SYSTEM

    MEDICAL CONDITIONS GENERALLY AGGRAVATED BY EXPOSURE
      NONE IDENTIFIED

    ROUTES OF ENTRY
      INHALATION, INGESTION, EYE CONTACT, SKIN CONTACT

    -------------------------------------------------------------------------
    MSDS for   SODIUM HYDROXIDE                            Page  3
    -------------------------------------------------------------------------

    EMERGENCY AND FIRST AID PROCEDURES
      CALL A PHYSICIAN.
      IF SWALLOWED, DO NOT INDUCE VOMITING; IF CONSCIOUS, GIVE LARGE AMOUNTS OF
      WATER.  FOLLOW WITH DILUTED VINEGAR, FRUIT JUICE OR WHITES OF EGGS, BEATEN
      WITH WATER.
```

FIGURE 11.1

(Continued).

IF INHALED, REMOVE TO FRESH AIR. IF NOT BREATHING, GIVE ARTIFICIAL
RESPIRATION. IF BREATHING IS DIFFICULT, GIVE OXYGEN.
IN CASE OF CONTACT, IMMEDIATELY FLUSH EYES OR SKIN WITH PLENTY OF WATER FOR
AT LEAST 15 MINUTES WHILE REMOVING CONTAMINATED CLOTHING AND SHOES.
WASH CLOTHING BEFORE RE-USE.

----
   6 - REACTIVITY DATA

STABILITY: STABLE   HAZARDOUS POLYMERIZATION: WILL NOT OCCUR

CONDITIONS TO AVOID: MOISTURE

INCOMPATIBLES: WATER, STRONG ACIDS, MOST COMMON METALS,
                       COMBUSTIBLE MATERIALS, ORGANIC MATERIALS,
                       ZINC, ALUMINUM, MAGNESIUM, HALOGENATED HYDROCARBONS

----
   7 - SPILL AND DISPOSAL PROCEDURES

STEPS TO BE TAKEN IN THE EVENT OF A SPILL OR DISCHARGE
   WEAR SELF-CONTAINED BREATHING APPARATUS AND FULL PROTECTIVE CLOTHING.
   WITH CLEAN SHOVEL, CAREFULLY PLACE MATERIAL INTO CLEAN, DRY CONTAINER AND
   COVER; REMOVE FROM AREA. FLUSH SPILL AREA WITH WATER.

   J. T. BAKER NEUTRACIT-2(R) CAUSTIC NEUTRALIZER IS RECOMMENDED
   FOR SPILLS OF THIS PRODUCT.

DISPOSAL PROCEDURE
   DISPOSE IN ACCORDANCE WITH ALL APPLICABLE FEDERAL, STATE, AND LOCAL
   ENVIRONMENTAL REGULATIONS.

EPA HAZARDOUS WASTE NUMBER: D002, D003 (CORROSIVE, REACTIVE WASTE)

----
   8 - PROTECTIVE EQUIPMENT

VENTILATION: USE GENERAL OR LOCAL EXHAUST VENTILATION TO MEET
                       TLV REQUIREMENTS.

RESPIRATORY PROTECTION: RESPIRATORY PROTECTION REQUIRED IF AIRBORNE
                       CONCENTRATION EXCEEDS TLV. AT CONCENTRATIONS UP
                       TO 60 PPM, A HIGH-EFFICIENCY PARTICULATE
                       RESPIRATOR IS RECOMMENDED. ABOVE THIS LEVEL, A
                       SELF-CONTAINED BREATHING APPARATUS IS ADVISED.

EYE/SKIN PROTECTION: SAFETY GOGGLES, UNIFORM, APRON, RUBBER GLOVES ARE
                       RECOMMENDED.

MSDS for   SODIUM HYDROXIDE   Page 4

----
   9 - STORAGE AND HANDLING PRECAUTIONS

SAF-T-DATA(TM) STORAGE COLOR CODE: WHITE STRIPE (STORE SEPARATELY)

SPECIAL PRECAUTIONS
   KEEP CONTAINER TIGHTLY CLOSED. STORE IN CORROSION-PROOF AREA.
   STORE IN A DRY AREA.

FIGURE 11.1

(Continued).

```
ISOLATE FROM INCOMPATIBLE MATERIALS.

-------------------------------------------------------------------------
10 - TRANSPORTATION DATA AND ADDITIONAL INFORMATION
-------------------------------------------------------------------------

DOMESTIC (D.O.T.)

PROPER SHIPPING NAME      SODIUM HYDROXIDE, DRY SOLID
HAZARD CLASS              CORROSIVE MATERIAL (SOLID)
UN/NA                     UN1823
LABELS                    CORROSIVE
REPORTABLE QUANTITY       1000 LBS.

INTERNATIONAL (I.M.O.)

PROPER SHIPPING NAME      SODIUM HYDROXIDE, SOLID
HAZARD CLASS             8
UN/NA                     UN1823
LABELS                    CORROSIVE
```

FIGURE 11.1

(Continued).

chemical formula and weight, followed by common synonyms: caustic soda, sodium hydrate, and lye.

Next is the Precautionary Labeling information, which assigns a standard hazard warning number of 0 (no hazard) to 4 (extreme hazard) for each of four standard hazard categories: Health, Flammability, Reactivity, and Contact. For sodium hydroxide, you'll find: "Health—3, severe (poison); Flammability—0, none; Reactivity—2, moderate; Contact—4, extreme (corrosive)."

Next comes Laboratory Protective Equipment. In this case the recommendation is for goggles, lab coat, vent hood, and proper gloves. The final section of category 1 is Precautionary Label Statements and the standard Storage Color Code. For sodium hydroxide, you'll find: "Poison Danger. Causes Severe Burns. May Be Fatal If Swallowed. Do Not Get In Eyes, On Skin, On Clothing. Avoid Spattering By Slowly Adding To Solution. Avoid Breathing Dust. Keep In Tightly Sealed Container. Use With Adequate Ventilation. Wash Thoroughly After Handling. Storage Color Code: White Stripe (Store Separately)." If you've ever worked with lye, you know these are not just idle warnings.

2. Hazardous Components and 3. Physical Data

Sections 2 and 3 list specific chemical information about the material. Section 2 tells you what the hazardous components are—in this case, only sodium hydroxide, but in many cases, a product will contain several potentially dangerous ingredients. Section 3 gives you the boiling point, melting point, and other chemical data, including the material's color and appearance.

4. Fire and Explosion Hazard Data

This section tells you how flammable and potentially explosive the material is and what fire-fighting steps to take. For sodium hydroxide, the warnings include: "flood with water, do not splatter or splash this material" and "reacts with most metals to produce hydrogen gas, which can form an explosive mixture with air."

5. Health Hazard Data

Section 5 discusses "Effects of Overexposure"—what can happen from excessive inhalation, contact with skin or eyes, or ingestion. It also lists "Target Organs," which are those organs most likely to be affected (in this case "Eyes, Skin, Respiratory System" and "Routes of Entry"), and the most common ways the material will enter your body (in this case "Inhalation, Ingestion, Eye Contact, Skin Contact").

Of extreme importance in this area is "Emergency And First Aid Procedures." Here you will find a complete and comprehensive list of exactly what to do if this material is swallowed, inhaled, or comes in contact with skin or eyes.

6. Reactivity Data and 7. Spill and Disposal Procedures

Section 6 describes other things this material reacts with (in this case water, most metals, and several other things). Section 7 tells you what to do in case of a spill and which EPA Hazardous Waste Numbers, if any, are assigned to this material.

8. Protective Equipment

Here you learn what types of safety gear and protective equipment you need. In the case of sodium hydroxide, you'll find advice about ventilating work areas and what "Eye/Skin Protection" equipment to be wearing: "Safety Goggles, Uniform, Apron, Rubber Gloves Are Recommended."

9. Storage and Handling Precautions and 10. Transportation Data

Section 9 gives you storage information: "Tightly Closed," "Corrosion-Proof Area," "Dry Area," and Section 10 gives you shipping information, including proper labeling information and which agencies, if any, have regulatory authority over shipping.

Remember to ask for an MSDS for any product you purchase that you have concerns about. Also, if you're an employer and your employees are required to use anything potentially dangerous—and that's virtually everyone in virtually any type of occupation—you are required by law to have an MSDS available for every product they use.

Recycling Materials

In many instances, it is to your advantage to reuse some of the materials you are removing. If you are working with an older home, for example, much of what you tear out might be difficult to match or, in some cases, might even be valuable.

Be especially careful in removing anything that might be of use. Even if you don't intend to reuse it, you might be able to sell it. Many cities have used-building-material outlets that will buy what you have, or you can place an advertisement in the local paper. Be sure to clarify with your clients who owns the materials being torn out of the house.

Wood Moldings

Some of the items most often saved during demolition work are wood moldings and trim. Reusing these moldings can save you money over having to purchase them new, and you might not always be able to match older patterns. Carefully examine any moldings you need to remove, and decide if they can be reused in the new addition.

If a molding has been painted several times, its joints might be obscured. Also, the paint acts as a binder to keep the molding stuck to the wall or other surface, a situation which can damage the molding or the surrounding area when you try to remove it. Furthermore, old paint typically contained lead, which leaves a hard, sharp edge that is very dangerous to handle and is also a serious health hazard if chewed or swallowed. If you suspect the presence of lead-based paint in the house, contact your local office of the Environmental Protection Agency for instructions on safe removal and handling.

To begin, use a utility knife or single-edge razor blade and cut through the paint at the joints. Also cut along the seam where the molding joins the wall or other surface. Work slowly, and be careful not to gouge into the molding or wall. Using a small, flat wrecking bar (Figure 11.2), work the molding away from the wall, starting at one of the joints. Pry the molding up slowly (Figure 11.3), a few inches at a time. You will find it easiest if you place the bar near each nail that fastens the molding.

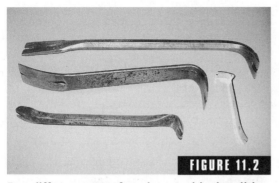

FIGURE 11.2

Four different types of pry bars used in demolition. The small one (right) is used for moldings, and the "cat's paw" (bottom left) is for pulling nails out of framing.

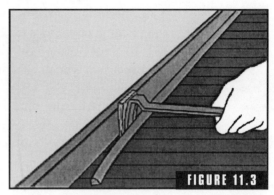

FIGURE 11.3

Using a small bar and a wood block to remove a piece of shoe molding. *(Courtesy of National Oak Flooring Manufacturer's Association.)*

When the molding has been removed, do not drive the nails back through to the front. This will cause the head to push up the surrounding wood, often splintering it. Instead, use a pair of end cutters (Figure 11.4) and work from the back. Grip the nail where it protrudes through the back of the molding, and with a rolling motion of the curved head of the end cutters, pull the nail through the molding from front to back.

These same procedures can be used for removing siding, paneling, trim, hardwood flooring, and other wooden components of the house.

Windows and Doors

The techniques for removing windows will vary depending on the type and style of window. In general, depending on whether the window has a wood or metal frame, one of two methods was probably used when it was installed. Reversing the installation methods will usually work to remove just about any type of window you encounter.

Most wood windows are built similarly to doors, and the sash is set in a frame to make up a one-piece unit. The window unit is placed in the wall opening, shimmed as necessary to make it plumb and level, then fastened by driving finish nails through the window frame into the

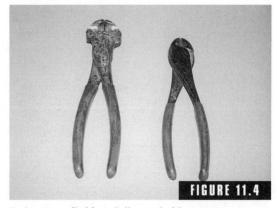

FIGURE 11.4

End cutters (left) and diagonal side cutters.

wall framing. The joint between the window frame and the wall opening is then covered with a molding.

To remove this type of window, first remove the moldings. Then, using a reciprocating saw equipped with a metal-cutting blade, cut between the window frame and the wall opening. This procedure will sever the nails and allow you to remove the entire window unit.

Metal and vinyl frame windows typically have an installation flange around the outside of the frame. Nails or screws are driven through the flange to secure the window to the outside of the wall framing, then the flange is covered with trim. Begin by removing the trim and exposing the flange. Then, working with a flat pry bar, get behind the flange and carefully pry it away from the wall. As the flange begins to come loose, work your bar or a pair of end cutters between the nail head and the flange and pull the nails.

Doors are removed pretty much like operable wood windows. Drive the hinge pins out and remove the door, then remove the door casings. It is then simply a matter of cutting between the doorjambs and the wall opening to sever the nails and remove the door frame in one piece.

Other Building Components

Other components of the building that are worth saving include just about anything bolted or screwed down and therefore easy to remove in an undamaged condition:

- Electrical appliances and fixtures, including lights, kitchen appliances, fans, heaters, and even old switches and switch plates.

- Bathroom and kitchen fixtures such as sinks, faucets, toilets, bathtubs, shower stalls, bidets, and a variety of chrome- or brass-plated pipes, valves, and water lines. It's not unusual for an old claw-foot bathtub in good condition to sell for $750 or more, and old porcelain pedestal sinks can sell for $500 or more.

- Kitchen and bathroom cabinets and preformed countertops. If you're tearing out a set of kitchen cabinets, there's a ready market for them among people who want them for use in garages and shops.

- Floor covering in good condition is also salable. If you're tearing out wall-to-wall carpet, for example, many people will buy it for use in rental houses or cabins. Hardwood flooring can typically be removed in a usable condition and also has a good resale market.

Bearing-Wall Removal

It's a virtual certainty that you will need to remove or alter a bearing wall at some point during the construction of a room addition. Even additions that are added on top of an existing house require that structural components such as ceiling joists and rafters be cut.

Bearing-wall removal is perfectly safe if done correctly, but it does present a definite hazard to both workers and the structure itself if it is undertaken improperly. Take your time, think through each step, and fully complete each phase of the work before moving on to the next.

The bearing-wall removal operation consists of four basic phases.

Phase 1: Determination of Load

Every house has two types of walls: weight-bearing walls and partition walls. A *weight-bearing wall* carries a load in addition to the weight of the wall itself, such as a ceiling joist resting on the wall's top plate or an exterior wall on a first story that has a second-story wall above it. *Partition walls,* also called *curtain walls,* carry only their own weight. A common example of a partition wall is seen in a house with manufactured roof trusses—the trusses are supported on the exterior walls, and the interior walls only serve to partition the space into individual rooms.

For a one-story house, or for walls on the upper floor of a multistory house, the best way to tell if a wall is weight-bearing is to look in the attic. Locate the top of the upper plate of the wall you're checking— you might have to move some insulation (Figures 11.5 and 11.6)—and study it carefully. Are ceiling joists spliced across the top of it? Do the rafters have vertical or diagonal bracing extending down onto the wall plates? Does the wall support any other weight, such as a roof air conditioner or solar panels? These are all obvious indications that a wall is weight-bearing.

In addition to loads that are clearly visible, certain assumptions must be made for those walls that cannot be checked. Exterior walls are always considered to be weight-bearing, because in all but a few cases they carry the weight of the roof structure. Also, because it's usually

FIGURE 11.5

A gas-powered vacuum for extracting loose-fill insulation from an attic.

impossible to check and verify without extensive demolition work, you should assume that every wall on the lower floors of a multistory house bears some of the weight of the upper floors.

As a general rule of thumb, if you can't positively verify that a wall is not weight-bearing, you should always assume that it is and proceed accordingly.

Phase 2: Temporary Bracing

Prior to actually cutting into or removing a bearing wall, it is necessary to construct some temporary bracing to support the load during the construction process. For an interior wall, start by cutting four 2 × 4s to the same length as the length of the wall you intend to remove. Nail one board to the ceiling on each side of the wall, about 2 feet out from the wall and parallel to it. Nail the other two to the floor directly under each of the ceiling boards, forming a temporary top and bottom plate (Figure 11.7).

Next, measure the distance between the two boards, and cut several 2 × 4s ⅛ of an inch longer than that measurement. Wedge these temporary studs between the plates about every 2½ feet, and toenail them to the plates to be sure they aren't inadvertently knocked loose.

For an exterior wall, you'll be able to place your temporary supports on only one side of the wall. Cut two plates and a series of studs as outlined previously, and erect the temporary frame on the inside of the exterior wall.

Phase 3: Wall Removal

Before proceeding with phase 3, take a moment to double-check that your temporary supports are securely fastened and firmly in place and that they are long enough and tight enough to be fully supporting the load on the wall you're going to remove. If you have any doubts about

FIGURE 11.6

The insulation is blown into a tarp-covered debris container.

the security or safety of your temporary supports, add additional bracing before moving on.

From the wall you're removing, measure out about 18 inches at
each end and make a mark on the ceiling. Snap a chalk line across
these two marks, and repeat the procedure on the other side of the
wall. Using a reciprocating saw or a small electric or battery-powered
circular saw, cut the drywall or plaster along the line and remove it. To
prevent possible damage to concealed wires or pipes, be sure your saw
is set only deep enough to cut through the drywall and no deeper.

Repeat for the ceiling on the other side of the wall. You will now
have two clean strips opened up on either side of the wall, exposing
the framing and leaving an area that will be easy to patch later.

Next, remove the drywall or siding from the wall itself. On dry-
walled areas, cut through the tape joints with a utility knife so that you
can remove the drywall with a minimum amount of damage to the surrounding surfaces. Siding should be cut back using a circular saw—
study the wall prior to cutting and try to cut and remove the siding in
a manner that is easy to patch into later if necessary.

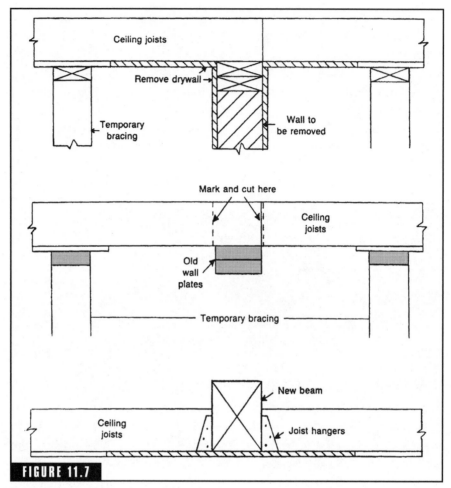

Ceiling joists

Remove drywall →

Temporary bracing

Wall to be removed

Mark and cut here

Ceiling joists

Old wall plates

Temporary bracing

New beam

Ceiling joists

Joist hangers

FIGURE 11.7

The three stages in bearing-wall removal: temporary bracing (top), removal of the wall (middle), and transfer of the wall's load to a new beam (bottom).

Immediately remove all of the debris from the area and sweep the floor. Discard it or stack it in a location that is out of your way. Don't be in a hurry—failure to get the debris out of your way presents a serious safety hazard for subsequent operations.

Now that the wall is stripped, examine it to determine any potential problems. If there is plumbing or electrical wiring to be removed, that must be completed prior to proceeding with removal of the wall. Safe removal is described later in this chapter.

Remove the wall studs one at a time, watching carefully to see that the temporary bracing is carrying the weight of the wall's load as you remove the individual studs. Using a reciprocating saw with a metal-cutting blade, cut carefully between the bottom of the stud and the top of the bottom plate, severing the nails that hold the stud in place. Pull the stud toward you at an angle to move it free of the bottom plate, then pull it sharply downward to loosen it from the nails in the top plate. Saw or snip off the nails in the upper plates—be sure to wear safety glasses. When all of the studs have been removed, pull up the bottom plate also.

If ceiling or upper-floor joists are resting on the top plate, they need to be cut back. Using a square, mark a vertical line on each of the ceiling joists, $\frac{1}{16}$ inch out from the top plates on each side of the wall, then remove the two top plates. Using a reciprocating saw with a sharp woodcutting blade—the space is too confined to use a circular saw—carefully cut along the lines and remove the ends of the ceiling joists. This work needs to be done on a ladder from below. Avoid the temptation to kneel on the ceiling joists from above, because this will put a dangerous amount of strain on the joists and their temporary supports.

Phase 4: Permanent Transfer of the Wall Load

The last step in this procedure is to transfer the load that had previously been supported by the old wall to the new, permanent supports. The most common method of doing this is to insert a beam into the opening and transfer the load onto it, which allows you to have an open, uninterrupted space where the wall used to be (Figure 11.8). Done correctly, the load will now be fully supported, and the finished ceiling and walls will show no evidence that a wall used to be in that location.

The size of the beam is critical to proper support. It must be matched to the span of the opening and be appropriate for the load it needs to support. Consult with your designer, the building department, or your local lumberyard for details on the support capabilities of the type of beam you're using and for help on determining the proper dimensions.

Measure the distance between the top plates of the two adjacent walls, outside to outside, and cut a beam to this length. Remember that

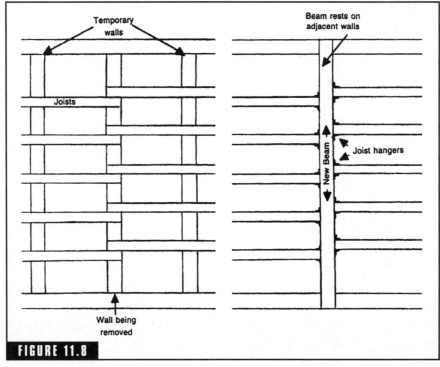

FIGURE 11.8

Top view of the same wall, showing the wall with the joists resting on it (left), then a new beam and hangers installed to support the ceiling joists once the wall is removed (right).

the opening you have formed in the ceiling by cutting back the joists along the old top plate is intended to fit a beam of the same width as the wall studs you removed—in other words, use a 3½-inch beam (a 4 × 8, 4 × 10, etc.) if you removed a 2 × 4 wall or a 5½-inch beam (a 6 × 8, 6 × 10, etc.) if you removed a 2 × 6 wall. If a thicker beam is required for your opening, cut the joists back accordingly.

Lift one end of the beam up through the gap between the joists and rest it on the adjacent wall plate. Lift the other end through the gap and slide it into position so that the beam is centered and resting fully on both plates. Toenail the beam to both of the plates.

Slide an appropriate-size joist hanger under each joist end, and nail it to the beam with approved joist-hanger nails. Be certain the bottom of the hanger does not extend past the bottom of the beam, which will cause problems with the drywall or plaster when you patch it back in. The joist hangers transfer the load, in this case the joists, onto the new beam.

Finally, gently remove the temporary supports and allow the joists to settle down into the hangers, then nail through the hangers into the joists. Watch for any sags or other signs of undue stress until the temporary bracing is removed.

Although placing the framing out of sight above the ceiling will always give the best finished appearance and avoid an "added-on" look, it might not always be possible. An alternative is to use a beam below the ceiling line. After you have erected the temporary braces as just outlined, completely remove the wall. Replace the wall framing with an appropriately sized beam, supporting it either with framing that is contained within the walls or with exposed posts that can be covered later. If you are using exposed posts, they must be attached to solid framing within the wall or extend down to the foundation. With either method, they must be secured in such a manner that they cannot become dislodged from the beam.

Removing Electrical Components

Quite often, opening up a wall will reveal electrical wires that need to be moved so that the wall framing can be removed. This is not a difficult procedure in most cases, but if you are not a licensed electrician in your state, or if you are not fully knowledgeable and comfortable with electrical work, then leave the wiring to a qualified, licensed electrician.

First, locate and disconnect the circuit you're going to be working on, which should actually be done in advance of any work on the wall, including removal of drywall. After closing the circuit, test the wiring to verify that you've disconnected the correct circuit (Figure 11.9), then place a note in the electrical panel and a piece of tape over the breaker to be certain someone doesn't turn it back on. Never assume

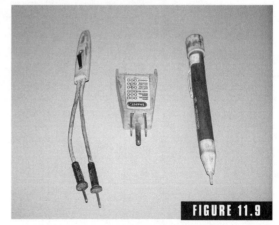

FIGURE 11.9

Electrical testers, including a two-lead tester for 120 volts (left), a plug-in tester for 120-volt outlets (middle), and a special tester that lights up in the presence of electrical current, even through an insulation jacket (right).

that the labeling in the electrical panel is correct—*always* test the circuit to be sure it's off.

If you are removing a wall containing outlets in the middle of a circuit, which is typically the case, you will need to reroute your wiring rather than just remove it—otherwise the other outlets and switches down line from where you're working will cease to function.

Rerouting 120-Volt Outlets and Switches

Once the wall has been stripped of drywall or plaster, the electrical cables will be visible. Trace where the cables enter and exit the outlet box you wish to remove. Follow the cables in each direction to a point in the attic (or under the floor if they come up that way) where they are out of the way of the wall being removed. Cut each cable at those points.

Attach a junction box to a convenient joist near each cut cable, again making sure it is out of the way of the wall being removed (Figure 11.10). Feed each cut cable into its respective junction box, run a new piece of cable between the two junction boxes, then color-match the wires and

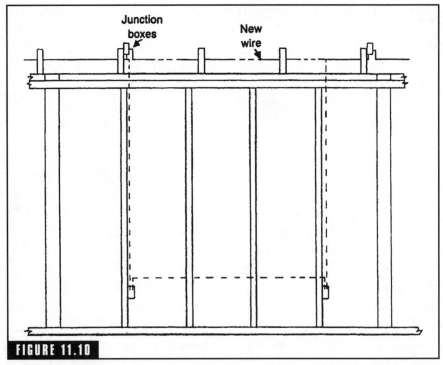

FIGURE 11.10

The typical procedure for rerouting an electrical cable to allow for removal of a wall.

connect them with wire nuts. Cover the new junction box with a blank cover and label the cover to indicate the circuit you've spliced.

In some instances, you might find an outlet in a wall at the end of the circuit run, which is indicated by its having only one cable entering the box. In this case, you can trace the cable back to the box it originated from and disconnect it there. You can also cut the cable and place the cut end in a junction box, cap the ends with wire nuts, then cover and label it. *Never* leave a live electrical cable loose in a wall, in an attic, or under the floor, even if the ends are capped.

Moving 240-Volt Wires

Note that 240-volt outlets, such as clothes dryers or other appliances, can be moved or disconnected but cannot be spliced. This type of cable contains three wires (two hot and one neutral), so splicing it in a junction box would make it possible for someone to later mistake the cable for one carrying two individual 120-volt circuits, and improper splicing into the 240-volt connection could be quite dangerous.

If you're going to move the outlet to a location closer to the service panel, you can use the same cable. Simply route it to the new location, feed it into a box, cut off the excess, and attach the appropriate receptacle. If the circuit is being removed, or if it's being extended to a new location farther from the service panel, the run must be traced back to the panel and disconnected there.

Disconnecting at the Panel

To disconnect the circuit at the panel, first shut off the main circuit breaker to disconnect the home's supply of electricity, then carefully remove the panel cover. Remember that the wires coming into the main breaker from the electric meter are still live, so work carefully. Locate the correct circuit breaker, and disconnect the two wires attached to it. Disconnect the ground and neutral wires from the neutral bar, and remove the cable from the panel.

If you are running a new circuit of the same amperage, bring the new cable into the panel and secure it to the existing breaker. If you're eliminating the circuit, remove the circuit breaker and close off the open slot in the panel cover to prevent possible accidental contact with the wires inside the panel—special plates are available from electrical supply stores.

The biggest problem occurs when the wall you're removing also contains the electrical service panel itself. This requires disconnection of the service drop or underground cable that serves the panel; then each of the circuits must be spliced or rerouted. I would strongly suggest that this operation be left to the skills of a qualified electrician, who cannot only do the work but can provide you with an accurate cost breakdown for inclusion in your estimate.

Removing Plumbing and Gas Lines

Galvanized plumbing lines in the wall must be traced back to a joint and disconnected, then rerouted if necessary. Locate the main water shutoff valve for the house and close it, then trace the pipe to the fixture it serves and disconnect it there. Working back from this fixture, disconnect and remove the pipe until you reach a point that is out of the way of the wall being removed. At that point you can splice onto the pipe and reroute it, or, if the pipe is under the house or in the attic, you can simply cap it. *Do not,* however, leave a live plumbing line capped in the wall—there is too high a potential for an undetected leak that could have disastrous results.

Copper and plastic pipe can usually be cut anywhere in the run, then disconnected and moved free of the wall. Again, you then have the option of splicing onto the pipe and rerouting it or else capping it anywhere except inside the wall.

Cast-iron drain lines can be disconnected at a fitting, or they can be cut using a special tool called a *chain cutter* or *soil line cutter.* Chain cutters, which you can rent, wrap around the pipe and, when the handles are closed, place pressure all around the pipe and snap it off at the point where the chain is connected. Once cut, you can splice onto the pipe using a rubber sleeve and worm-clamp device called a *band clamp.*

Gas lines are removed in the same manner as threaded-steel water pipe, after the gas supply has been shut off at the meter. Black pipe, or pipe with a yellow wrapping, is used for gas lines to distinguish them from the galvanized (silver) pipe used for water. When you are replacing gas line fittings or sections of pipe, always use black pipe, or cover it with a code-approved yellow wrapping.

When you have finished rerouting or capping the gas line, be sure to check all the connections for leaks. To do so, disconnect the meter from the main gas line that enters the house, then attach a pressure gauge, which can be rented, to the end of the gas line. Using a tire pump or a small compressor connected to the inlet on the pressure gauge, pressurize the line with air to about 10 pounds per square inch (psi).

Spray each connection with a solution of water mixed with a little dishwashing soap. If the solution bubbles around a connection, you have a leak. Tighten the fitting, repressurize the line, and test it again. Repeat this procedure until all of the connections test out okay. Once you are holding pressure, leave the pressure gauge in place until after the building inspectors have made their inspection of the lines—they will need to check the gauge and lines while they're still under pressure.

If you have any doubts about the procedures involved in dealing with a gas line, be sure to consult with a plumber or your gas company.

Scheduling Demolition

In most cases, demolition work is best left until the last possible moment in order to help avoid weather and security problems. The addition should be completely framed, roofed, and enclosed with siding, and the exterior windows and doors should be installed, before the walls connecting the addition with the existing house are removed.

Try to work in stages as much as possible, again doing only as much demolition work as is necessary for a particular phase of the construction. You may, for example, need to remove a small section of siding at the base of the wall in order to align the new foundation with the old one, or perhaps take down some drywall to line up the new ceiling joists. Even if it's all coming down eventually, it's best to remove only what you need to accomplish the task you are working on at the moment.

Weather and Security Precautions

Always remember that as the general contractor on a construction project such as a room addition, you are responsible for protecting the house and its contents from loss or damage. If it rains while you have the roof open, or if the house is burglarized because you've removed the windows and left them unprotected, you're the person that the homeowners and insurance companies will be coming after!

When you are cutting into an existing roof you should *always* have tarps or plastic sheeting available, even in the middle of summer (Figure 11.11). The house is extremely vulnerable when any section of roofing is off, and a sudden unexpected rainstorm can cause a considerable amount of interior damage. To a lesser degree, the same considerations apply when you remove windows, exterior doors, or sections of siding. Always plan ahead when doing any demolition work, and be prepared for the worst.

Besides the potential for weather-related problems, security and safety are always of major importance when cutting into someone's home (Figure 11.12). You'll need to have some scrap plywood handy whenever you open up a section of the house that is not otherwise secured. Work from the inside, and attach the plywood over the opening with long screws—screwing rather than nailing the panel in place makes it easier to open up each day.

Keep all boarded-up areas well lit at night, even if you must rig up portable lights with an extension cord. If the house will be unoccupied for an extended period of time, ask the homeowners to alert their

FIGURE 11.11

For weather protection, the roof has been "dried in" with 15-pound felt. Note the boards laid temporarily on the felt to keep it down until the shingles are installed.

FIGURE 11.12

For weather and security reasons, the walls of the existing house should be left intact until the addition is framed in and enclosed.

neighbors or the police to keep an eye on any vulnerable areas, even if you're working on it every day.

As demolition of the interconnecting walls proceeds, isolate the addition from the rest of the house as much as possible. Use 6-mil plastic sheeting and masking tape to seal off doorways, and keep furniture covered to protect it from dust. Turn off the furnace or air conditioning unless it is absolutely necessary to leave it on, and use plastic to seal off return-air grills and floor registers to prevent dust from being blown throughout the house. Remember to change the furnace filter when the demolition is complete and the debris has been cleaned up.

Living with a Partial House

One of the inescapable facts of building almost any addition is the disruption of the normal household routine. Water is unavailable at inconvenient times; the electricity is off at odd moments; entire rooms may be unusable for weeks at a time. There is no way around this, so you need to prepare your clients for what's ahead. Minimize their inconvenience as much as possible with good planning and scheduling; make sure your crew is sensitive to the homeowner's needs; and then ask your clients to extend you as much patience and understanding as possible.

Think ahead whenever you are turning off any of the home's utilities. Try to have all the necessary parts and tools on hand to complete the job you're working on, and allow yourself plenty of time. Don't shut off the electricity for a rewiring project with only an hour of daylight left or try to replumb the bathroom when guests are coming for dinner that evening.

If a room or section of a room is going to be lost during construction, prepare for it well in advance. Alert your clients to the construction schedule and ask them to clear out the room in advance—which is typically the client's responsibility unless your contract states otherwise. This saves a lot of confusion and disorganization and protects the room's contents from possible damage. An empty room is much easier to work in and speeds up the entire construction process.

Always keep one bathroom in operation if at all possible. If all of the bathrooms will be inoperable during any stage of construction, have your clients arrange to use the bathroom of a friend, neighbor, or family member, or encourage them to stay in a local motel until the bathrooms are back in operation. You must also rent a portable toilet for your crew's use while working on the job site (Figure 11.13).

No room is more difficult to do without than the kitchen. The loss of food storage and preparation facilities, dishes and utensils, and the family gathering place is usually quite disrupting. One way to minimize this is to help your client select a room away from the construction and set up a temporary kitchen.

FIGURE 11.13

Portable toilets can be rented inexpensively for use by construction crews or homeowners.

First, have them box up and store any appliances, dishes, glassware, and other kitchen items they don't actually need. Next, place sturdy wooden or cardboard boxes along one wall of the room for use as temporary storage for dishes and for food that doesn't require refrigeration. Move the refrigerator into the room if possible, or set it up in the garage or other out-of-the-way location. Finally, set up a small table to act as a countertop for food preparation. This small effort on your part will help the entire project run much more smoothly and with a lot less confusion and frustration.

Foundations and Floor Framing

The foundation is probably the single most important aspect of your addition in terms of getting it right the first time. It needs to be absolutely square and level in order to ensure that the rest of the addition will follow suit. If the foundation is poured wrong, you'll fight the rest of the construction all the way through.

Footings and Foundation Walls

The footing is the lowermost portion of the foundation and is designed and engineered to spread the downward weight of the addition over an area of ground that is wide enough to carry it (Figure 12.1). Footing widths vary, depending on soil conditions, but for most residential construction the footing is typically twice as wide as the foundation wall. The footing's thickness usually varies from 6 to 8 inches, depending on how many stories it must support, and it must be deeper than the average frost depth for your area. Your local building department will have specific information for footing sizes in your area.

Separate footings are used to carry the weight of any concentrated load such as a fireplace or spa. The size and design of special-purpose footings such as these will vary widely, depending on soil conditions, the depth of the frost line, and the total amount of weight they will need to support.

FIGURE 12.1

A typical footing and stem wall. Note the anchor bolts, and the forms still in place on the outside of the stem wall.

The foundation wall, also called a *stem wall,* rests directly on top of the footings and is usually constructed of poured concrete or concrete blocks. It can be poured continuously with the footing or poured separately after the footing has set. In houses having a crawl space, the foundation walls are relatively low, usually 18 to 24 inches high and 6 to 10 inches wide. If the addition is to have a basement, the basement walls will rest directly on the footings and will also serve as the foundation walls.

Concrete Slabs

If you are adding onto a house with a concrete slab floor, or if you wish the addition to be at a lower level than the floor of a house with an existing crawl space, then a slab floor is a good choice. It offers the advantages of low cost and faster construction time because no floor framing is needed. On the downside, it is rather cold and hard underfoot, and it offers no access to underfloor plumbing, wiring, and ducts.

As with the stem wall, the edges of the concrete slab need to rest on concrete footings in order to evenly distribute the weight of the walls. Most residential slabs are monolithic (Figure 12.2), meaning they are poured at the same time as the footings. After a period of curing, the slab is ready to accept the framing, and the smooth, hard surface forms a good underlayment for the floor coverings.

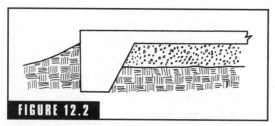

FIGURE 12.2

A typical monolithic concrete slab.

Laying Out the Foundation

Begin by clearing the ground where the addition is to be constructed. Trees and shrubbery need to be removed, and grass or weeds should be cleared back several feet in all directions from the intended addition.

Excavation

The amount of excavation needed for a particular foundation varies with the soil conditions and the depth of the crawl space. In all cases, though, the footings need to be deeper than the local frost line. As moisture in the soil freezes each winter, it can cause the ground to heave upward. Likewise, a sinking motion often occurs in the spring when the ground thaws. The frost line is the depth at which the earth is relatively safe from these movements, and this point varies depending on the climate conditions in different geographical areas. Bear in mind also that the footings must rest on undisturbed soil.

Excavation begins by pushing soil from the intended site. This process, typically done with a backhoe, clears and levels the land in the addition area and drops the grade to below the frost line. Once the footings and stem walls have been poured, the excavated soil is pushed back against the outside of the foundation, raising the grade to its original level and sloping it away from the addition, which protects the footings, provides proper drainage, and leaves the maximum amount of area exposed under the addition for ventilation and crawl space.

Pythagorean Theorem

Much of the layout work you'll be doing throughout the construction of the addition is based on the Pythagorean theorem of geometry (Figure 12.3), which in the building trades is commonly referred to as the 3:4:5. Simply stated, it means that if the base of a triangle is 3 units long (the units can be feet, inches, yards, etc.), the height is 4 units long, and the hypotenuse (the diagonal side) is 5 units long, then the corner of the triangle opposite the hypotenuse is exactly 90°.

Using the 3:4:5, you can quickly and easily lay out square corners for foundation walls, wall framing, cabinets, and a host of other construction applications. The theorem will work in any multiple of 3:4:5, such as 6:8:10 or 9:12:15, and the longer the distances you can use for the legs of the triangle, the more accurate the corner will be.

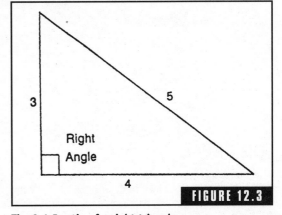

The 3:4:5 ratio of a right triangle.

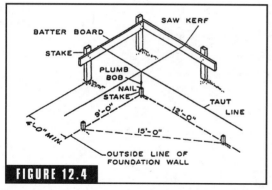

FIGURE 12.4

Batter boards set up to hold the strings that mark off lines for a foundation.

Initial Layout

The lines of the addition are laid out first, and these should correspond to the addition's finished outside size. If the building site for the addition is level, you can simply lay out the batter boards (Figure 12.4) and begin the form construction. If your site is on a low to medium slope, enough soil can usually be removed to create a level site, while on steep slopes, it will be necessary to step the foundation one or more times, then frame up from the foundation to create a level floor.

Starting against the existing house, mark the exact point where the addition will intersect the house wall (Figure 12.5). Measure along the house the length of the addition, and make a second mark. About 6 inches above ground level, drive a nail into the wall at each of these two marks. Finally, measure along the wall 6 feet from each of the original marks, and make a second mark.

Measure out from the house to the points where the addition's outside corners will be. Drive a stake into the ground at each of these points, and draw a line on top of each stake at the exact distance from the house (and parallel to it) where the back wall of the addition will be. Cut a saw kerf in the stakes at the pencil lines, and stretch a string between the two stakes, exactly parallel to the house.

Attach a string to one of the nails you drove into the house wall, and stretch it out beyond the string you just installed. While one person holds the string tight, make a pencil mark on the string 8 feet out from the house. Now measure the distance between the 6-foot mark you made on the

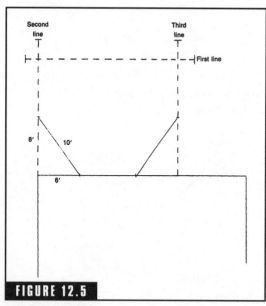

FIGURE 12.5

The typical sequence for laying out the foundation for a room addition. Note the use of the 3:4:5 ratio to square up the second line to the existing house.

house and the 8-foot mark on the string. If the diagonal distance between these two marks is 10 feet, then the string is square to the house wall. If it isn't, have the person holding the string move to left or right until the measurement is correct, and drive a stake at this point. Recheck your 10-foot measurement from house to string, and make a pencil mark at the exact point where the string crosses the stake. Make a saw kerf at this point, and secure the string to the stake. Repeat this procedure for the other side of the addition.

If your addition is to have any jogs in it, continue with the strings in the same manner until all of the outside walls have been laid out. Recheck all of the 3:4:5 measurements you made, and check that all the outside dimensions of the addition are correct as shown on the plans. As a final check, measure the diagonal distance between the corners of any square or rectangular areas—if the area is properly laid out, the diagonals will be equal.

Constructing the Forms

After the excavation is complete, forms will need to be erected to contain the concrete during the pouring operation. If your job requires footing forms, they will be the first to be built.

Building the Forms

For the footings, select straight, solid lumber of the same depth as the forms. For a 6-inch-deep footing, most inspectors allow 2 × 6 lumber, which is actually only 5½ inches deep (Figure 12.6). Working out from the house, begin by erecting the outside form. Use a plumb bob to take sightings from the strings on the batter boards, and measure out from these sightings the proper distance to establish the location of the form board. Drive a stake behind the board every 2 to 3 feet, using your spirit level or builder's level to be certain the forms are remaining true.

Duplex nails, which have two heads, are used to secure the stakes to the forms—the second head remains exposed, allowing for easy removal of the nail when the forms are disassembled (Figure 12.7). Remember to nail through the stake into the form, not the other way around. Continue around the footing trench in this manner, securing and leveling the form boards as you go. Securely nail the boards together at the corners, again

FIGURE 12.6

Footing forms laid out using 2 × 6 lumber.

using duplex nails driven in from the outside. Use the 3:4:5 method described previously to be certain the corners are square.

When the outside forms are in place, erect the inside forms in the same manner. Use precut spacers (Figure 12.8) nailed across the tops of the forms to maintain the correct distance between the forms, ensuring a consistent width for the footings. Check the inside forms for level, and level across the forms to be certain the inside and outside form boards are at the same level as well. Finally, construct any necessary forms for piers (Figure 12.9).

FIGURE 12.7

Metal stakes and duplex nails make for fast assembly and disassembly of the forms.

Footing Trenches

For smaller additions in solid soil, you may be able to dig foot trenches rather than construct forms. Following your layout strings, excavate the trenches to the exact size and depth needed for the footings. Use a square-point shovel to cut straight, vertical sides, and remove all loose dirt from the trench. The trenches should be relatively level, but the final leveling of the foundation will be done with stem-wall forms.

Leveling

If your foundation area is small, a spirit level might be enough to accurately level the forms. Select a good-quality level at least 48 inches in length for best results. Longer levels are also available and will

FIGURE 12.8

Reusable metal form ties make quick and easy work of spacing the form boards and holding them in place.

work even better for longer runs. On larger foundations, a builder's level or laser level is highly recommended, and they can be rented at any rental yard.

Both builder's levels and laser levels are mounted on a tripod that is set up either outside the addition's foundation area or, for large additions, in the center of the push-out. Once on the tripod, the instrument is positioned using three or four leveling screws in the base until the built-in leveling vial indicates it is perfectly level. The instrument then can be rotated on its base without disturbing its level.

A builder's level uses a type of telescope with crosshairs, through which the object to be leveled is sighted. While one person looks through the telescope, a second positions a leveling rod (a straight pole precisely marked in graduations of feet and inches) at various points on the foundation form. The crosshairs inside the telescope allow you to accurately judge where your line of sight is hitting the rod, and by then moving the leveling rod to another point on the form and resighting it through the telescope, you can tell if this point on the form is high or low relative to the first sighting you took.

A laser level is even more accurate, and it can be used by one person. Once

FIGURE 12.9

A form for a large pier pad, with rebar.

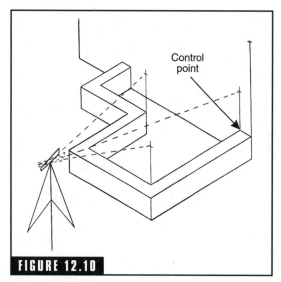

Control
point

FIGURE 12.10

Using a builder's level to check the level of the foundation forms at various points.

the level is set up and turned on, it rotates, sweeping the site with a safe, low-intensity laser beam. The leveling rod has a receiver on it that indicates its position, high or low, relative to the laser beam, which in turn tells the operator if the rod—and by extension, the form you're holding it on—needs to go up or down to be level.

Leveling begins at a point on the footing or stem wall form that is easy to establish (Figure 12.10). This point, called the *control point,* is usually where the addition meets the existing house, since it's important that the floor levels match up. Leveling then proceeds around the foundation by placing the leveling rod on top of the form, then raising or lowering the forms as necessary to meet the same level established by the control point.

Concrete

Concrete is actually a mixture of four materials: portland cement (named for its resemblance to an English limestone); coarse aggregate, which is any of a variety of rocks in different sizes, depending on the intended application; fine aggregate, usually sand; and clean water. The exact ratio of these materials varies with the concrete's intended use. One part cement to two parts sand to four parts rock is the most common mixture, with enough water added to make the mixture liquid enough to pour.

You can purchase ready-mixed concrete in a cart that can be towed behind a pickup truck. This is limited to 1-yard quantities, but is a convenient method for getting quality concrete for small areas.

Much more common is to have the ready-mixed concrete delivered to your site by truck. Most concrete trucks can handle about 7 yards at a time, and the concrete can be mixed to your specifications before leaving the yard. Purchasing ready-mixed concrete assures you that it will be thoroughly mixed and correctly proportioned for your application. It saves you from any guesswork about the ratios of materials.

Be certain that you have completely prepared your site, that all necessary forms are in place and fully secured, that you have all of the necessary tools ready and waiting, that you have enough people to help you place the concrete before it hardens, and that you have ordered the correct amount.

Most concrete companies will charge extra for standing time if the truck and driver must wait while you finish your site preparations. You'll also have to pay for all the concrete you order, even if it's more then you need for your job. You also might be faced with the need to get rid of the excess in the event the driver can't take it to his or her next job, so it definitely pays to plan carefully before you order a delivery.

Pouring the Footings

For most jobs, the footings are poured first. Then the stem-wall forms are erected and poured separately. If possible, arrange to have the concrete truck back up to the area where the foundation is being constructed—you can then use the truck's chute to place the concrete directly into the forms with a minimum of extra labor.

If the truck cannot get close enough, you will need to bring the concrete to the site in wheelbarrows and shovel or pour the concrete into place. If you have a lot to pour, consider hiring a concrete-pumping company. The concrete is poured directly into a special truck- or trailer-mounted machine, then pumped out through a hose, allowing you to easily direct the concrete into your forms with a minimum of additional labor.

Pour or shovel the wet concrete into the forms. As you work, tamp the concrete down with a shovel to be sure it is worked evenly into the forms, with no voids. Tap the outsides of the forms with a hammer to help the concrete settle and to avoid hollows on the finished edges.

Lay a 2 × 4 across the forms, starting at one end. With one person on each side, slide the board back and forth across the forms, scraping off the excess concrete as you work your way to the other end of the forms. This process is called *screeding* or *striking off*. Using your shovel or a piece of lumber, tamp the concrete into the forms to level and settle the wet mix.

For the footings, the concrete is rough-finished using a wooden trowel called a *float.* The surface should be level but not too smooth, providing a good bond for the concrete in the wall forms. For an even better bond between the footing and the foundation wall, rebar can be inserted into the footings, or a keyway can be created by embedding a strip of 1×2 lumber in the wet concrete. Remove the board after the concrete has set.

Stem Walls

After you allow the footings to cure for about 48 hours, you can erect the stem-wall forms. Replace the strings on the batter boards, and use them as guides for laying out the form boards. Take sightings from the strings with a plumb bob in several places, and mark the top of the footings. Then snap a chalk line across the marks to show the line the forms will follow. Mark off the width of the foundation wall on each footing, and snap a second chalk line to show where the inside form will be.

Plywood is the most common material for building the forms. Each sheet is ripped as needed to create a stem-wall height matching that of the house. Then the sheets are coated with motor oil, diesel oil, or a commercial form-release compound to help prevent them from sticking to the concrete.

Following the chalk lines on the footings, begin erecting the plywood panels. The panels may be secured to the footings using wooden cleats or special metal ties that support the bottom of the form while automatically establishing the spacing. The ties or cleats can be secured to the footing using special nails for hardened concrete. Erect the outside forms first; then do the inside panels. As with the footing forms, carefully square all the corners, and then secure them with duplex nails.

As the forms are erected, stakes are driven into the ground at an angle from the top of the form about every 2 to 3 feet to brace the top of the forms and prevent them from spreading when the concrete is placed. Use wooden spacers or metal ties to maintain the correct spacing between the tops of the forms. After all the forms are in place, check them carefully to be certain they are level, square, and well secured.

Pouring the Stem Walls

Place the concrete in the forms as described for the footings, pouring to a height of about half the forms. Carefully watch for spreading of the forms as you pour, and quickly add more stakes if necessary. When you have filled the entire run of forms half full, return to where you started and fill the forms to the top.

Carefully pack and tamp the concrete into place to prevent voids. If the wall forms are quite deep, rent a vibrator (a small motor with a vibrating rod at the end of a long cable), which is pushed down into the wet concrete at regular intervals to make the concrete more liquid, allowing it to flow into the forms more evenly. Screed the forms as noted previously, and finish the concrete smooth with a steel trowel.

FIGURE 12.11

Foundation bolts poured into the stem wall.

Anchor Bolts

Anchor or foundation bolts (Figure 12.11) are used to provide a means of transition between the foundation and the sill plate, which is the first piece of floor framing. Anchor bolts are typically ½ inch in diameter and 10 inches long, with one end threaded and the other end bent at a right angle. They are placed into the wet concrete a maximum of 6 feet apart and should protrude approximately 2 inches above the top of the stem wall.

Concrete Block Walls

Concrete blocks present an alternative to poured concrete for the stem walls or basement walls, and they are erected on poured concrete footings. They offer the advantages of not needing forms and of allowing you to construct the foundation in slower stages if desired, but laying blocks is fairly labor intensive for anyone who doesn't do it frequently.

Concrete blocks come in certain standard shapes and sizes, and they are designated by their nominal size, which makes an allowance for mortar joints. The common block for foundation work is usually designated as being 8 inches wide by 8 inches high by 16 inches long; the actual size is $7\frac{5}{8} \times 7\frac{5}{8} \times 15\frac{5}{8}$, allowing for a $\frac{3}{8}$-inch mortar joint.

Rebar must be installed in the footing when it is first poured, and the size and number you need will be specified by the building department. Wherever the hollow area in a concrete block coincides with the rebar, that hollow is filled solid with concrete, forming a positive tie between the footing and the block wall. Lay the blocks in a common bond so that each subsequent course overlaps the joints in the course below it. Anchor bolts are set in the hollows of the top course of blocks, and those hollows also are filled solid.

Concrete Slabs

Two types of slabs are commonly used for residential construction: floating and monolithic. The *floating slab* uses a conventional footing with a short stem wall. The concrete slab is then poured within the enclosure formed by the stem walls, but is not tied into them. Somewhat more common is the *monolithic slab,* which is poured in one continuous operation with the footings.

After the footings are dug and all underfloor wiring, plumbing, and heat ducts are installed, the ground where the slab is to be poured is compacted, and perimeter forms are set so that the finished slab is level with the existing finished floor of the house. A layer of rigid foam insulation is placed down—use an insulation that's approved for below-grade use—along with a layer of sand or gravel.

The concrete slab, usually 3 to 4 inches thick, is then poured directly on the insulation. A thick wire mesh, usually in 6-inch squares, is embedded in the concrete before or during the pour to reinforce the slab, and anchor bolts are set in the wet concrete around the perimeter as needed. The concrete is screeded off in sections, then hand- or machine-finished to a hard, smooth surface.

Ventilation

Moisture can enter the crawl space area from the soil and from the house, and if it is not removed it can cause serious damage to wood members. The building codes require that underfloor ventilation be provided as a means of getting rid of this moisture.

Code typically recommends a minimum of 1½ square feet of ventilation per 25 linear feet of exterior wall. You can also figure ventilation based on 1 square foot of vent for every 300 square feet of floor area for homes with dry soil in the crawl space, or 1 square foot per 150 square feet for homes with damp soil. Position the vents near the corners of the stem walls first, then equally space the rest around the perimeter. Vents should always be placed to allow a good cross flow of ventilation through the crawl space.

FIGURE 12.12

A plastic foundation vent, set in place as the stem wall is being poured.

A variety of prefabricated vents are available. Some types are meant to be cut into the rim joist, and these are installed at the time the floor is framed. Other types need to be installed in the stem wall itself, and these must be placed in the stem-wall forms prior to pouring the concrete (Figure 12.12).

Vents are designated by size, which refers to their overall outside dimensions, and by net free area (NFA). Since a certain portion of every vent is screened to keep insects and small animals out and a certain portion is solid material that supports the screen, the entire dimension of the vent cannot be counted in calculating how much air will flow through it.

Instead, the vent is designated by the manufacturer with an NFA rating, which tells you exactly how much of the vent's total area is open for airflow. When calculating your ventilation needs, always use the NFA designation—which is stamped on the frame of the vent—rather than the overall vent size.

In colder climates, closable foundation vents are available to help keep the crawl space warmer in winter and reduce the risk of frozen water pipes. Some types have a lever-operated shutter to close off the screened portion (Figure 12.13), while

FIGURE 12.13

A louvered metal foundation vent. The handle in the center activates a movable plate behind the louvers that allows the vent to be closed off in the winter.

FIGURE 12.14

Foam blocks used to seal off a plastic foundation vent in the winter.

others have precut foam blocks to seal the vent openings (Figure 12.14).

Vapor Barriers

In addition to underfloor ventilation, vapor barriers are typically required by code as well. Most vapor barriers are formed from sheets of 6-mil black plastic (1 mil = $\frac{1}{1000}$ inch). The plastic is simply laid out on the ground, with sheets overlapping by at least 12 inches. Lap the plastic 6 inches up the stem walls also, but do not allow it to contact wood members.

Floor Framing with Joists

Platform framing is the method used for residential and light commercial construction. It consists of three separate, interconnected framing stages: the floor framing and subfloor, which forms the platform; interior and exterior wall framing; and roof framing. In the case of an addition with a concrete slab floor, the slab takes the place of the floor framing and creates the platform.

Understanding Deflection

The underfloor framing consists of a carefully designed system of posts, girders, and joists, designed to equally distribute load over the entire floor area, with adequate additional support for any specific, unusually heavy "point loads." Done correctly, it creates a solid, squeak-free floor that is one of the most frequently mentioned items of customer satisfaction in surveys of new-home buyers.

Constructing a solid floor is not difficult if you have good materials, good construction techniques, and an understanding of the structural concept of live load deflection. *Deflection* is the total distance that a structural member such as a floor joist will sag down off the horizontal, measured at the center point between two supports. *Live load* is the load placed on a structure by the weight of its occupants and furnishings, typically figured at 40 pounds per square foot for residential applications. Live load deflection, therefore, is simply a calculation of how much the floor is going to sag under the weight of the people who live on it.

Deflection in a structural member is expressed by the formula L/x, where L is the length of the joist and x is the deflection factor. The deflection factor used under most current building codes is 360, so the formula would be written as $L/360$, calculated as follows: the length of the member between supports (in inches) divided by 360 equals the maximum allowable deflection (in inches).

Suppose you have a floor joist that is spanning a total of 16 feet between supports. First, convert 16 feet to inches ($16 \times 12 = 192$ inches). Then, apply the formula $L/360$ ($192 \div 360 = 0.53$). Therefore, according to current building code standards, your joist could sag a maximum of 0.53 inches at the center under a live load of 40 pounds per square foot.

Increasing the deflection formula you use will decrease the allowable deflection, resulting in a stiffer floor. For example, most of the charts and software programs used for sizing floor-framing members provide at least two possible deflection options: the code minimum of $L/360$ and an optional formula of $L/480$. Applying the second formula to the same example, your deflection would be 0.40 inches instead of 0.53 inches ($192 \div 480 = 0.40$). You've reduced the midpoint deflection of that 16-foot joist by about ⅛ inch—almost a 25 percent improvement—which will obviously result in a stronger floor with less bounce.

When working with your clients on their addition design, floor strength is something worth discussing. There are a variety of ways to create a stiffer floor, but remember that these reductions in deflection usually come with an increase in construction costs:

- *Use deeper joists.* Select a deeper joist that meets the stiffer $L/480$ deflection criteria (most lumberyards have standard span charts to help you), which is usually one lumber size larger than the $L/360$ (a 2×10 joist instead of a 2×8, for example).

- *Use engineered I-joists instead of solid lumber.* With the growing popularity of I-joists (Figure 12.15), costs have come down considerably in the last few years. You may be able to substitute an engineered I-joist for your solid lumber joist and improve floor performance without significantly affecting the price.

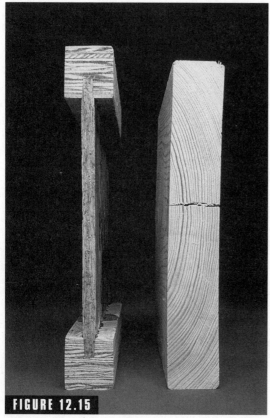

FIGURE 12.15

An example of the uniformity and dimensional stability of an engineered I-joist (left) compared to a piece of solid sawn lumber of the same dimension. *(Courtesy of Trus Joist MacMillan.)*

■ *Reduce the center-to-center spacing.* The closer the joists are to one another, the more they will share the overall load that's placed on the floor. As you increase the load sharing, you create a floor that acts more like a single member and less like a combination of individual pieces. As load sharing is increased, deflection is reduced.

■ *Use thicker subfloor.* Increasing the thickness of the material you use for the subfloor will once again improve the load-sharing capabilities of the overall floor system, reducing deflection.

■ *Decrease support beam spacing.* By decreasing the distance between the beams or girders that support the joists, you decrease the joist's span and improve its deflection. This may offer an easy and inexpensive solution in some of the additions, but it may be impractical in others.

Sill Plates

The first framing members installed are the sill plates, also called a *sill* or *mudsill,* typically consisting of 2 × 6 or 2 × 8 pressure-treated lumber (do not use untreated lumber, because the moisture in the concrete stem wall will cause it to rot) attached directly to the foundation to serve as a transition between the concrete of the foundation and the subsequent wooden framing.

To prevent cold air and insects from moving under the sill plate, use a sill sealer first. The sealer can be in the form of caulking, but most builders use foam sealers designed for this purpose (Figure 12.16). Sill sealers are simple and inexpensive to install before the sill plates are laid down—just roll it out on top of the stem wall, cutting it to go over the anchor bolts—and can add greatly to the energy efficiency of the addition.

If you live in an area where termites are a problem, you might wish to consider installing a termite shield. Made of galvanized sheet metal, the termite shield is installed under the sill plate so that it overlaps the stem wall on both sides. Angle the sheet metal down so that any termites coming up the stemwall cannot make their way out and around the shield.

After installing the sill sealer, start the sill plate installation at one corner of the addition. Set a section of sill plate on the foundation and butt it against the anchor bolts. Placing a square against each side of the first bolt, mark the bolt's location on the board. Measure from the outside of the stem wall to the center of the bolt at each location, then transfer this measurement to the sill plate to give you the exact location of each bolt.

FIGURE 12.16

A foam sill sealer, visible at right between the bottom of the sill plate and the top of the stem wall.

Drill a hole at each marked location on the plate, using a bit that's about ¼ inch larger in diameter than the diameter of the bolt to allow movement for ease of alignment. Set the plate over the bolts, and loosely secure it with the nuts and washers. Cut each subsequent section of sill plate to length and repeat the marking and drilling procedure until you have installed the entire run of plates. If necessary, shim under the sill plates to bring them level. Check that the corners are square and that the boards are correctly aligned with respect to the stem wall, then securely tighten all the nuts (Figure 12.17).

Ledgers

A common situation that arises in the framing of a room-addition floor is the need to extend directly off the existing house. This extension is accomplished through the use of a ledger, which is secured directly to the home's existing floor framing (Figure 12.18).

FIGURE 12.17

A typical anchor bolt, nut, and washer used to secure the sill plate to the stem wall.

FIGURE 12.18

Floor framing for an addition. Note the ledger attached to the house below the windows, which aligns with the floor of the existing house. *(Courtesy of Senco Products.)*

The height of the ledger is set so that when the subflooring is installed over it, the addition's floor will match up exactly with the floor of the existing house. Time and care need to be taken with the placement of the ledger to ensure that this transition is smooth.

The ledger is attached to the existing house by setting nails or lag bolts into the existing framing. For long spans or for floors that will carry a substantial load, it might be necessary to attach the ledger to the existing framing with bolts, nuts, and washers. For additional load-bearing capacity, install 2 × 4 or 2 × 6 pressure-treated kickers from the underside of the ledger down to the top of the original footings. If the ledger cannot be installed in one piece, be sure to reinforce the splices with a wooden plate that extends at least 1 foot beyond the joint in each direction.

Installing the Floor Joists

Floor joist size and spacing depends on the length of the area the joist needs to span. Joist-size information will be included on your plans, or the building department will have span tables available that will show you the size and spacing necessary to span a given area at a given amount of deflection.

Joists should be laid out parallel to the shortest dimension of the floor in order to minimize the span. If the span is still too great to be handled by a joist in one piece, the span is divided up through the use of girders, posts, and piers.

Framing begins from the existing house and works outward. If the joists run perpendicular to the house, they are attached to the ledger using joist hangers. If they are parallel with the house, count the ledger as your first joist and begin your spacing layout from there.

The first joists to be installed are the rim joists, which are installed on the walls perpendicular to the directional run of the joists. The rim joists are installed flush with the outside of the sill plates, and they're marked with the joist spacing layout starting from the house (Figure 12.19).

Install the joists one at a time (Figure 12.20), checking each to see if there is any up or down warp along the edge. This warp, called a *crown,* should always be placed up so that the weight of the floor load will push it down. The load will tend to worsen the crown if it is installed in the down position.

Nail through the rim joist into each joist using three 16d nails. If the joists must be spliced, secure overlapping splices by nailing through the two boards with 16d nails. Butt splices are joined using a wooden splice plate, secured with 8d nails for 1-inch lumber or 16d nails for 2-inch

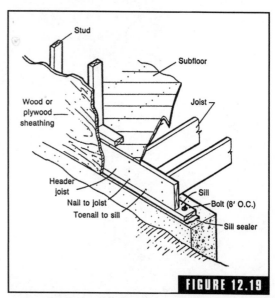

FIGURE 12.19

A typical floor-framing situation, showing the stem wall, sill sealer, sill, rim joist, floor joists, and subfloor.

FIGURE 12.20

An engineered I-joist resting on the sill plate, along with an engineered lumber rim joist.

lumber. In either case, toenail the spliced boards down into the supporting girder.

In order to stiffen the joists over long spans, bridging is necessary. There are two types of bridging: solid and cross. *Solid bridging* consists of solid blocks of lumber of the same dimension as the joists (Figure 12.21). The blocks are cut to fit between the joists and are secured using 16d nails driven into the blocks through the sides of the joists. Staggering the bridging makes nailing considerably easier.

Cross bridging is installed between the joists in the form of an X, extending from the inside top of one joist to the inside bottom of the adjacent joist and vice versa. Cross bridging can be hand-cut from 1×2 or 1×3 stock and secured to the joists with 8d nails, or you may prefer to use prefabricated metal bridging, which is manufactured to the proper length to fit a given joist size on a given center. Teeth on the upper end of the metal bridging are driven into the top of the joist, then the angled bottom is driven into the joist bottom.

Bridging should be installed wherever the joists are spliced, and then should be placed approximately every 8 to 10 feet, or as specified by the building department. Either type of bridging can use up a lot of lumber, so remember to take that into consideration when you are estimating and ordering.

Engineered Lumber Joists

Engineered lumber is a concept that has gained considerable acceptance and widespread use in recent years. Instead of using solid sawn lumber, which is diminishing in supply and quality, small second- and third-growth trees are chipped, peeled, or sliced into pieces and then reassembled into a variety of solid structural members (Figure 12.22).

FIGURE 12.21

Solid blocking used between I-joists, directly over a supporting girder.

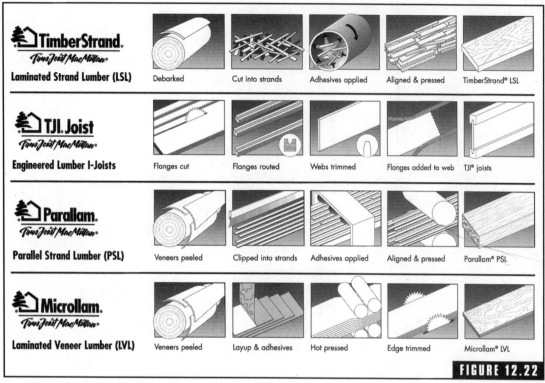

FIGURE 12.22

The manufacturing processes involved in four types of innovative engineered lumber products. *(Courtesy of Trus Joist MacMillan.)*

One of the most common and popular of the engineered lumber products is the I-joist, which consists of a central web of oriented strand board (OSB) or plywood that is glued under heat and pressure to top and bottom chords of lumber, plywood, or other engineered lumber products. The result is a joist that is light but extremely resistant to deflection. I-joists can span long distances without additional support, and they are dry and dimensionally stable as well, virtually eliminating warping and splitting.

Most lumberyards now stock I-joists and other engineered lumber products, and a growing number have on-site designers and product-specific computer programs that will design your entire floor system at no charge (Figure 12.23). The resulting design will specify the size and type of I-joist for a given span, the recommended spacing, blocking

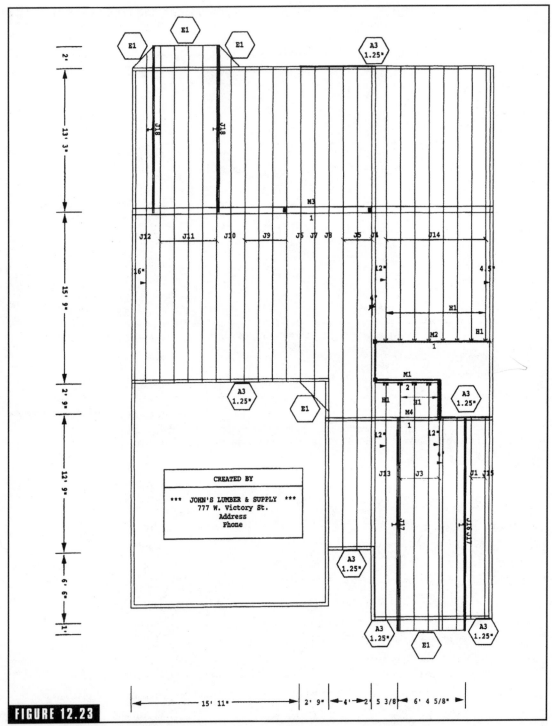

FIGURE 12.23

An example of a computer-generated floor joist layout, using I-joists and other engineered lumber products. *(Courtesy of Trus Joist MacMillan.)*

and other supports, hangers and other hardware, and complete nailing and installation instructions.

Post-and-Beam Construction

Also called *pier-and-beam* and *pier-and-post,* post-and-beam framing is another method of underfloor framing (Figure 12.24). It uses a series of beams, called *girders,* typically placed on 4-foot centers and parallel with the shorter dimension of the foundation. The ends of the girders rest either on the sill plate or in beam pockets that were cast into the stem walls when they were poured. The girders are then supported approximately every 5 feet by 4 × 4 posts, which in turn rest on concrete piers. The piers may be precast and set on undisturbed soil, or they may be cast in place in excavated holes or in forms set directly on the ground.

This framing method uses a minimum of materials and therefore assembles fairly quickly, but requires thicker subflooring than joist framing and is a little more difficult to insulate. Post-and-beam construction can be used only on the first floor of a building—floor joists

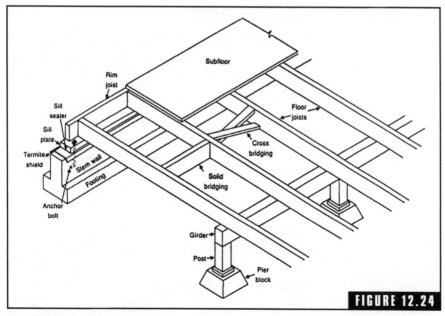

FIGURE 12.24

Typical post-and-beam construction.

are necessary for each subsequent floor. If post-and-beam construction is being used, the pier layout will be indicated on the foundation plan and should be poured at the same time as the rest of the foundation.

Install the rim joists as described previously, perpendicular to the run of the girders. Measure in 4 feet from the outside edge of the foundation to locate the center of the first run, which should fall directly over the run of piers. Mark the centers of the girders on the sill plates. Stretch a string tightly between the marks so that it is lying directly on the sill plates—this indicates the bottom of the girders and is used in determining the length of the supporting posts.

Carefully measure from the top of each pier to the string, and cut a post to this length. Code requires either that a waterproof barrier be placed between the post and the concrete of the pier or that pressure-treated posts be used. A scrap of asphalt roofing shingle is a common choice to rest the post on, and its thickness must be taken into consideration when you are measuring for the post length.

Toenail each girder to the supporting posts and to the sill plates. Nail a 2-foot piece of 1×6 or 2×6 lumber to the sides of the girders over each splice to lock them together.

Special Floor-Framing Situations

In some instances, the layout of the addition might require special framing in addition to the simple joist or girder layout. Care must be taken that these situations are well thought out and planned for during the framing operation to provide the proper support.

Openings

Common floor-framing situations are openings, such as those for crawl-space access or stairwells between floors.

First, install the joists that will form the sides of the opening. These two joists, called *trimmers,* run parallel to the direction of the other joists. Next, install a crosspiece, called a *header,* between the trimmers at each end of the opening. Then extend short joists, called *tail joists,* off the headers to complete the framing. If only one joist space is being spanned by the opening, this framing will be sufficient. For larger openings, it is necessary to double both the trimmers and the headers to provide adequate support. Remember to allow for this second piece of lumber when you are initially framing the opening so that the opening will be the correct size when all of the boards are in place.

Extensions

Another common framing situation arises when one section of the floor is to extend out past the foundation or lower story of the house, as in the case of a bay window (Figure 12.25).

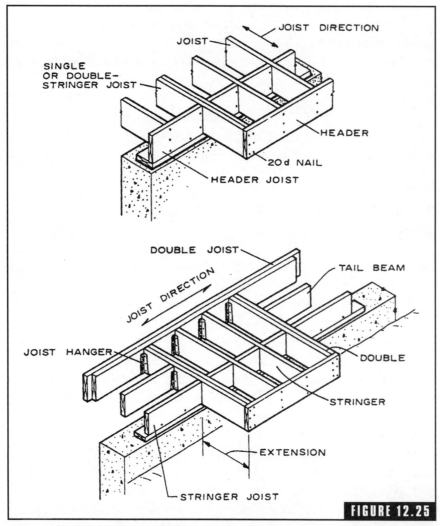

FIGURE 12.25

Standard framing for floor extensions past the foundation wall, running parallel with the joists (top) and perpendicular to the joists (bottom).

If the extension occurs in the same direction as the run of the joists or girders, it is simply necessary to extend the joists out past the foundation or wall the necessary distance. Then secure another rim joist to the ends of the joists and place solid blocking between the joists at the line of the foundation or wall.

For extensions that run perpendicular to the joists, a cantilever must be framed. If the extension is for floor space that will support a standard live load, you can apply the "one out, two in" rule so that the joists supporting the extension extend inward at least twice the distance that they overhang outside—for example, a 2-foot extension requires that the joists extend back into the addition at least 4 feet. Double the joists at the outside of the extension to provide an adequate bearing surface for the walls, and also double the regular joist where the extension joists intersect it.

Extensions that will support concentrated point loads, such as a woodstove or a bathtub, should be designed by an architect or engineer to ensure safe and proper framing.

Dropped Floors

In some instances it might be necessary to have one portion of the floor lower than the surrounding area. This situation might occur when two finish-flooring materials of substantially different heights will intersect, or it might be a desired architectural feature (as in the case of a sunken living room).

If the dropped area makes up a large part of the floor area, it might be necessary to step down the foundation. This is an important consideration in the early planning stages, because the drop must obviously be built into the foundation when it is first poured.

Another method is to use joists that have a smaller height than the surrounding joists. This method will work only if the lower area is small enough that the shorter joists are adequate for the span. Consult a span table to determine the smallest joist you can safely use for the intended span. In order to gain adequate support for the smaller lumber, it might be necessary to decrease the spacing between the joists or add additional posts and beams to shorten the span.

For post-and-beam construction, using a beam pocket in the foundation will enable the girders in one area to be set lower.

Subflooring

The last step in constructing the floor platform is the installation of the subfloor. Subfloor materials and thicknesses, which vary widely with the intended application, must be matched to the size and type of floor framing that supports the subfloor.

Most applications over floor joists use 4 × 8 sheets of ¾-inch tongue-and-groove plywood, OSB, or com-ply (a material with an OSB core and plywood face veneers). Subflooring should be installed using adhesive on top of the joists, then secured with hand- or air-driven nails or staples (Figure 12.26).

For post-and-beam framing, thicker subfloor is required to handle the greater spans between support. The old method was to use 2 × 6 or 2 × 8 tongue-and-groove

FIGURE 12.26

Fastening sheets of tongue-and-groove OSB subfloor with an air-powered nail gun. *(Courtesy of Senco Products.)*

lumber, and if the floor of the original house was built this way, you need to be aware of it so that your new subfloor will line up with the old one. Today, the most common material is 1⅛-inch plywood, which is rated for a 48-inch span.

Wall and Roof Framing

There are two basic types of wall framing: platform and balloon. With *balloon framing* (Figure 13.1), which is rarely used anymore for walls, the sill plates are first secured to the foundation, then the wall studs are erected one at a time, extending full length to the roof. You will still see some modified examples of balloon framing in new houses, particularly in areas where a half story is being framed, or in soffits and some other types of special situations.

In *platform framing* (Figure 13.2), the walls are framed while they are lying on the subfloor; then they are stood up, moved into position, and secured. This procedure, which is the same for both slab floors and floors over a crawl space, is the accepted method for virtually all residential framing.

If you are adding onto a house that was constructed using the balloon framing method (or any method of framing other than platform framing), you can easily adapt platform framing to it. Once the foundation has been poured at the correct level and the underfloor framing and subfloor have been constructed, the only other real framing considerations are building the walls to the correct height and matching up the roof framing.

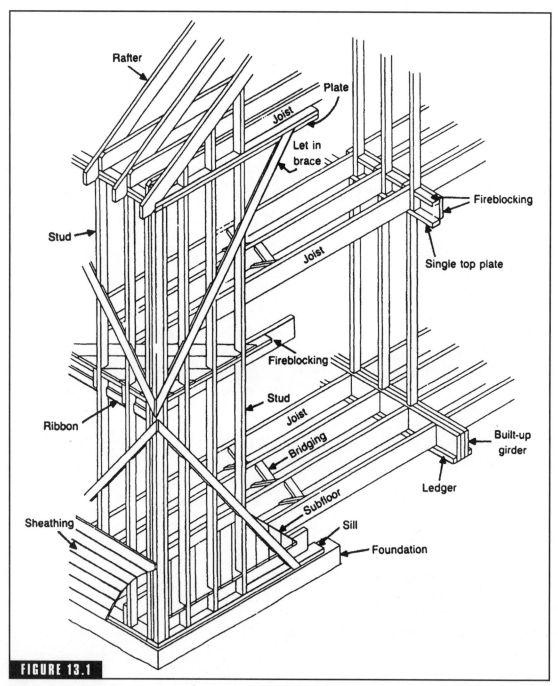

FIGURE 13.1

Typical balloon framing, with the studs extending all the way to the foundation. *(Courtesy of the National Forest Products Association.)*

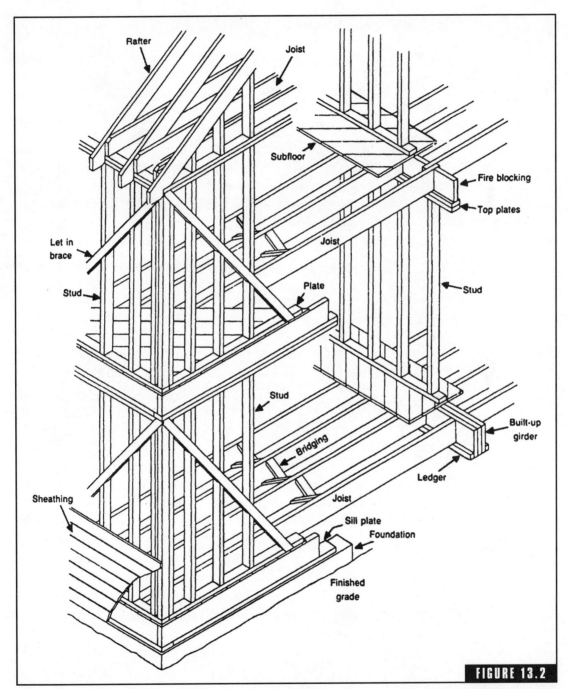

Typical platform framing, with the joists and subfloor creating a platform on top of the foundation. *(Courtesy of the National Forest Products Association.)*

Matching Framing-Lumber Sizes

For many years, 2 × 4s were the overwhelming choice for wall studs and plates. However, energy codes have changed, making 2 × 6 framing (which accommodates thicker insulation) mandatory for exterior walls almost everywhere.

The problem arises when attempting to align the new 2 × 6 walls of the addition with the 2 × 4 walls of the existing house. If your addition is such that the new walls are not a direct extension of the old walls, as in a second-story addition, or one that does not directly align with the old walls, 2 × 6 construction works fine. For first-story walls that must be a direct extension off an existing wall, talk to the building department about alternative insulation methods. By using rigid foam insulation in place of standard fiberglass batts, you can usually achieve the necessary R-19 or R-21 insulation values in a 2 × 4 wall.

Another trick is to make a jog in the addition as quickly as possible. This could be a closet, a pantry, or simply a cross wall for another room—anything that allows you to transition from the old 2 × 4 to the new 2 × 6 without having a major alignment problem or visual irregularity.

When adding onto older houses, you may also find that the 2 × 4 lumber in the walls is literally that—2 inches by 4 inches (as opposed to the 1½ by 3½ inches that is the actual size of today's surfaced lumber). While the thickness doesn't usually matter, the depth of the old lumber presents a wall-alignment problem. You can use 2 × 6 lumber and rip it down to the exact width of the old studs, but a more economical solution is to simply furr out standard 2 × 4s with strips of ½-inch plywood to match up to the dimension of the old wood.

Another framing consideration is ceiling height. For most new construction, the use of precut studs is a great labor saver. The studs are precut to length, usually 92¼ inches, and when combined with 1½-inch lumber on the bottom and two top plates, the total wall height is 96¾ inches. With ½-inch drywall on the ceiling, you can use standard 8-foot sheets of drywall or paneling on the walls with ¼ inch of play, which is later covered by the baseboards.

However, matching up to the old ceiling heights is essential, and if the original house was not framed with precut studs, you're stuck with having to cut each stud from 8-foot or even 10-foot material in order to match up to the old ceiling.

Wall-Framing Techniques

In order to accurately lay out the wall prior to framing, several items need to be established first, including the type of corners and intersections being used, the stud spacing, and the rough-opening sizes for windows, doors, and other wall openings.

While some framing is now being done with studs on 24-inch centers, the most common spacing is 16 inches. If you're considering 24-inch spacing, make sure the siding you intend to use is rated for this type of spacing.

Openings

When you are framing the walls, you will need to know the exact size of any openings such as doors or windows. At the framing stage, this is known as a *rough opening,* since it needs to be large enough to accept the finished door or window unit (Figure 13.3).

Rough-opening sizes sometimes are listed on the plans. If they aren't, you'll need to request them from your supplier before framing begins. As a general rule of thumb, rough openings for doors are framed 2 inches larger than the finished unit in both directions. For example, if you're using a door 3 feet wide by 6 feet 8 inches high, the rough-opening size would be 3 feet 2 inches wide by 6 feet 10 inches high. This extra space in the opening allows room for the doorjambs and any shimming that is needed to plumb the door frame. What's left of the opening is then covered by trim.

Window openings are usually framed to the actual size being used. A 4 × 3 window, therefore, would require a 4-foot-wide by 3-foot-high rough opening. The manufacturer makes the necessary size adjustment when the window is built, usually making the actual window frame ¼ inch smaller in each direction.

FIGURE 13.3

Standard wall framing, including two headered openings for windows.

Corners and Intersections

Wall corners can be framed using three studs, which was common for many years, or by utilizing the more popular two-stud method, which saves lumber and allows for insulation to be placed in the corners (Figure 13.4).

There are also two ways to frame the area where one wall intersects another (Figure 13.5). One method is to assemble three studs, nailing two of the studs to the edges of the third (center) stud, which provides a solid point of attachment for the intersecting wall and a nailing surface on each side of the wall for the attachment of the interior finish.

An easier method is to simply frame the first wall with the studs on regular centers, then block between two studs wherever an intersection is needed. This method allows for faster framing, less lumber, insulation at the intersection, and more flexibility in the exact alignment of the cross wall. To provide a backing for the wall finish, use 6-inch lumber (either 6 × 1 or 6 × 2) or, if you prefer, drywall dips.

Laying Out the Wall

Wall framing begins by making a full-size layout of the stud and opening locations directly on the top and bottom plates. Cut the bottom plate and one top plate to the desired length and lay them out side by side. Starting at one end of the plate, make a mark at 15¼ inches, which is the edge of the first regular stud in the wall (assuming 16 OC spacing). Draw a pencil line at that mark, then place an X on the side of the line away from the end from which you started measuring—this sets the center of the first

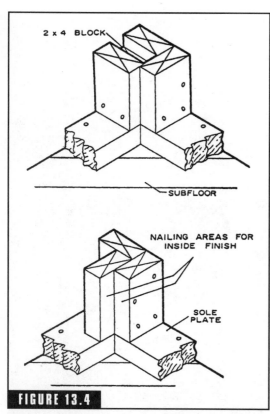

FIGURE 13.4

Two types of outside corner framing—two studs with blocking, also called a *three-stud corner* (top), and a *two-stud corner* (bottom).

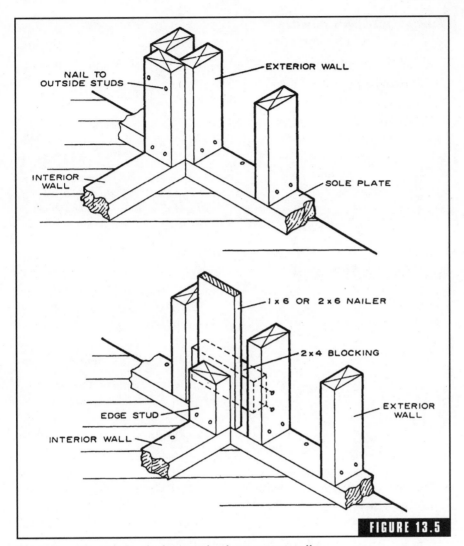

FIGURE 13.5

Labels: NAIL TO OUTSIDE STUDS · EXTERIOR WALL · INTERIOR WALL · SOLE PLATE · 1 x 6 OR 2 x 6 NAILER · 2 x 4 BLOCKING · EDGE STUD · INTERIOR WALL · EXTERIOR WALL

Two types of framing for the intersection between two walls.

stud 16 inches from the end of the wall. From this first stud line, measure off and mark the remaining stud locations for the entire wall in 16-inch increments. For 24 OC framing, mark the edge of the first stud at 23¼ inches, then space the lines 24 inches apart from there.

Openings are noted on plans by the distance from the end of the wall to the center of the opening. After determining the center location of the opening, measure one-half of the rough opening width from that point to locate where the opening starts, then measure an additional 1½ inches to indicate the trimmer, then another 1½ inches to indicate the king stud. Do the same on the other side of the opening.

If you mark the trimmer location with a T, it helps to avoid confusing the trimmer's location from those of the studs, marked with an X. You'll also notice that the stud spacing continues across the opening, even though there will be no studs there. For window openings, just leave those marks in place—they'll indicate the location of the cripples under the windowsill. If they fall within a door opening, it's best to scribble them out so a stud isn't inadvertently placed in the opening.

Assembling the Wall

Place the two plates on edge, marks facing each other. Place a corner assembly at the end, then set all of the regular, full-length studs in place on the X side of the line. If two or more plates are being joined to make up the full length of the wall, the splice must fall over a stud.

Next, assemble the studs and trimmers that make up each side of the openings (Figure 13.6). The king studs for the openings are full-length, while the trimmers need to be cut to proper length for the height of the door or window header. Nail the plates to the studs and trimmers using 16d nails.

Header stock is made up from single or doubled 2× lumber (Figure 13.7), from solid-stock 4× or 6× lumber, or by using one of the new engineered lumber beam and header products now on the market (Figure 13.8). The size and type of the material you use is based on the size of the opening and the load above it, and this can be determined from a span table or by using a computer program for engineered lumber, a service that's available at most lumberyards.

For window openings, install the sill next. Measure down from the bottom of the header to the correct rough opening height. Cut the sill to length and install it between the trimmers, then install all of the necessary cripples to complete the framing under the window. The bottom plate is left in place across all door openings and is cut out later, after the walls are up (Figure 13.9).

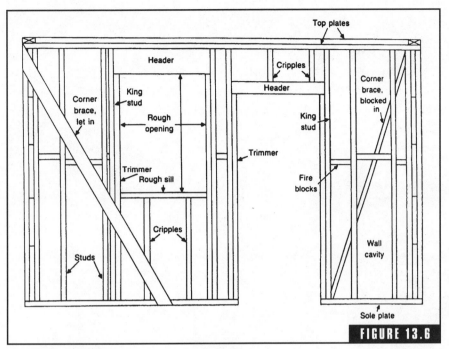

FIGURE 13.6

The basic components of a platform-framed wall.

Standing the Wall

When you are raising the wall sections into place, use enough people to comfortably lift the section and keep it under control. Have nails and extra lumber close by for temporary bracing.

For the side walls that attach to the existing house, care must be taken with the alignment so that the finished wall surfaces will be flush. You will need to know what material will be used for both the siding and sheathing, if any, on the new walls so you can determine at this point how they will align with the existing walls.

With one or more people steadying the wall, install temporary diagonal braces between the floor and the top of the wall (Figure 13.10). Check the outside of the wall

FIGURE 13.7

A header made from a single piece of 2x lumber.

FIGURE 13.8

An engineered lumber header. *(Courtesy of Trus Joist MacMillan.)*

FIGURE 13.9

Bottom plates are left in place across doorways as the walls are raised, then cut out afterward.

FIGURE 13.10

Temporary bracing is used to hold a wall plumb and square until after completion of the sheathing.

with a level as the braces are installed to be certain it is plumb. As each outside wall is added, nail the corners together (Figures 13.11 and 13.12).

Permanent Bracing

To prevent side-to-side movement in the wall (called *lateral movement,* or *racking*), permanent bracing needs to be installed. If the walls are to be sheathed with plywood or covered with plywood siding, these panels will provide the necessary bracing. In this case, 1 × 4s are nailed diagonally to the inside of the studs in one or more corners to hold the wall plumb until the sheathing or siding is installed; then the braces are removed. If you are using a nonstructural insulated sheath-

FIGURE 13.11

After standing and plumbing an intersecting interior wall, it is fastened to the framing in the exterior wall. *(Courtesy of Senco Products.)*

FIGURE 13.12

Using an air-powered framing nailer to secure a wall plate to the subfloor. *(Courtesy of Senco Products.)*

ing, you can use plywood of the same thickness at the wall corners to serve as permanent bracing.

For unsheathed walls being covered with vertical or horizontal siding boards, or with stucco or other masonry, diagonal bracing must be installed in the wall itself. The easiest way is to use a perforated metal strap, specially manufactured for this application. Nail through one of the holes in the strap at the top plate on the outside of the wall, extend the strap down at approximately 45°, then nail the strap to each stud that it crosses. Wooden braces, placed so that they don't interfere with the exterior wall covering, can also used. They can either be let-in (recessed into the wall studs) or blocked in between the studs.

Top Plates and Blocking

After all the walls are standing, including the short walls that form the closets and smaller interior spaces, add the second top plate. Install these plates in such a way that they overlap the first top plate of each intersecting wall, locking the two walls together.

As the final step in the wall-framing stage of the addition, take a moment to consider where blocking might be needed. Examine all the wall/ceiling and wall/wall intersections, and make sure you have backing for the drywall. A prefabricated shower stall or bathtub often requires blocking around its perimeter for support or to provide a point of attachment. Cabinets, towel bars, shelving, fixtures, curtain rods—all these items and many others might require some additional support within the wall. Installing the blocking now will make the later installation of these items much easier.

Sheathing

Many types of siding require the installation of sheathing before the finish siding material is put in place. Most types of masonry and individual board siding will require sheathing for structural support and backing and as a nailing surface. Plywood and other solid-sheet siding typically does not.

In today's construction, plywood and oriented strand board (OSB) (Figure 13.13) has replaced individual boards as a sheathing material.

FIGURE 13.13

OSB sheets being used as wall sheathing.

Since appearance is not a concern, lower plywood grades such as C-D-X are most commonly used.

One common problem is matching new sheathing to existing sheathing. Older houses often used ¾-inch surfaced boards, or even rough boards measuring a full 1 inch thick. Sheathing an entire addition with ¾-inch plywood or two layers of ½-inch plywood adds unnecessarily to the cost of the building, so consider some alternatives instead.

If you are extending a wall where a jog or interior partition makes alignment of the interior walls unnecessary, the new wall framing can be set to whatever sheathing thickness you wish. For example, suppose the existing house is sided with ¾-inch boards over ¾-inch sheathing and the wall of the addition does not need to align with an existing interior wall. If you intend to side with ¾-inch boards over ½-inch sheathing, simply set your wall framing in 1¼ inches (rather than a full 1½ inches) from the face of the existing wall.

If the new walls are a direct continuation of the old walls, making alignment of both the interior and exterior surfaces necessary, stick with a minimum sheathing thickness on the exterior, then shim the interior walls as necessary to complete the alignment (Figure 13.14).

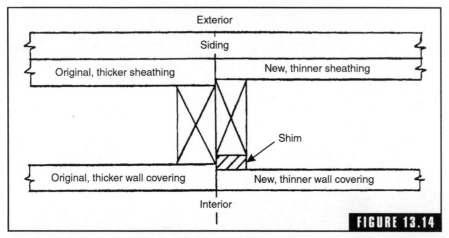

An example of how a combination of offsetting the new studs and installing shims over them (shaded area) can be used to align both the interior and exterior wall surfaces, even though both the sheathing and the interior wall covering is thinner on the addition (right) than it was in the original house (left).

Remember that it's not necessary to sheath the entire addition with the same thickness of material. If only one wall requires a facing of ¾-inch material in order to align it with the old wall, the rest of the addition can be sheathed in ½-inch material.

Wall sheathing is applied starting from the same corner where your stud layout began so that the sheets will fall over the center of a stud. Nail the sheathing directly to the studs with 6d or 8d nails, or use a pneumatic sheathing stapler. You can make cutouts for windows, doors, and other openings as you install each sheet, or you can cut them out later (Figure 13.15) with a reciprocating saw.

Ceiling and Roof Framing

The most difficult part of framing any house is the roof, and this is even more difficult with a room addition. Calculation of the angles, determination of rafter lengths, design of the cornices—everything must be carefully thought out and constructed so that the new roof blends in naturally with the old one.

All roof framing is based on the geometric formula for right triangles, called the Pythagorean theorem. The formula is $a^2 + b^2 = c^2$, where a is one leg of the triangle, b is the other leg, and c is the sloping side opposite the right angle, called the *hypotenuse.* If you imagine looking at a cross section of a roof, you'll see that a is the horizontal distance from the outside of the wall to the center of the ridge, b is the vertical distance from the top of the wall to the center of the ridge, and c is the roof.

FIGURE 13.15

For speed and greater stability, the sheathing can be installed over the rough window openings and then be cut out later.

Roof Types

There are a number of different roof shapes and designs used in residential construction (Figure 13.16), and sometimes a combination of two or more might be employed on the same house. The appropriate choice of roof type for an addition is usually dictated by the existing design, although in some cases a different

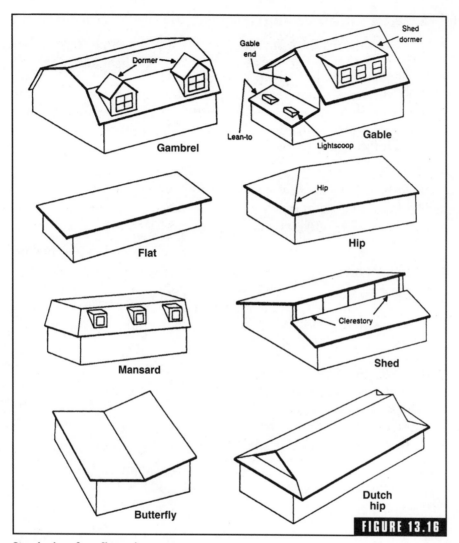

FIGURE 13.16

Standard roof configurations.

roof type will blend very nicely with the architecture of the existing building. Most roof types are some variation of the following basic configurations.

■ *Gable:* The most commonly used of all the roof types, gable roofs have two sloping surfaces extending down to two sides from a central ridge. Gable ends, which are extensions of the wall surface, make up the other two ends.

■ *Hip:* Hip roofs slope in all four directions, with no gable ends.

■ *Flat:* Technically, a flat roof is one having no slope at all, but in actual practice, flat roofs have a slight slope (usually no greater than 1:12) to allow for water drainage.

■ *Dutch hip:* The Dutch hip is a combination of the gable and hip styles, in which a slight hip is added to the two gable ends for architectural interest and to provide an overhang on all four sides.

■ *Shed:* Shed roofs slope in one direction only, and they are the easiest of all roof types to construct. When attached to the side of a building, this type of roof is also referred to as a *lean-to*.

■ *Gambrel:* The traditional "barn" roof, gambrels are identified by their double-sloping roof lines. The upper slope is relatively flat, usually about 2/12 or 3/12, while the lower slopes are steeper, often 12/12 or greater. Gambrel roofs offer good interior headroom on the upper story, and they are often used in conjunction with dormers.

■ *Mansard:* Similar to both the hip and the gambrel, mansard roofs have a double slope, with the upper slope being almost completely flat and the lower slope being almost vertical. Mansard roofs offer the greatest amount of interior headroom when they are used to enclose a second story.

■ *Butterfly:* The opposite of a gable roof, butterfly roofs slope down from the walls to a lower central valley. This type of roof is rarely seen in residential construction.

Roof-Framing Terminology

There are a number of terms associated with roof framing that you should understand before beginning your project (Figure 13.17). This knowledge will make the layout and construction of the roof easier and will enable you to make framing decisions based on your particular roof.

bird's-mouth A notch cut in the bottom side of a rafter so that it will sit down over the wall plate.

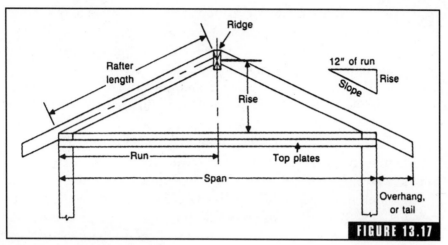

The parts of a typical roof frame.

cornice   The section of the roof that overhangs the side wall.

jack rafters   Shorter rafters that do not go all the way from ridge to plate. *Hip jacks* connect the hip rafter to the plate; *valley jacks* extend between the ridge and the valley rafter; *cripple jacks* connect a hip rafter with a valley rafter.

level cut   An angled cut that will be horizontal when the rafter is installed in its diagonal position. Also referred to as a *seat cut*.

overhang   The horizontal distance that the roof extends out past the walls.

plumb cut   An angled cut on the end of a rafter that will be vertical when the rafter is installed in its diagonal position.

rafter length   The total length of a rafter, measured diagonally from the centerline of the ridge to the outside of the plate, exclusive of overhangs.

rafters   There are three types of full-length rafters that make up a roof frame. *Common rafters* extend diagonally from the ridge to the plate. *Valley rafters* extend from the ridge to an inside corner of two intersecting walls. *Hip rafters,* found only on a hip roof, extend from the end of the ridge to the outside corners of the walls.

rafter tail   The portion of a rafter extending past the walls to form the overhang.

ridge   The highest horizontal member of the roof frame, to which one end of all the full-length rafters are attached.

rise The vertical distance from the top of the wall plates to the center of the ridge.

run The horizontal distance from the outside of the wall plate to the center of the ridge, equal to one-half the span.

slope The ratio between the unit rise and the unit run. Slope is commonly designated simply by referring to that ratio (a 4/12 roof, a 6/12 roof, etc.).

span The total width of the building, from the outside of one wall plate to the outside of the opposite wall plate.

unit rise and run The angle of the roof is expressed as a ratio between one unit of run, which is always 12 inches, and one unit of rise, which is the vertical distance that the roof rises within those 12 inches of run. For example, a 6 in 12 roof would rise 6 inches vertically for each 12 inches it extends out horizontally.

Roof-Framing Tools

One tool that is virtually indispensable for roof framing is the framing square, also called a *rafter square*. It consists of a one-piece, L-shaped frame. The shorter side of the frame, 16 inches long, is called the *tongue*, and the longer side, 24 inches long, is the *body*. The square is ruled on the face side in ⅛- and ¹⁄₁₆-inch measurements, and on the back side in ¹⁄₁₀- and ¹⁄₁₂-inch measurements. In addition, it is printed or stamped with rafter-length tables and other useful information.

In addition to the rafter square, other marking and measuring tools are quite helpful in cutting a roof (Figure 13.18). Speed Squares are marked with a variety of common rafter angles as well as plumb and level cuts. Another is the sliding T bevel, used for duplicating angles.

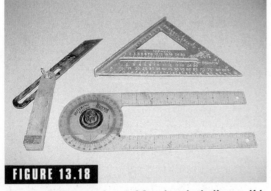

FIGURE 13.18

Three helpful tools for roof framing, including a sliding T bevel (left), a Speed Square (top right), and an adjustable angle gauge (bottom right).

Determining Existing Slope

When you are framing the roof for a room addition, it's crucial to know the slope of the existing roof. If the drawings of the original house are not available, then you'll need to take measurements from the actual roof.

If the existing house has a fairly accessible attic, you can take your measurements there. Using a framing square, place the 24-inch mark on the body against the underside of a common rafter (Figure 13.19). Holding a level on the body to be certain it's perfectly horizontal, read the number on the tongue where it meets the rafter. Because you are measuring to the 24-inch mark on the body, you have doubled the unit run. You must therefore divide the rise number on the tongue by 2 to determine the unit rise. If, for example, with the square held level and at 24, the 12 on the tongue is adjacent to the rafter, this would be a 12/24, or 6/12, slope.

You can also take the measurements on the roof using two levels. Place the end of a 24-inch level against the roof and hold it so it's level. Place a second level against the other end of the first level and hold it so it's plumb. Have a second person measure from the bottom of the horizontal level to the roof, using the vertical level as a guide. Once again, because the level is 24 inches long, the measurement must be divided by 2 to determine the actual unit rise.

If you have access to an electronic level, this is the easiest method of all (Figure 13.20). Place the level flat on the roof, activate it and set it to read in degrees, then simply read the roof pitch in degrees on the screen.

Ceiling Joists

Framing begins with the layout and installation of the ceiling joists. The ceiling

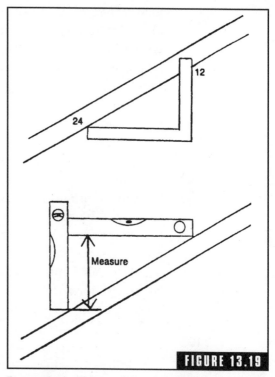

FIGURE 13.19

Two methods of determining the pitch of the existing roof: using a framing square (top) or two 24-inch levels (bottom).

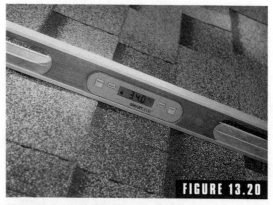

FIGURE 13.20

The use of an electronic level makes determining roof pitch both easier and more accurate.

joists act to tie the outside walls together and ensure that they are parallel to each other. They also serve as a stable working platform from which the roof can be framed.

Once again, a span table is necessary as a reference for selecting the size of the ceiling joists. Joist size is directly dependent on the length of the area the joists must span. In some cases, the joists will need to be spliced over interior partition walls in order to reduce their overall span. Those partition walls then become load-bearing, and any openings in the walls must have correctly sized headers.

Ceiling joists are installed parallel to the shortest dimension of the building, again to reduce the span. In some instances, the joists in one section of the house might run at right angles to joists in another section, depending on how the bearing partitions are laid out. If necessary, a beam can be run between the plates, then the joists can be extended out from the side walls in each direction and attached to the beam with joist hangers. This method reduces the overall distance the joists must span while eliminating the need for a partition wall.

The ceiling joists are laid out in the same manner as were the wall studs. If the joist spacing is 16 inches OC, measure in from one end of the wall 15¼ inches to locate the first joist, then simply lay out the joists every 16 inches.

With a hip roof, the first ceiling joist sometimes must be eliminated if its height will interfere with the rafters. In this case, set the edge of the first joist at 31¼ inches (15¼ + 16), then continue on with 16-inch spacing from there. After the rafters are in place, short tail joists are extended out perpendicular to this first joist to span the distance between it and the plate.

The ends of the joists must be flush with the outside edge of the plates. Because all of the joists are cut to the same length, if they are not flush with the outside of the walls, the walls will lean in or out. To correct this situation, place temporary diagonal bracing against the walls. Secure the joists by toenailing them into the plates.

Openings

Openings in the ceiling (Figure 13.21), such as those for a stairwell or skylight shaft, are framed exactly like those in the floor. Place double trimmer joists on each side of the opening and doubled headers at each end. Shorter tail joists finish the frame by extending out from the head-

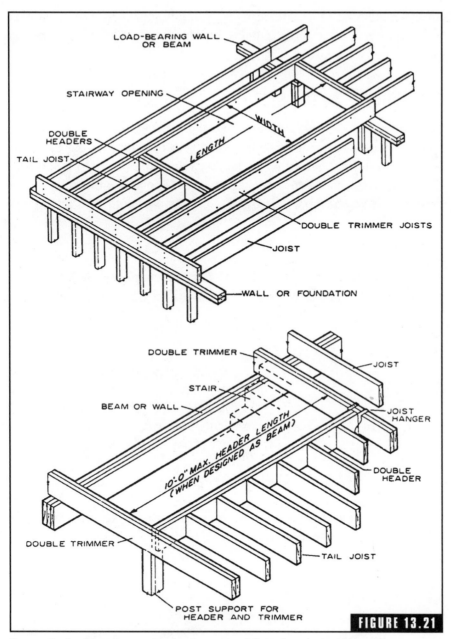

FIGURE 13.21

Two methods of framing an opening in a second floor for a stairwell.

ers in each direction. Smaller openings, such as those for an attic access hatch, can be framed by simply boxing in between the joists with single headers.

Determining Rafter Size

The size of the material that will be used for the rafters is determined from the span table. Rafter size is based on the slope of the roof, the length of the rafter, and the spacing between the rafters. To determine the length of the common rafters, apply the Pythagorean theorem. These calculations can be done very quickly on any calculator equipped with a square root key.

EXAMPLE

Assume you're working with a roof that has a span of 30 feet and a slope of 4 in 12. First, determine the total run (run = ½ the span):

$$30\text{-ft span} \times 0.5 = 15\text{-ft total run}$$

With a 4/12 roof, the roof rises 4 inches (unit rise) for each 12 inches it extends horizontally, so determine the total rise (unit rise × total run = total rise):

$$4\text{-in unit rise} \times 15\text{-in total run} = 60 \text{ inches total rise}$$

Convert total rise in inches to total rise in feet:

$$60 \text{ in} \div 12 = 5\text{-ft total rise}$$

You now have the base of the triangle (15-ft total run) and the height of the triangle (5-ft total rise). Apply the Pythagorean theorem formula $a^2 + b^2 = c^2$.

$$a^2 = 15^2 = 225$$

$$b^2 = 5^2 = 25$$

$$225 + 25 = 250$$

Square root of 250 = 15.81

Total rafter length is 15.81 feet

Next, convert 15.81 feet into feet, inches, and fractions of an inch so that the length can be accurately laid out on the board. Convert 0.81 foot into inches:

$$0.81 \times 12 = 9.72 \text{ in}$$

A simple method of converting the decimal into a fraction is to multiply the decimal by the accuracy of the fraction to which you wish it converted. In any framing, ⅛ inch is usually considered accurate enough, since there are disparities in the lumber and the practicalities of job-site applications. Convert 0.72 inch into eighths of an inch:

$$0.72 \times 8 = 5.76 \text{ (round off to 6)}$$

$$0.72 \text{ inch} = ⅝ \text{ or } ¾ \text{ in}$$

Each common rafter in this example is 15 feet 9¾ inches long. When you are ordering lumber for the rafters, be sure to add in the length of the overhangs as well as a waste allowance for the plumb cuts at each end of the rafter to determine the total length of the boards you'll need.

If you are doing a lot of roof framing, there are a growing number of books, computer programs, and specialized framing calculators that will greatly simplify calculations such as rafter length.

Building a Gable Roof

The first rafter is placed directly at the end of the wall, then each subsequent rafter is laid out according to the chosen spacing. Continue with the layout along the top of the plate until you reach the intersection with the existing house, making a pencil line and an X on the appropriate side of it, as was done during the wall layout. The last rafter sits at the end of the wall, regardless of the spacing between it and the rafter preceding it.

To stay accurate on your layout for the use of 4 × 8 sheathing, remember to subtract one-half the thickness of the rafter from the first layout, making it 15¼ inches in from the end for 16-inch spacing, or 23¼ inches in for 24-inch spacing.

Cutting Common Rafters

Common rafters are the first rafters to be cut and assembled on the roof (Figure 13.22). The first rafter must be accurately laid out and cut; it can then be used as a pattern for cutting all other common rafters of the same size.

Select a straight piece of lumber for the pattern rafter and lay it out across two sawhorses. Place the framing square on the board so that the unit rise on the tongue and the unit run on the body are both against the top edge of the board.

Using the preceding example for a 4/12 roof, these points would be the 4 on the tongue and, as always, the 12 on the body. Mark a pencil line along the outside edge of the tongue to indicate the centerline of the ridge.

Measure off 15 feet 9¾ inches from this point (the calculated rafter length), and repeat the procedure with the square, drawing a line to indicate the outside wall of the building. Form the bird's-mouth by using the square to draw a line perpendicular to the outside wall line.

FIGURE 13.22

Common rafters, for a gable roof, in this case engineered I-joists, connected to a ridge beam. *(Courtesy of Trus Joist MacMillan.)*

This line should be positioned so that it is approximately as wide as the wall plates. Finally, subtract half the thickness of the ridge from your first line, and the pattern rafter is ready to cut. Let the overhang end run long—it will be cut after the rafters are set.

Erecting the Intersecting Ridge

If the addition is perpendicular to the existing house, you will need to frame an intersection where the new roof ties into the old one (Figure 13.23*a, b*).

The first step is to erect the ridge. Begin by attaching some temporary supports to the ceiling joists to clamp the ridge to. Measure along the new ceiling joist closest to the existing house and mark the exact center of span. Measure over from this mark one-half the thickness of the board being used for the ridge. Select a straight 2 × 4, and nail or clamp it vertically to the rafter along this second mark. Use a level to be certain the board is plumb. Repeat this procedure, standing another 2 × 4 at the last joist and at as many intermediate joists as necessary to support the ridge board.

FIGURE 13.23A

Trusses being used to frame an intersecting roof for the addition of a garage.

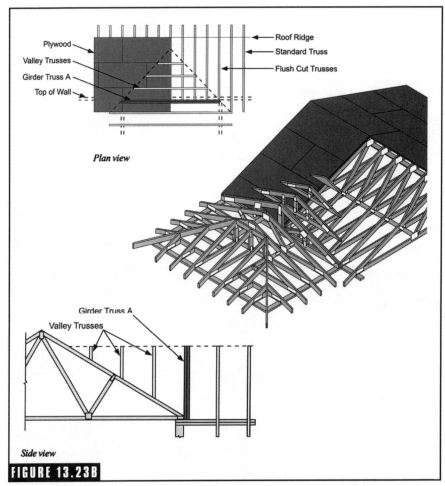

Plywood
Valley Trusses
Girder Truss A
Top of Wall

Roof Ridge
Standard Truss
Flush Cut Trusses

Plan view

Girder Truss A
Valley Trusses

Side view

FIGURE 13.23B

An example of how roof trusses are used to form an intersecting roof between an existing house and a room addition. *(Courtesy of Wood Truss Council of America.)*

Using the total rise figures calculated earlier, determine how high the bottom of the ridge will be and mark this point on each of the upright supports. Clamp a block of wood to each upright to support the ridge.

Cut the ridge board to length, using a board that is one size wider than the rafters—a 2×8 if you're using 2×6 rafters. If the ridge is to be made up of two or more pieces, you must splice them where a pair of rafters join in order to provide adequate support. Finally, cut an angle on one end of the ridge to match the slope of the existing roof.

Lift the ridge board and set it on the blocks. Carefully slide it along the blocks until it intersects the existing roof, and mark the intersection. Set the ridge back down on the ceiling joists. Snap a chalk line between this intersection point and the point where the addition meets the existing house. Repeat on both sides.

Using the line as a guide, tear off the old roofing within this triangular area. Replace the ridge board, clamping it securely to the uprights and nailing it to the roof sheathing at the intersection. Check it to be sure it's level, and adjust it as necessary by moving the clamps.

Gable Roof Framing

Referring to the rafter layout marks on the plates, mark the ridge where each rafter will join to it. Stand the common rafters up on each side of the building where they can be reached easily.

Lift the rafter closest to the existing house into place—the plumb cut on the end of the rafter should meet the ridge; the top of the rafter should be even with the top of the ridge; and the bird's-mouth should drop into place over the plate. Toenail the rafter to the plate, then nail through the ridge into the other end. Repeat with the remaining rafters, and remove the temporary supports.

Framing the Intersection

Measure along the ridge from the last common rafter and lay out the spacing for the jack rafters. Each jack rafter will have a plumb cut at one end where it meets the ridge and a seat cut at the other end where it sits on the old roof. In addition, the seat cut will be beveled to match the slope of the existing roof.

Snap new chalk lines from the point where the ridge intersects the roof to the point where the new wall plates meet the house. These lines indicate the angle of the valley formed by the two intersecting roofs.

You can determine the length of the jack rafters by referring to the tables printed on the face of the framing square or by using a rafter table or a framing calculator. On the square, refer to the line marked "diff in length of jacks 16 inch centers" (or the next table down, "diff in length of jacks 24 inch centers" if your rafters are on 24-inch centers). Look under the number on the outer edge of the body of the square that corresponds to the unit rise of your roof. Read down to the line on the table, and you will see a number indicating the amount by which each succeeding jack rafter will be reduced.

Start by laying out the length of a common rafter, marking the location of the ridge cut and the bird's-mouth. From that layout, subtract the measurement found on the rafter square table to determine the length of the jack rafter. Reading the fifth line down on the tables, you will see "side cut of jacks use." Again looking under the unit rise number, find the appropriate number from the table. Turn the rafter on its side, and hold the square against the edge of the board so that this number on the tongue is against the edge of the board, as is the 12 on the body. This will give you the angle of the bevel.

Using a circular saw, set the appropriate angle and cut along the seat cut mark you made earlier. Reset the saw for a straight cut and cut the plumb cut at the other end. Test-fit the jack rafter to see that it meets the ridge and the chalk line and that it is parallel with the last common rafter. If it isn't, make any necessary adjustments and cut a new one. When the cut is correct, cut a second one for the other side. Continue cutting the jack rafters, reducing the length of each pair, until you reach the intersection. Secure the jacks by nailing them to the ridge and toenailing them to the roof sheathing.

Extending an Existing Gable Roof

If the addition simply extends out from an existing gable end, the framing is considerably simplified by the elimination of any intersections. The main consideration is that the two roofs align exactly with each other so that the transition between them is unnoticeable.

First, remove any existing gable end overhang—new common rafters thus can join directly to the existing framing, and the framing and standing of the walls will be easier.

Connect the ridge board to the end of the existing ridge, and support it on temporary uprights as described previously. The first two common rafters should be installed directly against the last two existing rafters, and the tops of the new rafters should be exactly flush with the tops of the existing ones. By placing the first rafters directly against the old ones, you are assured of an exact transition between the roofs and adequate support for the end of the new ridge. Continue out from the house with the rest of the rafters until you reach the new gable end.

Gable End Framing

After all of the rafters are in place, gable end framing must be added. Since the gable end is actually an extension of the wall below it, the framing is essentially the same.

Using the layout of the wall framing as a guide, transfer the layout to the top of the top plate so that the gable end studs are directly above the wall studs. Hold a piece of stud lumber upright on the top plate at one of the marks, place a level against it to be certain it's plumb, then draw a line along both the top and the underside of the gable end rafter where it crosses the stud.

Cut the stud off straight at the lower end of the angled upper pencil mark. Set the depth of a circular saw to 1½ inches, then cut along the lower line. From the end of the stud, cut along a line that is 1½ inches in from the face of the stud. The resulting cuts will form a notch with an angled bottom. Toenail the stud to the top plate at the layout mark, then nail through the back of the notch into the gable end rafter. Remember that if a gable end vent is being used, you'll need to box in an opening between the studs as necessary.

Gable End Overhangs

Planning for an overhang should be decided on at the time the ridge is set. The ridge board should overhang the gable end wall by an amount equal to the width of the overhang minus the thickness of the rafter material.

The overhang is formed from horizontal supports, called *lookouts,* that are attached to the last regular rafters. Two more rafters, called *barge* or *fly rafters,* are attached to the lookouts. These boards should be carefully chosen for appearance, and they are usually one size wider than the stock used for the main rafters.

The 2 × 4 lookouts normally are placed 4 feet on center, measuring up from the fascia so that they fall in line with the 4-foot sheets of plywood used for the sheathing. Measure to the center of each lookout and mark this spot on both the gable end rafter and the next rafter in. From this mark, measure out 1¾ inches in each direction to make up the width of a 2 × 4.

With a circular saw set at a depth of 1½ inches, cut through the top of the gable end rafter on the two marks, then at several places

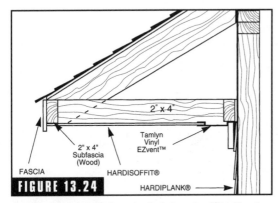

2" x 4"

2" x 4"
Subfascia
(Wood)

FASCIA

Tamlyn
Vinyl
EZvent™

HARDISOFFIT®

HARDIPLANK®

FIGURE 13.24

Construction details for a typical closed soffit. *(Courtesy of James Hardie Building Products.)*

between the marks to create a notch. Do not cut the next rafter in. Cut the lookouts to length so that they will reach from the inside of the second rafter to the inside of the barge rafter. Set them in the notches, then nail down into the gable end rafter and also through the second rafter into the end of the lookout. Cut the barge rafters to the same length as the common rafters, and nail them to the lookouts.

Once all of the roof and barge rafters are in place, you can add the fascia board. Fascias are normally made from 2-inch lumber, one size wider than the width of the rafters. Some types of cornices require slotted or other specially prepared fascia boards (Figure 13.24). Refer to the fascia drawings on the plans for details and specifications.

Measure and mark the overhang length at each end of the roof, and snap a chalk line between the two marks. This method ensures that the fascia will be straight and parallel with the house—simply cut a plumb cut on each rafter tail at the mark (Figure 13.25). Install the fascia directly to the ends of the rafters, using two 16d galvanized nails. Joints in the fascia should fall over a rafter, and they should be scarfed for best appearance.

FIGURE 13.25

Rafter tails extended past the wall with both plumb and level cuts for a closed soffit. Note the notched blocking between the rafters, which provides both support and ventilation. *(Courtesy of Trus Joist MacMillan.)*

Building a Hip Roof

Hip roof frames employ the same common rafters as on a gable roof, with the addition of hip rafters and hip jacks (Figure 13.26). After the common rafters are in place, cut the ridge off flush with the outside of the last common rafters. Then install one additional common rafter from the end of the ridge to the center of the end wall.

Since the last three common rafters form two squares when viewed from below, the hip rafters—which extend from

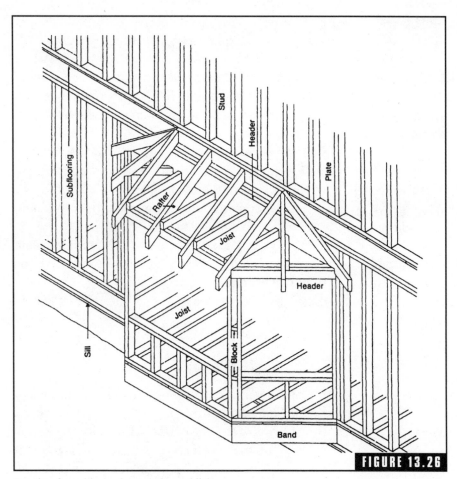

Framing for a hip roof over a bay addition.

the end of the ridge to the corner of the wall—are actually diagonals of those squares. Using the Pythagorean theorem, you can easily calculate the length of the hip rafter—a being the distance from the common rafter in the center of the end wall to the outside of the wall, b the length of the common rafter, and c (which you are calculating) the length of the hip rafter.

Lay out the hip rafter as was done for the common rafters, using the length just calculated. Because the hip rafter is the diagonal of a square, the ends will be cut at 45° to the other rafters. Just as the calculated length of the common rafters was reduced by half the thickness of the ridge, the hip rafter is reduced by half the thickness of the ridge measured on a 45° angle. With the saw blade set at 45°, make a plumb cut on the end of the rafter from both sides, forming a point. Cut a bird's-mouth at the other end.

The hip jacks are similar to the valley jacks cut earlier for the intersection. At the lower end, the bird's-mouth, tail length, and plumb cut are the same as for a common rafter. At the upper end, where the jack meets the hip rafter, make a beveled plumb cut.

After you have marked the tail and bird's-mouth cuts on the board, lay out the length as for a common rafter. Determine the common difference in length from the rafter tables on the square, as you did for the valley jacks. Subtract this difference from the length of the rafter, and also subtract half the 45° thickness of the hip rafter.

As with the other jacks, the angle of the cut can be determined from the fifth table on the framing square. Mark a plumb cut and, with the saw set at the appropriate angle, cut the top end of the rafter. Each subsequent rafter is reduced by the same common difference to ensure that the spacing layout on the plate is consistent.

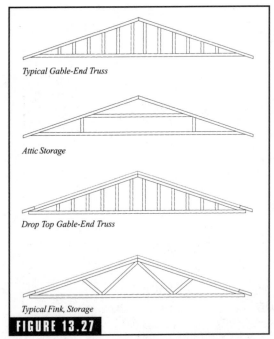

Typical Gable-End Truss

Attic Storage

Drop Top Gable-End Truss

Typical Fink, Storage

FIGURE 13.27

Four standard types of manufactured roof trusses.
(Courtesy of Wood Truss Council of America.)

Roof Trusses

A very popular alternative to all of the layout and cutting involved in constructing a roof is the use of prefabricated roof trusses. A truss is constructed in such a way that it forms a series of triangles (Figure 13.27), and as such is quite structurally rigid. It can span the distance between the outside walls with no additional support, eliminating the need for weight-bearing interior partition walls and allowing greater freedom in the layout of the interior.

The truss consists of the upper members, called the *top chords,* which form the roof line. *Lower chords,* which can be horizontal or angled as desired, act in place of the ceiling joists to support the finish-ceiling material. A number of engineering calculations are required for a truss to be properly weight-bearing and self-supporting, and documentation of these calculations (available from the company that is manufacturing the trusses for you) is required by most building departments prior to issuing building permits (Figure 13.28).

To order trusses, you will need to know the following things, all of which the truss company should be able to take from your plans: the total span from the outside of one exterior wall to outside of the opposite exterior wall, the slope of the roof, the size of the overhangs, and the desired configuration of the ceiling. Trusses take several days to several weeks to prepare, depending on their complexity and the back-

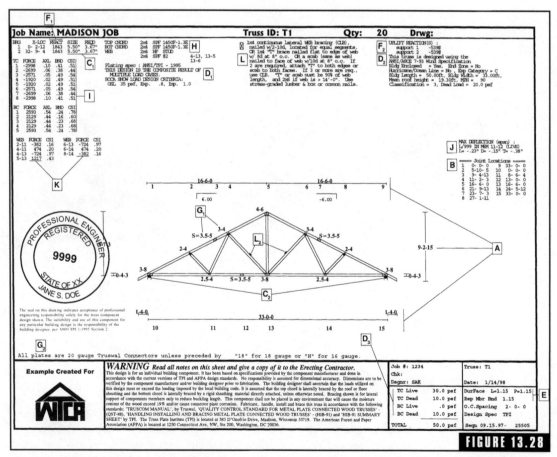

A typical engineering report and drawing for a manufactured roof truss. Note the engineer's stamp at left. *(Courtesy of Wood Truss Council of America.)*

FIGURE 13.28

log at the truss company. Order them at about the same time the floor framing is being done to ensure they will be ready when you need them.

Each truss takes the place of one pair of common rafters and one ceiling joist. For a gable roof, order a gable truss for each gable end. Gable trusses are constructed with vertical studding instead of the intermediate diagonal chords, making it easier to apply the siding. For hip roofs and intersections, the truss company can supply precut hip and valley rafters and jacks, or you can cut your own as described previously.

Install the trusses as soon as you have completed and braced the walls. Trusses are usually set 24 inches OC, and you should have the plates marked before the trusses are delivered.

Arrange with the truss company for plate-top delivery (Figure 13.29). A truck equipped with a small crane will deliver them to the site and set them in one or more bundles on top of the wall plates. For

FIGURE 13.29

Roof trusses that have been delivered to the job site and set by crane on the top plates. Note the temporary brace (left) holding them upright.

large or awkward trusses, you can hire the truss company to swing each truss into place individually and hold it with the crane while your carpenters secure it into place. Depending on the size and complexity of the roof structure, this service might be well worth the extra money.

Begin installation with the gable end truss or, for a hip roof, with the last common truss before the hip. Set the truss on the plate marks and toenail it down to the plates. Special framing anchors may also be used if desired. Place a long diagonal brace from the truss to the ground or to any other solid spot, and brace the truss in a plumb position.

Continue placing the trusses according to the spacing on the plates. Measure the distance between the trusses at the top, and nail a temporary board across them to hold them at the correct spacing until the sheathing is set. Usually, a 2×4 or 2×6 is nailed across the top of the bottom chords to keep the spacing consistent and to provide a walkway between the trusses.

SpaceMaker™ Trusses

A recent innovation in trusses, very helpful for the remodeler and room addition contractor, is the SpaceMaker™ Truss (Figure 13.30) from Trus Joist MacMillan (see Sources). It is a site-assembled truss (Figure 13.31) that's designed to create additional living space over any framed area.

The truss is constructed from a very strong and stably engineered wood called Timberstrand® laminated stand lumber. It is fully engineered, precut, and predrilled at the factory, and it comes with all the necessary assembly hardware and instructions. Assembly takes only a few minutes with a standard socket wrench (Figure 13.32).

The completed trusses are lifted into place and erected as described previously. As with any type of truss, they form both the roof and ceiling joist, but their open interior design also creates additional living space that can be finished off at any time in the future.

Sizes are limited to 22 to 28 feet in width, with roof pitches of 10/12 or 12/12, but if they work for your addition, it's a quick and easy way of gaining both a roof structure and a bonus room.

FIGURE 13.30

SpaceMaker™ Trusses, which simplify creating additional living space on a second floor. *(Courtesy of Trus Joist MacMillan.)*

Attic Ventilation

Attic ventilation is necessary to allow moisture from the house to be exhausted to the outside. Allowed to collect in the attic, this moisture will do serious damage to the wooden framing members. Properly installed attic ventilation has the added benefit of removing hot air from the attic during the summer, which helps keep the house cooler and prolongs shingle life.

A simple formula for calculating ventilation requirements is 1 square foot of net free area (NFA) (Figure 13.33) of ventilation for each 300 square feet of ceiling area. Thus, for a 1500-square-foot house, 5

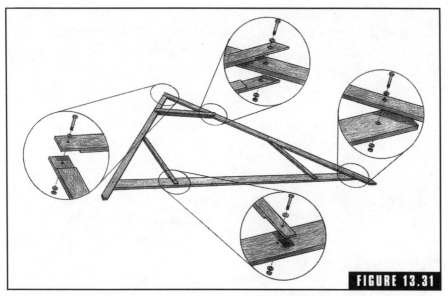

The assembly sequence for the SpaceMaker truss. *(Courtesy of Trus Joist MacMillan.)*

The SpaceMaker truss uses a carefully designed assembly of engineered lumber, connected with steel spacers, bolts, washers, and locknuts. *(Courtesy of Trus Joist MacMillan.)*

The NFA for a vent, in this case 50 square inches, is printed on the vent housing.

square feet of ventilation would be required. The vents should be placed so that half of them are low on the roof, typically in the soffits, and half are high, as close to the ridge as possible. Through the natural rising of warm air, this placement will allow cool air to be drawn in through the low vents, while hot air is exhausted out the high vents (Figure 13.34).

A number of different types of vents are available, including screened soffit vents, vents for the gable end, top vents, and continuous-ridge vents (Figure 13.35). You can purchase vents with wood, metal, or vinyl frames, and in different angles and configurations (circles, octagons, and other shapes). You can also construct your own soffit vents through the use of screened holes or slots (Figure 13.36).

Attic Access

Building codes require that most attics have some means of access. To do this, you can install an additional ceiling access hole in a closet or

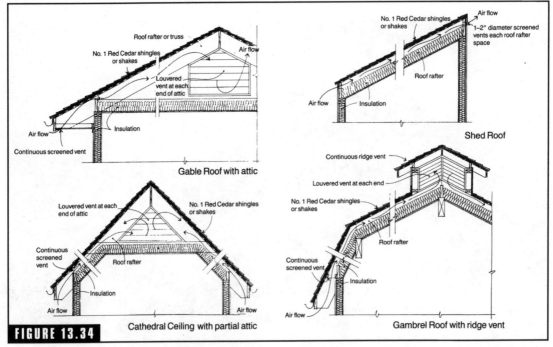

FIGURE 13.34

Ventilation airflow for four different kinds of roof construction. *(Courtesy of Cedar Shake and Shingle Bureau.)*

FIGURE 13.35

Roof vents set over an attic space to provide high (exhaust) ventilation.

other unobtrusive area, or you can cut an opening in the attic to provide a passageway between the existing attic and the addition, usually by cutting through the old roof sheathing and then boxing in between two rafters.

Adding a connection between the two attics allows easy access to the addition and provides a better cross flow of ventilation. If the addition is large, you should plan on providing both a new ceiling access and a passageway between the attics—this will greatly simplify access to the addition attic in the future.

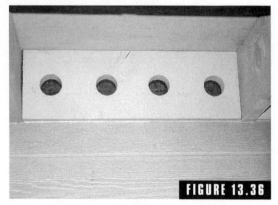

FIGURE 13.36

A site-drilled, screened block between rafters to provide low (intake) ventilation.

Roofing

With the framing done, the next step is to begin enclosing the addition, and that begins with the roofing.

Roof Sheathing

Before the roofing materials are applied, the roof frame must be sheathed. There are two types of sheathing: *solid-sheet sheathing* and *spaced sheathing* (also called *skip* or *open sheathing*).

Spaced sheathing is usually done with 1 × 4 lumber spaced the width of one board apart. The boards are attached using two 8d nails in each rafter. Spaced sheathing can be used only with certain types of roofing materials, and the spacing of the boards should be coordinated with the kind of roofing being used. Check with the manufacturer or supplier for recommendations.

Solid sheathing is considerably faster to install, and it adds lateral strength to the entire roof frame. Plywood has long been the most popular material for solid sheathing. For plywood, the most common grade choice for all areas of the roof that cannot be seen from underneath is C-D-X, meaning the panel has one C face, one D face, and is laminated with exterior glue. For exposed cornices, C-C plugged is a good choice. It offers one C face in which the defects have been removed and plugged with solid veneer, which offers a good surface for painting. The most common thickness is ½ inch, but ⅝ inch or even ¾ inch is used in certain high-load applications.

A less expensive and very popular alternative to plywood is oriented strand board (OSB). OSB panels are manufactured from long, thin strands of wood, oriented so that their grains are all running the same direction. The strands then are mixed with waterproof resin and cured under heat and pressure into a stable, uniform board. It is available in 4 × 8 panels, and the most common sheathing thickness is ⁷⁄₁₆ inch. When you are using OSB for sheathing, be sure that you still use plywood for exposed cornices.

First apply the panels to the overhang, using the C-C plugged grade if necessary. Start the first course with a full panel, continuing with full panels for the entire length of the roof. Start the second course with a half panel, so that the joints are staggered over different rafters, then continue with full panels to the end. Continue staggering the joints of each course by alternating full and half panels to start each course, making certain that the joints always fall over a rafter. Nail the panels to the rafters with 6d or 8d nails. Space the nails 6 inches apart along the edges and 12 inches apart everywhere else.

Reroofing

You'll find a wide variety of roofing materials on the market today, and several considerations must go into choosing the right one for your addition. If the primary goal is to match the existing roof, then that will certainly be a limiting factor.

A major remodeling project such as a room addition is also a perfect time to discuss a complete reroofing with your clients. A complete reroofing offers a number of benefits:

- Problems with matching the exact style and color of the existing roof are eliminated.

- Clean transitions and interweaving between old and new are no longer an issue.

- You can typically do the reroofing less expensively as part of the addition package than for the reroofing project by itself.

- All of the roofing will all age at the same rate.

- Warranty issues that may arise from integrating an old roof with a new one are avoided.

- Best of all, it gives the entire project a finished look—badly blended roofing is one of the biggest giveaways to an addition.

Evaluating the Existing Roof

Now is the time to take a good look at the existing roof to decide if reroofing is necessary (Figure 14.1). Begin the inspection by looking closely at the ceilings to see if there are any water stains. Since water will tend to run down the rafters to the lowest point of the roof no matter where the leak originated, pay particular attention to the areas where the ceiling intersects the outside walls.

If water stains are present, go up to the attic and use a bright light to examine the rafters. Look for dark streaks along the sides of the

Begin inspection inside the roof for hidden leaks and stains.

Cedar shakes may split and dislodge when aged.

FIGURE 14.1

Typical warning signs of deteriorating roofing that is due for replacement. *(Courtesy of Cedar Shake and Shingle Bureau.)*

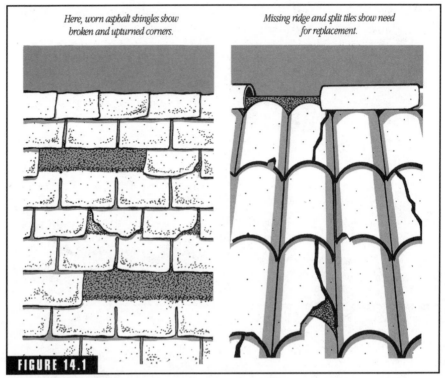

Here, worn asphalt shingles show broken and upturned corners.

Missing ridge and split tiles show need for replacement.

FIGURE 14.1

(Continued).

wood, especially in the areas where the ceiling stain was noticed. Try to trace any stains up the rafters and pinpoint their entry point. Use a tape measure to take measurements from the point of entry to any objects that will be readily identifiable on the roof, such as a chimney, vent pipe, or roof vent. Also, measure down from the ridge and up and over from the outside walls.

A close inspection of the roof itself is next. Begin with a look at the roof in general, paying particular attention to obvious signs of deterioration. If the roof has been covered with composition shingles or roll roofing, check to see if the shingles have begun to curl up at the edges. Another indicator of wear is the condition of the mineral granules that cover the shingles—if a considerable amount of them are gone, showing large portions of the black part of the shingle, a new roof is needed.

For wood shingles and shakes, look for large cracks in the wood and for loose shingles where the nails have begun to work loose. Look at the hip and ridge shingles for signs of deterioration. Signs of mildew growth on wood shingles and shakes is another sign of trouble, and one that also indicates a serious lack of attic ventilation. Built-up roofing, commonly used on flat roofs, should be checked for signs of cracking, particularly around the edges and where flashings are embedded. If gravel or mineral surfacing was used on the top layer, it should be checked as the composition shingles were for obvious signs of loose and missing material.

Now transfer your attic measurements to the roof, and look for signs of where the water stains on the rafters might have originated. Check around pipe and vent flashings, around roof jacks, and along the perimeter of the chimney. Examine the flashings around skylights, and check the skylights themselves.

Another good indicator of roof problems is the age of the house itself or the time that has elapsed since the last reroofing. Most composition shingle and built-up roofs have a life expectancy of 20 to 25 years. Wood shingles are about the same, while wood shakes can last anywhere from 25 to 35 years or even longer in some areas. Metal and tile roofs kept in good repair should last the life of the house. If the roof is approaching the end of its life expectancy or if you observe any of the conditions just described, a complete reroofing is well worth discussing with your clients.

Roofing Materials

Each roofing material has its own advantages and disadvantages, and some can be used only with certain types of roofs. When considering a complete reroofing, discuss the pros and cons of each type with your clients.

Composition Roofing

Composition roofing is made up of a thick asphalt felt or asphalt-impregnated fiberglass mat. Mineral granules in a variety of colors are embedded in the asphalt, increasing the wear resistance and providing architectural appeal.

Composition roofing is available in two forms: rolls and shingles. Roll roofing is available in 36-inch-wide rolls, usually in 36-foot lengths. Shingles are available in a variety of shapes and sizes, typically 36 to 39 inches long and 12 inches wide. Most composition shingles are manufactured with a strip of asphalt adhesive on the back. As the shingle warms in the sun after installation, the strip affixes the top shingle to the shingle below it for greater wind resistance.

Of particular popularity today is the laminated shingle, which is actually two shingle layers laminated together. The bottom layer (a rectangle) and the top layer (with several cutout areas in it), when bonded together, create a shingle that is heavier, flatter, and has more depth and shadow lines than the traditional single-layer, three-tab shingles.

- *Applications:* Composition shingles, applied over a solid roof deck such as plywood, are limited to roof slopes of 4/12 and above. (With special installation procedures, they can be installed on slopes lower than that.) Weather exposure is 4 to 6 inches, depending on the style, and weight varies from under 200 pounds to almost 400 pounds per square. Roll roofing also is applied over a solid deck and, depending on the amount of overlap, can be used on roofs as flat as 1/12. Weather exposure varies from 16 inches for low slopes to 34 inches for most other types. Double-coverage rolls cover ½ square; all others cover one square per roll. Weight varies from 75 to 90 pounds per roll.

- *Advantages:* Lower cost than most other roofing. Wide variety of colors and patterns available. Very wind-resistant. Class A fire rating (the best). Fairly resistant to ice-damming problems. Fast and easy to install.

- *Disadvantages:* Some view it as a "low-end" roofing that lacks richness and texture. Three-tab shingles do not have a lot of architectural appeal, and roll roofing has none whatsoever.

Wood

Wood shingles and shakes usually are manufactured from cedar, but cypress or redwood are occasionally used. The wood is yellowish or reddish in tone when it is first applied, weathering to a moderate gray after several years. Wood shingles are produced by sawing, leaving a uniform taper and width. Shakes are hand-split, providing less uniformity and more surface texture, and they are longer and thicker than shingles. Shingles are rated as follows: No. 1, a clear and premium grade; No. 2, a slightly lower grade; No. 3, an economy grade used primarily for outbuildings; and No. 4, used only for undercourses. Shakes are No. 1 only.

- *Applications:* Wood shingles and shakes are installed over a solid deck or spaced sheathing boards, and they're limited to roofs of 4/12 slope or greater. Sizes range from 16 to 24 inches in length, depending on type, with weather exposures of 5 to 7½ inches. Weight is approximately 150 to 200 pounds per square.

- *Advantages:* Warm, natural appearance. Complements and blends with virtually any type of architecture. Installation is fairly straightforward. Can sometimes be installed directly over old wood or composition shingles, eliminating the need to tear off the old roofing.

- *Disadvantages:* Class C fire rating (the worst). Treated wood can reach a Class B, but this is more expensive. Installed cost can be two to four times that of composition. Very prone to lifting and subsequent damage from ice damming—shakes in particular.

Metal

Metal roofing has been around a long time, but is only now beginning to enjoy an increase in popularity. The most common metals are aluminum and galvanized steel, although other metals are used. Metal roofing is available in long strips, usually 2 to 3 feet wide, in several styles: corrugated; high rib, which overlaps and interlocks with the previous sheet; and stamped, in patterns resembling wood shakes or individual tiles. Individual metal and aluminum tiles are also available. All types are available in several different colors, and the sheet metal can be purchased unpainted.

- *Applications:* Sheet metal can be applied over a solid deck or spaced sheathing and can be used on slopes down to 3/12. Aluminum shingles should be installed only over a solid deck, and on slopes down to 4/12. The exposure, packaging, and weight vary with the manufacturer, but the panels are relatively light when compared with other types of roofing.

- *Advantages:* Lightweight and completely fireproof. Virtually indestructible and should last the life of the structure. Increasing number of colors and types available for better compatibility with different house styles. Sheets are continuous from eave to ridge. Sheds snow quickly with little buildup. Virtually impervious to ice damming.

- *Disadvantages:* Relatively expensive compared to most other roofing. More difficult to install, especially on complex roofs. Some types require special tools. Somewhat difficult to walk on. Sometimes difficult to flash and seal, and difficult to cut into for remodeling. May be noisy during rain- or hailstorms.

Tile

Tile roofing, like metal, has been introduced in new styles and colors in recent years, and its popularity is increasing. Most tile roofing is made of shale or shale mixtures, which is then formed in molds and burned. Some new, lightweight types are also made of cement and other materials. Most types are left unglazed. Color is added before the burning; therefore it is uniform and baked into the entire tile.

- *Applications:* Tiles may be installed over solid decking or over spaced sheathing, although the second application varies with the type of tile. They should be installed only on roofs with a 4/12 or greater pitch. Exposure is approximately the same as for composition shingles. Weight varies with tile size and type, but most are quite heavy—some types weigh as much as 800 pounds per square.

- *Advantages:* Completely fireproof. Should outlive the building itself. Many styles and colors available, with a warm, shakelike appearance. Compatible with virtually any architectural style.

- *Disadvantages:* Typically the most expensive of all roofing types. Most tiles are very heavy, and may require structural reinforcement of the roof (the newer lightweight tiles have overcome most of this problem). Similar to shakes in amount of labor to install. Requires special cutting tools. Hard to walk on and difficult to cut through. Some types require special flashing.

Installing Composition Shingles

Composition shingles are installed with flat-headed, galvanized roofing nails, either hand- or air-driven, or with wide-crown, air-driven galvanized staples. Use 1¼- or 1½-inch-long nails for new work, 1¾-inch or longer nails for reroofing, except on exposed cornices where the fastener length must be carefully chosen so that the points do not protrude through the exposed plywood sheathing.

Underlayment

After the sheathing is completed, it is covered with an underlayment of 15-pound, asphalt-impregnated felt (Figure 14.2)—the "15-pound" designation refers to the felt's weight per square. The waterproof felt provides an additional layer of protection against leaks, and should never be omitted when shingling over new sheathing.

To help the roof shed water away from the cornices and overhangs, a drip edge is often installed along with the felt. Galvanized sheet-metal drip edges in a preformed L shape are available in various sizes to accommodate the thickness of new roofing or reroofing. Install one at the eaves, directly on the roof sheathing, and cover it with the felt. Install the side drip edges on top of the felt.

The bottom edge of the roof is covered with at least one layer of 15-pound felt, which is secured with staples. Subsequent rows of felt are then installed all the way to the ridge, with the upper row overlapping the previous row at least 2 inches, and 4 inches at the sides if the felt needs to be spliced.

In colder areas where winter icing is a problem, the installation of protection against ice damming is typically required by the building codes. This can usually be in the form of an extra layer of 15- or 30-pound felt, extending up far enough so that it overlaps the line of the outside wall. In areas with severe icing problems, 90-pound roll roofing or a specialized ice-protection membrane is highly recommended.

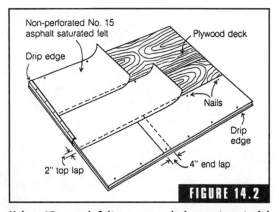

FIGURE 14.2

Using 15-pound felt as an underlayment material over roof sheathing prior to installation of composition shingles.

Shingles

A starter course of shingles is installed at the eave line first. This can be in the form of a special starter shingle or a standard three-tab shingle with the tabs facing up. This shingle is installed flush with the side and bottom drip caps.

The first course begins with a full shingle, aligned to overlap the side and bottom drip cap edges to shed water, and then continues along the first course with each shingle butting the one before it. The last shingle is cut off flush with the drip cap.

Four fasteners—nails or air-gun staples (Figure 14.3)—are installed in each shingle above the line of the sealant, with two of them about 1 inch in from each end and the other two approximately one-third of the way in from each end.

For the second course, the first shingle is shortened by 6 inches (Figure 14.4), ensuring that the butt joints of one course do not fall over the joints in the course below. Each succeeding course is shortened by an additional 6 inches until getting back to a full shingle again—the cutoff pieces are used at the other end of the course. A chalk line is typically used for alignment of each course (refer to the manufacturer's recommendations for the correct amount of weather exposure).

Valleys

A 36-inch-wide strip of 50- or 90-pound roll roofing or ice and water membrane is typically installed in the valleys, on top of the underlayment felt. Shingles are nailed at the outer edges only, with care taken not to nail into the central portion of the valley.

Shingling continues on one side of the valley, allowing the shingles to extend at least 12 inches past the valley centerline and onto the other side of the valley. The roofing on the other side of the valley is installed next, overlapping the singles from the other side. The exposed second layer of shingles is then cut on an angle that follows the line of the valley (Figure 14.5).

Vent Flashings

Any protrusion through the roof requires the installation of flashing to prevent the roof from leaking at that point, typically in the form of a

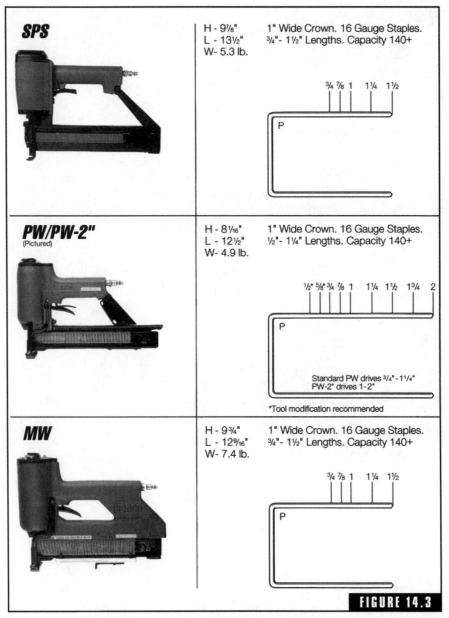

SPS

H - 9⅞"
L - 13½"
W- 5.3 lb.

1" Wide Crown. 16 Gauge Staples.
¾"- 1½" Lengths. Capacity 140+

¾ ⅞ 1   1¼   1½

P

PW/PW-2"
(Pictured)

H - 8¹⁄₁₆"
L - 12½"
W- 4.9 lb.

1" Wide Crown. 16 Gauge Staples.
½"- 1¼" Lengths. Capacity 140+

½* ⅝* ¾ ⅞ 1   1¼   1½   1¾   2

P

Standard PW drives ¾"-1¼"
PW-2" drives 1-2"

*Tool modification recommended

MW

H - 9¾"
L - 12⁹⁄₁₆"
W- 7.4 lb.

1" Wide Crown. 16 Gauge Staples.
¾"- 1½" Lengths. Capacity 140+

¾ ⅞ 1   1¼   1½

P

FIGURE 14.3

Three types of air-powered roofing staplers and the sizes of wide-crown staples each will shoot. *(Courtesy of Senco Products.)*

FIGURE 14.4

Installation procedure for three-tab composition shingles. Note how each course is staggered back from the preceding one by 6 inches.

FIGURE 14.5

Composition shingles overlapped and cut in a valley.

prefabricated aluminum, plastic, rubber, or sheet-metal flashing (Figure 14.6). Plumbing vents are left open on top, while mechanical vents and flues use a two- or three-piece flashing with a cap. All penetrations of the roof must be complete before roofing begins.

Step Flashings

Flashings also are required where the shingles meet a vertical surface, such as a wall, a chimney, or a skylight curb (Figure 14.7). These flashings, called *step flashings,* are approximately 7 inches long and 10 inches wide, folded along the 7-inch dimension into an L shape.

Starting from the bottom, one piece of flashing is set so that it sits on the roof deck and also extends up the wall. It is secured by driving one or two nails into the sheathing at the top, then extending the roofing course over the flashing up to the wall. A dab of roofing cement placed between the bottom of the shingle and the top of the flashing will improve the shingle's wind resistance. Siding should be held above the angle of the step flashings by about 1 inch to allow for good drainage.

For skylights and masonry chimneys, cap and base flashings must also be used. The base flashing is installed first, set so that it is on top of the lower courses of shingles. Step flashings are installed up the sides, and a cap flashing is installed overlapping the top step flashings. The upper row of shingles covers the roof deck flange of the cap flashing.

FIGURE 14.6

A metal roof flashing with a rubber insert for use with an ABS vent pipe.

FIGURE 14.7

Step flashings used where a roof meets a side wall.

Hips and Ridges

Hips and ridges are finished off with hip and ridge shingles (Figure 14.8). These can be made by cutting regular three-tab shingles into pieces or by using shingles manufactured for this purpose.

Hips are covered first, working from the bottom up, so that the ridge shingles will overlap the tops of the hips. Each shingle is centered on the hip and secured with two nails, one on each side about 5½ inches up from the bottom and 1 inch in from the sides. Each succeeding hip shingle covers the fasteners in the one preceding it.

Installing Wood Shingles and Shakes

While there are similarities between the installation of composition shingles and wood, there is also a number of differences. Wood is not as uniform, especially in the case of shakes, and it is not self-aligning, as are composition shingles. The smaller size of wood shingles and shakes means a much greater number of pieces per square, and their random widths require more installation time.

FIGURE 14.8

Composition hip and ridge shingles.

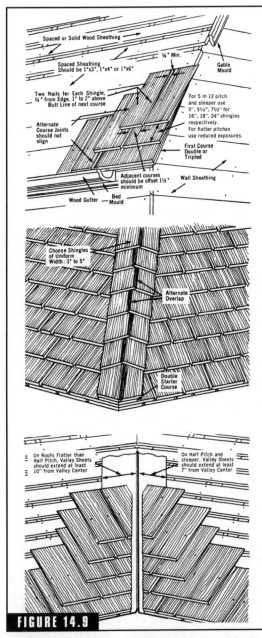

Spaced or Solid Wood Sheathing

¼" Min.

Gable Mould

Spaced Sheathing Should be 1"x3", 1"x4" or 1"x6"

Two Nails for Each Shingle, ¾" from Edge, 1" to 2" above Butt Line of next course

For 5 in 12 pitch and steeper use 5", 5½", 7½" for 16", 18", 24" shingles respectively. For flatter pitches use reduced exposures.

Alternate Course Joints should not align

First Course Double or Tripled

Adjacent courses should be offset 1½" minimum

Wall Sheathing

Wood Gutter

Bed Mould

Choose Shingles of Uniform Width: 3" to 5"

Alternate Overlap

Double Starter Course

On Roofs Flatter than Half Pitch, Valley Sheets should extend at least 10" from Valley Center

On Half Pitch and steeper, Valley Sheets should extend at least 7" from Valley Center

FIGURE 14.9

Standard installation procedures for wood shingles, including installation of the shingles (top), installation of hip and ridge shingles (middle), and installation of valley flashing (bottom). *(Courtesy of Cedar Shake and Shingle Bureau.)*

Wood shingles are installed using 3d box nails for the 16- and 18-inch shingles, and 4d for 24-inch shingles. Use 6d nails with wood shakes. Each square will require 2 to 2½ pounds of nails.

Installing Wood Shingles

Wood shingles are installed without underlayment felt or drip caps (Figure 14.9). Installation begins at the bottom edge of the roof with a starter course of No. 4 shingles, overlapping the eaves by about 1 inch to ensure good drainage over the cornice. Space shingles approximately ¼ inch apart to allow for expansion, and secure them with two nails driven about ¾ inch in from each side.

Completely cover the starter course with the first course of regular shingles. Pay close attention to the joints between the shingles to ensure that each one falls over a solid shingle below. Place each shingle to offset the joints by at least 1½ inches from the joints in the course below it. At least two rows of shingles should separate the courses before the joints begin to fall in line again. Choose shingles carefully from among the different widths in the bundle to find the proper combinations of overlaps.

The weather exposure of the shingles varies with the length of the shingle being used. Use some sort of guide to keep the shingles straight—a length of board temporarily tacked to the roof works best, enabling rapid installation of the shingles by simply butting them against the board. Snapping a chalk line for each course also works well.

Installing Wood Shakes

Shakes are installed essentially the same as wood shingles, except that an 18-inch-wide strip of 30-pound felt, called a *shaker liner,* is used between the courses.

Install a strip of 36-inch wide, 30-pound ice and water membrane at the eaves first, followed by a strip of 18-inch wide shake liner, positioned up from the eaves a distance equal to twice the weather exposure of the shakes (Figure 14.10). For example, for 24-inch shakes with a 10-inch weather exposure, which is fairly common, position the felt 20 inches up from the eaves. The bottom edge of the next strip will be 10 inches up from the first, as will each succeeding row. Several rows of felt are usually rolled out at once, with the felt tacked down only at the top edge, so that the shakes can slide under it.

Install the shakes in the same manner as the wood shingles, paying close attention to the positioning of the joints between the shakes. Space the shakes about ¼ to ⅜ inch apart, and secure them with two nails each. As you install each course, position it so that the shakes go over one layer of felt and under the layer above that. Approximately the top 4 inches of the shake should be covered by the felt.

Valleys

Prefabricated, galvanized sheet-metal valleys are used with both wood shingles and shakes (Figure 14.11). The valley sheets are 10 feet long, and are nailed to the sheathing starting from the bottom up. Each sheet is overlapped by at least 2 inches, and nails are held back at least 6 inches from the centerline of the valley.

Cut the shingles at an angle as they reach the valley, matching the angle so that it parallels the centerline of the valley metal. Approximately 1 to 2 inches of metal should remain exposed on either side of the centerline.

Flashings

The procedure for installing flashings is the same for wood as for composition. Cut the shingles neatly around the vent pipes, and install them so that the bottom part of the flange is on top of the shingles and the upper part is beneath the shingles. Step, cap, and base flashings are all used in the same manner (Figures 14.12 and 14.13). In areas with

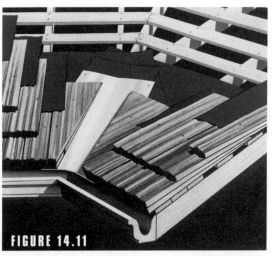

Standard installation procedure for cedar shakes. Note the staggering of the shingles and the use of individual courses of 30-pound shake liner felt. *(Courtesy of Cedar Shake and Shingle Bureau.)*

The installation of galvanized metal valley flashing with wood shakes. *(Courtesy of Cedar Shake and Shingle Bureau.)*

severe winter weather, you'll need to take precautions to prevent the formation of ice dams at the eaves.

Hips and Ridges

The easiest and best-looking way to cover hips and ridges is with pre-assembled hip and ridge shingles (Figure 14.14). They consist of two uniform-width, tapered shakes, overlapped along one edge and nailed together to form a V. The overlapped area is then beveled for a finished appearance.

Install the hip and ridge shingles so that the overlaps alternate. The bundles are packaged this way at the factory, making selection of alternating laps quick and easy. Wood hip and ridge shingles are installed in the same manner as the composition ones, doing the hips first and working from the bottom up. The exposure to the weather should be the same as for the rest of the shingles.

Connecting to an Existing Roof

In cases where the existing roofing is still in good condition, you may choose to tie the old shingles in with the new ones. If the old roof is

FIGURE 14.12

Individual step flashings and counterflashings to seal the joint between a shake roof and a brick chimney. *(Courtesy of Cedar Shake and Shingle Bureau.)*

FIGURE 14.13

Bottom flashings and counterflashings on a brick chimney. *(Courtesy of Cedar Shake and Shingle Bureau.)*

only one layer thick, position the top of the sheathing on the addition to be flush with the top of the existing sheathing.

If the old roof has two or three layers, patching in is not recommended. The problem is that it will be necessary to raise the sheathing to a point where the new shingles and the top layer of the old shingles will coincide. This can be done at the time of framing by one of several methods: raising the new ridge and rafters; shimming between the rafters and the roof sheathing; or raising the level of the new roofing by first laying down one or two layers of 90-pound roll roofing with butted (not overlapping) seams and applying the new shingles over it. While any of these procedures will work to align the new and old layers of shingles at the time of the addition's construction, serious alignment problems will be presented when it comes time to reroof and all of the layers of roofing are stripped off.

Starting from the top and working out from the intersection of the addition and the existing house, tear back each course

FIGURE 14.14

Wood hip and ridge shingles. Note the alternating overlaps where the two shingles are attached to each other to form the hip shingle. *(Courtesy of Cedar Shake and Shingle Bureau.)*

of existing roofing to expose a shorter section of the course below it. When you reach the bottom of the roof, the old roofing will have the appearance of a set of stairs, with each course of roofing torn back a little farther than one before it.

From this point, roofing proceeds as if it were a new roof. Underlay the new deck as required, then place the necessary starter course. Begin roofing by butting to the end of the first existing course and working out to the edge of the addition. Each succeeding course will in this manner cover the transition seam in the course below it. The whole key to reroofing properly is the proper alignment of the roof decks to make the level of the new roofing even with the level of the old one.

Skylights

Skylights have grown in popularity in the last decade or two, and advancement in design and construction has made installation easy and leakproof. Adding one or more to the addition, or to the existing house, can be done easily at the time of roofing.

There are two basic styles of skylights. *Flat skylights* are flat, tempered glass sheets set in a wood, metal, or vinyl frame, while *domed skylights* are made from convex molded acrylic sheets set in a metal frame. The domed models offer more surface area, resulting in a greater amount of light entering into the room, and their domed shaped makes them somewhat "self-cleaning" in the rain. Circular and pyramid shapes are variations of the domed style.

Flat skylights offer the advantage of being less obtrusive on the roof because of their lower profile. The glass will not yellow or scratch the way acrylic can, and a number of options are available with flat glass skylights that can't be found in acrylic, including shades, blinds, and the ability to open for ventilation.

Single, dual, and triple glazing are available in both styles from most manufacturers, but remember that skylights, like windows, must comply with energy codes in your area.

Average sizes range from a 12-inch square to a 48- by 96-inch rectangle, with a variety of sizes in between. The heights of the domes range from about 4 to 8 inches. If the house has a trussed roof, the skylight cannot be wider than the spacing between the trusses—usually

24 inches—because each truss is engineered as a self-supporting unit and cannot be cut or altered in any way.

In choosing a skylight, use the smallest size that will do the job. This practice saves on the initial purchase price, and most important, it saves energy. A dual-glazed skylight is rated at less than R-2, so it becomes a rather large cold spot in a ceiling rated at R-38.

Flat glass skylights can be purchased in operable models as well. While more expensive than fixed units, the operable type can be opened in the summer to allow hot air trapped at the ceiling to escape. Choices among operable skylights include manual operation, usually via a crank, or electric operation from a remote switch, with a manual override in case of emergency. Some types of electrically operated skylights also have optional rain sensors that will close the skylight automatically in the event of wet weather.

Most skylights are available in the following shades:

- Clear glazing, which offers the most light but also has the greatest amount of heat loss and gain

- Translucent white, which offers a more subdued light and a slightly better resistance to heat loss

- Tinted, usually a gray or bronze shade, which reduces glare but also reduces the amount of incoming light and also colors the light to some degree

Light Shafts

If the room that you intend to illuminate with the skylight has an open ceiling (one that is simply the underside of the actual roof), you can install the skylight without needing to construct a light shaft. This is by far the simplest installation, and it offers the maximum amount of light and view of the sky. Operable units are usually recommended, especially for a second-floor room, because these direct skylights often add a considerable amount of heat to the room on a summer day.

For conventional ceilings with an attic above, you must construct a light shaft to connect the skylight to the room (Figures 14.15 and 14.16). The light shaft is usually constructed of 2 × 4 or 2 × 6 lumber, and is covered on the inside with wood or drywall. Painting the drywall with glossy white paint will reflect even more light into the room. These shafts take one of three forms:

FIGURE 14.15

A cutaway view of a typical operable skylight and light shaft. *(Courtesy of Velux-America.)*

- *Straight,* in which the shaft drops vertically from the roof to the ceiling and is the same dimension as the skylight itself. This type is the easiest to construct, but, because of its offset angle to the skylight, offers the least amount of light.

- *Angled,* where the shaft is parallel to the pitch of the skylight. It, too, is the same dimension as the skylight, but its straight-in angle offers more light than a straight shaft. Angled shafts also are used to connect two locations that cannot otherwise be aligned—that is, when the skylight must be installed in a particular spot (e.g., between two trusses) and the shaft opening is likewise limited to a particular location on the ceiling.

- *Splayed,* or *pyramid,* in which the ceiling opening is larger than the skylight opening in width, in length, or in both. This type, although slightly more difficult to construct, is the most popular, simply because it allows a smaller skylight to illuminate a larger area.

CONSTRUCTING A LIGHT SHAFT

First, decide on the desired ceiling opening. Take into consideration the overall room size and how much light is needed, and select an opening of appropriate size. Remember, an opening that will lay in between the ceiling joists will require the least amount of framing.

Mark the opening on the ceiling, using a framing square and straightedge to ensure a square, accurate layout. Drive a small nail through the drywall at each corner, then go up into the attic and check for obstructions such as electrical wires and pipes. While you're up there, move the insulation away from the area of the opening.

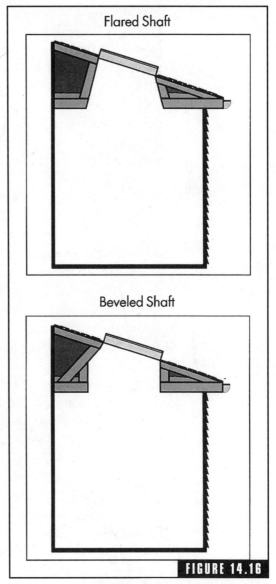

Two types of skylight light shafts. *(Courtesy of Velux-America.)*

The next step is to mark the underside of the roof for the skylight opening. Use a plumb bob to transfer each corner of the ceiling opening up to the roof sheathing. Refer to the manufacturer's specifications for the proper roof opening for your skylight, and mark this opening size on the sheathing also. Use the ceiling opening marks as a guide for laying out the roof opening, aligning the second opening to the first in accordance with the type of shaft you intend to use. Drive a 16d nail up through each corner of the roof layout.

From below, use a drywall saw to cut out the ceiling opening. If the opening falls directly between the two joists, use lumber of the same dimension as the joists and install a cross piece between the joists at each end of the ceiling cutout. Be sure the crosspieces are installed square to the joists.

If the opening necessitates cutting a joist, first construct temporary supports between the floor and the ceiling to carry the cut joists during framing. Cut and box the joists with headers and trimmers as with any other ceiling opening.

Locate the four protruding nails on the roof, and carefully remove the shingles in an area 12 inches beyond these marks. Cut out the roof sheathing between the four corner marks; then use lumber of the same size as the rafters and frame in the opening, using the same procedures as for the ceiling opening.

Flat glass skylights are installed directly onto the roof sheathing, using the L-brackets provided with the kit. Simply attach the clips to the sides of the skylight, center it over the opening, then secure the clips to the sheathing with screws.

For a domed skylight, you will need to construct a wooden box called a *curb*. Using 2 × 6 or 2 × 8 lumber on edge, frame the box around the opening, with the inside edges of the curb aligning with the inside edges of the hole in the roof. Apply a thick coating of waterproof roof mastic to the sheathing around the opening and secure the curb to the roof, toenailing it down to the rafters. Also seal the corner joints in the curb with roof mastic.

Many manufacturers offer flashing kits to fit the size of the skylight frame or curb, and this is the best way to go. If a kit is not available, you will need to have the flashing components made up at a sheet-metal shop.

The flashing consists of a top and bottom flashing and a series of step flashings. Install them as described earlier in this chapter under Installing Composition Shingles, patching in the roofing as you go. For a curbed skylight, the last installation step is to secure the skylight on top of the curb and seal it in place.

Construct the shaft simply by connecting the opening in the roof with the one in the ceiling. Use 2 × 6 lumber, cut at the appropriate angles, to complete the connection. The inside of the shaft is typically covered with drywall, although wood or other materials can be used as well. On the attic side, insulate the shaft with fiberglass batt insulation to at least an R-21.

Doors, Windows, and Siding

Windows and doors make a major contribution to the architectural style of a home, and their selection is not something that should be taken lightly. There is a large selection of doors and windows, and, when choosing among them, you should consider energy efficiency, cost, appearance, and style.

The style of the windows and doors should be consistent with the rest of the house. The wrong window can ruin the look of a carefully planned and constructed addition, and doors that don't match the rest of the house tend to point out which areas have been added.

Door Styles and Materials

Selecting doors for the addition is a little easier than selecting windows, because the door style of the existing house is probably still around today. Door styles (Figure 15.1) have not changed to any great degree in many years. The big changes are in the materials, and this stems from the growing interest in energy efficiency and alternatives to solid wood.

Wood Doors

There are two basic door styles: flush and panel (Figure 15.2). A *flush door* consists of a four- or five-piece framework onto which sheets of various materials, called *door skins,* are glued. The skins might be

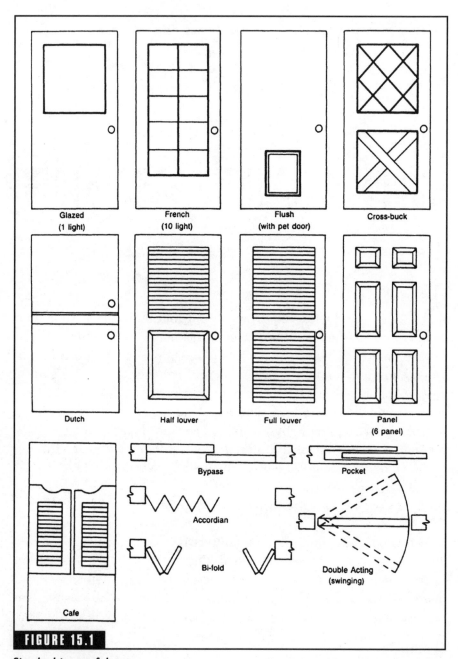

FIGURE 15.1

Standard types of doors.

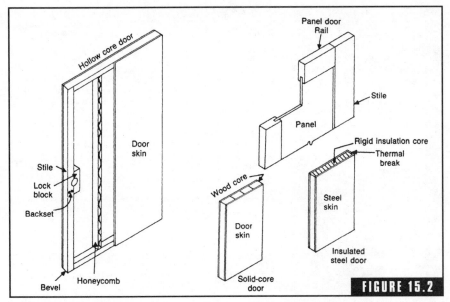

FIGURE 15.2

Typical construction of hollow-core, solid-core, and foam-core doors.

a wood veneer—oak and birch are two of the most popular—or hardboard that's embossed with a grain pattern or covered with a photographic paper that simulates the look of wood grain.

Flush doors can be *solid core,* meaning that the space between the door skins is solid lumber or particleboard, or *hollow core,* with a void space between the veneers except for strips of corrugated material that give some rigidity to the skins. Solid-core doors can be used inside or out, while hollow-core doors are intended for interior applications only.

Panel doors contain four or more slotted, interlocking frame pieces assembled around one or more central wood panels (Figure 15.3). Panel doors are designated by the number of panels they contain (a

FIGURE 15.3

A four-panel wooden prehung door.

FIGURE 15.4

Another carved wooden prehung door, with a pair of wood panel and leaded-glass sidelights.

one-panel door, a four-panel door, etc.). The panels can be either flat or beveled (to give a raised appearance). A number of styles are available, including ones with carved panels and other decorative effects (Figure 15.4), and a variety of hardwoods and softwoods are used.

One of the most popular innovations in recent years is the raised-panel hardboard door (Figures 15.5 and 15.6). For this type of door, a face panel is manufactured from thick, resin-coated hardboard that is formed and pressed to resemble a four- or six-panel door, with either a smooth or wood-grained surface texture. The appearance is very realistic, even down to duplicating the look of the joints where the frame pieces are normally joined. These are hollow-core, interior doors, intended for paint-grade use.

French doors, a variation of the panel door, contain one or more panes of glass in place of the wood panels. French doors are made up in pairs, with doors hinged at the outer jambs and closing against one another in the middle. Center-swing doors are also made up in pairs, but one glass panel is fixed in place (inoperable) and the other is hinged against the edge of the fixed one and latches against the outer frame.

Louvered doors are also a form of panel door, having a series of angled slats between the vertical stiles of the door. *Half-louver doors* have a solid panel in the bottom and open louvers above.

Insulated Metal Doors

Another variation is the insulated exterior door, which provides a higher R-value than standard wood doors. Something of a cross between traditional flush and panel doors, most insulated doors are constructed from a two-piece stamped-steel frame. The two sections of steel are separated by a strip of material that does not readily conduct heat, usually wood, rubber, or plastic, called a *thermal break.* The

FIGURE 15.5

A hardboard interior door, pressed into a six-panel configuration.

FIGURE 15.6

Another hardboard six-panel door, in this case set up in pairs for use as a bifold closet door.

thermal break reduces the natural tendency of metal to conduct heat, thereby improving the performance of the door. Sandwiched between the steel panels is a solid core of rigid-foam insulation.

Insulated steel doors are supplied with a thick bulb or magnetic weatherstripping, creating a good, airtight seal. The steel panels are either flat, like a flush door, or stamped with a raised panel effect, and these doors offer excellent security. Metal doors are paint-grade only.

Fiberglass Doors

Fiberglass doors offer a nice compromise between wood and steel. They contain a solid foam core like the steel doors, but with face panels that have been carefully detailed to look like real wood. The fiberglass will accept stain almost like wood, allowing it to be customized to match the home's existing doors. Although still rather expensive, it does offer one more choice for some applications.

Standard Door Sizes

Doors are manufactured in two standard thicknesses: 1¾ inches for interior or exterior use, and 1⅜ inches for interior use only. The standard manufactured height is 6 feet 8 inches, although 7-foot doors are also readily available. In addition to these standard heights and thicknesses, certain standard widths are also commonly available: 2-foot, 2-2, 2-4, 2-6, 2-8, 2-10, 3-0, and 3-6. Not all dealers carry all sizes, although 2-6 through 3-0 are almost universally stocked. Other sizes are available by special order, but as with any nonstandard item, the cost jumps considerably. For economy and to ensure easy availability, always plan to use standard sizes.

When you are ordering prehung doors (already hinged onto a preassembled frame), you will have three other considerations in addition to door size. One is the boring you wish for the lockset. The standard is a 2⅛-inch-diameter hole, centered 40 inches down from the top of the door and 2 inches in from the face (called the *backset*). Any deviation from these standards will need to be specified.

Second, you will need to specify the jamb width. Jamb width varies with the type of wall construction, and must be equal to the thickness of the wall studs plus the combined thicknesses of the finished wall-covering materials. One of the most common jamb sizes is 4⁹⁄₁₆ inches, which allows for a 2 × 4 stud (3½ inches) and a layer of ½-inch drywall on each face, plus an additional ¹⁄₁₆ of an inch of play.

The final consideration is which way you want the door to swing, which is specified as a right-hand or a left-hand door. Visualize yourself standing in front of the door and having it swing out and away from you. If the hinges are on the right, it's a right-hand door; if they're on the left, it's a left-hand door.

Installing a Prehung Door

To install a prehung door unit, first remove the temporary nails or plastic fasteners that hold the door to the jamb during shipping.

Without removing the door from the frame, slide the unit into the opening. Use a level to check that the floor in the opening is level. If it isn't, insert a shim under one of the jamb legs to raise it. Place the level against the underside of the head jamb, and tap the shim in until the frame is level.

Next, place the level against the hinge jamb leg and check to see if the frame is plumb. Use shims as necessary between the jamb leg and the trimmer stud to bring the entire leg into plumb. Plumb the entire hinge leg first. When that side is plumb, work on the strike leg, using both the level and a visual sighting of the gap between the door and the jamb legs as a guide. A uniform space of approximately ⅛ inch should exist all the way around between the door and the frame.

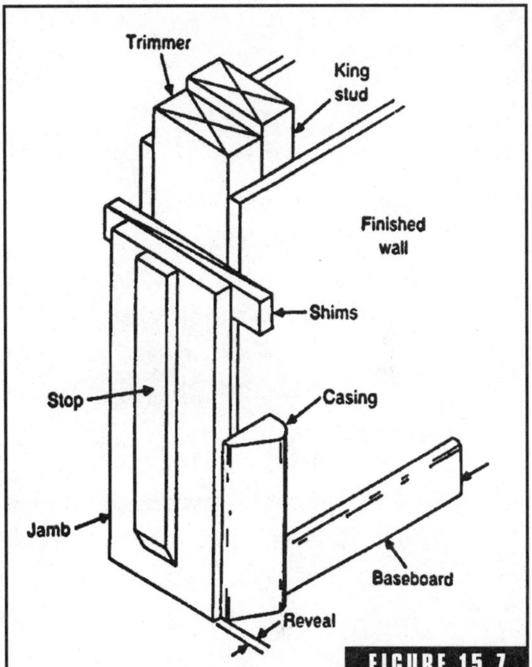

If a large amount of shimming is necessary between the jamb and the stud, you should install the shims from both sides so that they overlap and slide over each other (Figure 15.7). This method shims both edges of the frame equally, preventing the framing from being twisted. When the door and frame are positioned correctly, nail through the jamb and shim into the trimmer studs on each side, using hand- or air-driven 8d or 10d finishing nails. Open and close the door to check its operation. Use a sharp handsaw to cut the protruding ends of the shims off flush with the face of the wall.

FIGURE 15.7

The use of doubled shims for installing a prehung door frame.

Windows

At first glance, the number of window choices might seem a bit bewildering. However, as with doors, there are certain standard materials and configurations, and making the basic choices one at a time will make the whole selection process easier (Figure 15.8).

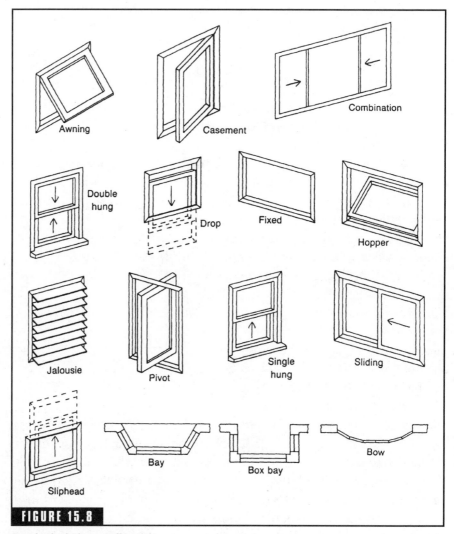

FIGURE 15.8

Standard window configurations.

Probably the biggest difference between the windows you'll be looking at and the ones that are already in the house is energy efficiency. In the last decade or so, window manufacturers have made great strides to improve the performance of their windows. As with doors, the window styles themselves have not really changed, so the chances are quite good of finding a new, energy-efficient window that offers a visually pleasing match with those in the existing house.

Window Materials

The three most common materials for window frames are vinyl, aluminum, and wood. Each has its strengths and weaknesses, and the advantages of one are the disadvantages of the other.

VINYL

Vinyl windows (Figure 15.9) are made by extruding molten vinyl in certain cross-sectional shapes and cutting it into standard lengths. The pieces are assembled into a frame, and a matching sash of vinyl and glass is added in one of various configurations.

It is this fast, standardized manufacturing process that keeps the cost of vinyl windows relatively low. In addition, the windows are very easy to install, never need painting, and weather the elements virtually forever with no deterioration of the frames or sashes.

For vinyl windows, you will have a choice between white and almond. The vinyl itself is colored prior to the extruding process, so the color permeates the entire frame. If you scratch a vinyl frame, you will see the same color underneath, which is not true for aluminum frames.

Vinyl windows are very tough and solid, and they perform well in all weather conditions, both physically and from an energy-efficiency standpoint. They are available in literally hundreds of standard and custom sizes and configurations, and they are one of the all-around most popular windows on the market today.

FIGURE 15.9

A vinyl single-hung window with decorative grids installed between the two layers of insulated glass.

FIGURE 15.10

A pair of fixed, aluminum-frame windows, trimmed with wood.

ALUMINUM

As with the vinyl, aluminum windows (Figure 15.10) are extruded by drawing molten aluminum through a die, then cutting the pieces and assembling a solid aluminum frame and sash. Aluminum windows can be left in their original silver color, called a *mill finish,* or colored by painting or a chemical process called *anodizing.* Bronze is probably the most widely used standard color for aluminum, but virtually any color is available by special order.

Like vinyl windows, aluminum windows are relatively low-priced, come in a wide variety of shapes and sizes (including custom ones), are very tough and sturdy, and weather a variety of climatic conditions with virtually no maintenance or deterioration.

Aluminum windows have the drawback of comparatively poor energy performance, although manufacturers have gone a long way in recent years to overcome that. As with all metals, aluminum is an extremely good conductor of heat. During cold weather, the temperature of the aluminum frame drops rapidly, and any moisture in the house will readily condense on the cold frame, often forming frost or even ice.

To counter this problem, manufacturers of aluminum windows have introduced thermally broken frames. The frame is actually two pieces of aluminum separated by a strip of rubber, plastic, or other material that resists heat movement. These types of frames perform well and have all but replaced standard one-piece frames.

WOOD

Wood windows are still constructed in virtually the same manner as they always were (Figure 15.11), except that modern manufacturing techniques have replaced much of the hand labor in an effort to keep costs down. Clear grades of softwoods, especially pine, fir, and hemlock, are used almost exclusively in today's windows. Several styles are available, with casement and single-hung windows being the most popular.

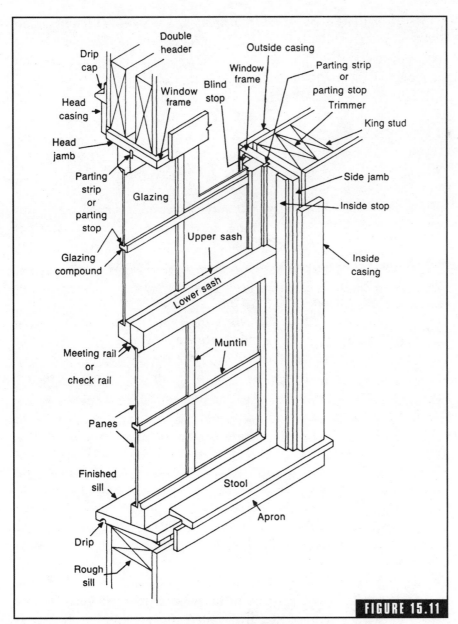

FIGURE 15.11

A cutaway view of the construction of a typical double-hung wood window.

The advantages of wood windows are energy efficiency and appearance. Wood is naturally low in heat conductance, so the frame stays much warmer than an aluminum one. Although condensation may still appear on the glass itself, it is eliminated on the frame. As far as appearance is concerned, few materials, if any, can match natural wood for warmth, style, and beauty.

Wood, however, is not naturally resistant to weather, as are aluminum and vinyl, and must be protected in some way to ensure long life and good performance. Painting the exteriors is one way of providing protection, but this method is time-consuming and must be redone every few years. Many wood windows are also available with an exterior cladding of aluminum or vinyl, which offers excellent weather protection and maintenance-free color on the exterior while maintaining the beauty of natural wood on the interior. This method adds considerably to the cost of the window, however, and wood windows are already more expensive than vinyl or aluminum.

You will probably find that vinyl or aluminum windows can be installed in an addition to a house with existing wood windows and still be a good blend, while wood windows are often not a very good match with the basic, lower-cost, sliding aluminum windows used on many houses in the last two decades or so.

Energy-Efficient Windows

Frame material is only one consideration in the energy efficiency of a window. Glass, which is used in windows because it does not obstruct or discolor visible light, is a naturally poor insulator and does little to obstruct heat flow. With the increased emphasis on energy efficiency in all aspects of building design and construction, it is only natural that window manufacturers look at ways of improving the performance of the glass itself.

The first major improvement was double glazing, which today is virtually standard and is required by most building codes. Double glazing is achieved by setting two panes of glass in a common seal with a space between them that contains a vacuum. This dead-air space acts as an insulator between the glass panes, keeping the inner pane warmer and slowing the loss of heat through the glazing.

Triple glazing is available in some windows, which improves thermal performance over double glazing, but slightly blocks some of the visible light. Quad-pane glazing, which incorporates two thin panels of transparent plastic or other material between two panes of glass, further improves the performance while affecting the visible light about as much as triple glazing, but weight becomes a factor in how well the window will operate.

Today, one of the most popular alternatives is a glass coating known as *low emissivity* (low-e) (Figure 15.12). Low-e coating does not affect the amount or color of the light rays passing through the glass into the house, but it does reduce the amount of heat that the window emits (loses).

Recently, many manufacturers have begun filling the dead-air space between the panes of glass with argon, a clear and inert gas that has also been shown to block the radiation waves of heat from passing out of the house. Combined with low-e glass, the argon has contributed to some very reasonably priced, high-performance windows that meet or exceed all of today's strict energy codes.

Window Styles

Wood, vinyl, and aluminum windows are all available in a variety of styles, which makes matching your existing windows a lot easier. Remember that with vinyl and aluminum windows, you need to trim out the inside window openings afterward with individual pieces of wood or drywall. With wood windows, it's often necessary to order attached jambs of the proper width, as with prehung doors. Be sure to ask your supplier about the jamb details when you are purchasing wood windows.

Some of the most common window styles follow.

FIGURE 15.12

The designation between two layers of insulated glass indicating that the window has a low-e coating.

- *Single- and double-hung:* Double-hung windows were the standard in wood windows for many years. In the traditional double-hung style, two vertically sliding sashes were fixed in tracks in a wood frame. The lower sash slides up and to the inside of the upper sash, while the upper sash slides down on the outside.

The sashes were connected by cords to iron weights suspended in a cavity in the wall. The weights counterbalanced the weight of the sash to prevent it from dropping. In later years, different sash-holding methods were used in place of the weights to make the construction and installation of the windows easier. Today, while double-hung styles are still available, most windows of this type are single-hung—the lower sash opens vertically over and to the inside of the upper sash, which remains fixed. In most cases, single-hung windows will match well with older-style double-hungs.

- *Sliding:* This style consists of two equally sized sash units, one of which slides horizontally over and to the inside of the other one, which is fixed. In larger units, a fixed center panel is used, with two sliding sashes opening over it from each side.

- *Casement:* A casement window contains a sash that is hinged on pins at the top and bottom corners of one side of the frame. A crank is used to open these windows outward, pivoting them on these pins. Steel was a fairly common material for earlier casement windows. As with doors, casement windows close tightly against a frame and can be very effectively weather-stripped.

- *Awning and hopper:* Awning windows have a sash that hinges on pins at the two top corners, while hopper windows hinge at the two bottom corners; both styles open outward. Most awning and hopper windows use a fairly small operable sash combined with a larger, fixed sash above.

- *Bay and bow windows:* These types of windows are actually composed of several window units that project out from the face of the wall. A bay window contains three units, one of which is parallel to the wall. The other two are set at an angle to the back one, usually 30 or 45°. A variation of this window is the box bay, in which the three units are at right angles to each other. Bay windows can be factory-constructed as a three-window unit ready for installation, or can simply be three individual windows set separately into framed openings. In most cases, the back window is fixed and the two side units are casement, but a number of different combinations are available.

A bow window is similar to a bay window, except it is made up at the factory from several narrow sashes set at slight angles to each other to form a curve. Bow windows usually contain all fixed sashes, although sometimes the first sash on each side is a casement.

Bay windows remain a very popular item in residential construction, adding light, floor space and architectural interest. In a room-addition situation, you can use a bay just about anywhere. By matching the windows and the siding used in the bay to that of the existing house, bays will blend very nicely with any style of home.

Egress and Tempered-Glass Codes

In addition to the interior door that opens into a bedroom, building codes specify that every bedroom or other area used for sleeping must have an emergency exit, called an *egress,* that opens directly to the outside of the house. Egress codes are very strict and will be checked by the plans examiner and the on-site inspectors, so this is an important consideration when selecting the size of the windows you're going to use.

Having an exterior door in the bedroom in addition to the interior door satisfies the egress code, allowing you to do anything you want with the window sizes. But lacking this extra door, at least one window in the room must be large enough to allow someone to exit through it in an emergency.

The 1995 CABO code, for example, lists, in part, the following specifications:

Where windows are provided as a means of egress or rescue they shall have a sill height of not more than 44 inches above the floor. All egress or rescue windows from sleeping rooms must have a net clear opening of 5.7 square feet. The minimum net clear opening height shall be 22 inches. The minimum net clear opening width shall be 20 inches.

There are also building codes that require tempered or other safety glass in certain areas. These include glass in doors, in windows within 12 inches of a door, in windows that are located within a tub or shower enclosure, and in windows that come within 18 inches of the floor.

Be sure you read and understand the specific egress and tempered-glass codes that are in effect in your area.

Installing Windows

Most windows are designed to be installed on the rough framing or wall sheathing before the installation of the finished siding. Make certain the rough opening is square and of the correct size before you begin the installation of the window.

Aluminum and vinyl windows come equipped with a flange around the outside, called a *nailing fin.* Apply a bead of caulk to the inside face of this flange, and then set the window into the opening from the outside. Check the window from the inside to confirm that it's centered in the opening (Figure 15.13) and that it's plumb, level, and square. You can use shims as necessary to support the window in the desired location.

Secure the window by simply nailing through the fin into the wall framing. Use a nail that is long enough to penetrate through the fin and the sheathing and into the framing by at least 1 inch. Nail the two sides and the bottom, placing the nails about 2 to 4 inches from the corners and 12 inches apart after that. Do not nail the top fin, because distortions of the header under load could be transferred to the window and possibly break the glass.

Wood windows are installed in much the same way. Most wood windows come with a finish molding attached to the outside of the window frame. This molding acts in the same manner as the nailing fin on the aluminum window, providing a stop against the wall and a surface for nailing. Caulk around the inside surface of the molding, then install the window in the opening and position it. Nail through the molding with 8d or 10d galvanized fin-

FIGURE 15.13

Fitting an aluminum window into an opening.

ishing nails. Remember that the molding will remain visible as a finished trim piece, so take care that it isn't damaged.

Siding

With the framing and roofing complete and the widows and exterior doors in place, the last stage of enclosing and weatherproofing the addition is the installation of the exterior siding. Here again, proper selection and installation of the siding material is crucial to achieving an addition that blends in with the rest of the house. No single step in the process of constructing a room addition has more visual impact than the installation of the siding.

The first step in selecting the siding for your addition is to accurately identify the existing siding and decide if you will match it or re-side the entire house. Re-siding is a big job and is usually necessary only if the existing siding has deteriorated to a point beyond repair. In most cases, repair, washing, and repainting will be sufficient.

Board Siding

Wood has always been a popular material for siding. It is durable, attractive, and available in many patterns and styles. Properly maintained, it will last for years. A huge variety of styles, sizes, and patterns of siding boards have been manufactured over the years, and matching old to new sometimes takes a little work.

If the pattern is really difficult to find, you might want to check with suppliers of used building materials, or perhaps with older carpenters who have been building in the area for a long time. They can often lead you to obscure sources for matching your siding. In some instances, you might need to have a quantity of the siding specially milled in order to get an exact match—this can take a couple of weeks or more, and it will typically add substantially to the cost of the siding.

In recent years, many of the more popular siding styles have been duplicated in wood-composite materials such as OSB, hardboard, and medium-density fiberboard (MDF), as well as in nonwood materials such as fiber-cement. The composite material is formed and cut into standard siding widths and is typically made in 16-foot lengths for convenient installation with a minimum of joints. A smooth or wood-grained resin coating is applied to the face of the board under heat and pressure, then primed. The result is a hard, durable siding board that is void of imperfections and dimensionally very stable.

All composite siding boards come with a factory warranty against such common problems as warping, cupping, and splitting (Figure 15.14). However, there are typically some very strict guidelines that must be followed in the installation and finishing of these composite sidings, so be sure to read all of the manufacturer's instructions carefully.

Siding Styles (Figure 15.15)

- *Boards:* These are square-edged boards available in a variety of widths and thicknesses, with either a smooth or rough-sawn face. They are applied vertically using one of three methods: (1) board and batt (or batten), in which you place wide boards on the wall and cover the joints with narrow boards called *batts;* (2) batten and board, which is the reverse of the previous pattern, with the narrow boards put up first; and (3) board on board, which uses wide boards of equal width.

- *Channel:* These boards are milled in a variety of widths with a wide rabbet along one face edge and a narrower rabbet along the opposite back edge. They can be installed vertically or horizontally, producing a 1¼-inch-wide channel, similar to a batten-and-board style, when the edge rabbets are overlapped.

- *Drop:* This popular horizontal siding has developed in a number of styles over the years. Some types have tongue-and-groove edges; other types are shiplap. When installed, the edges overlap and form a slightly curved or beveled surface along one face edge.

- *Bevel, bungalow:* Bevel siding boards vary from 4 to 6 inches in width, tapering in thickness from bottom to top. They typically have one smooth face and one rough face, and either face can be exposed for the desired decorative effect. This type of siding is designed for horizontal use, with the thick bottom edge of one board overlapping the thinner top edge of the preceding board by about 1 inch. Bungalow siding is the same as bevel, but the boards are wider, ranging from 8 to 12 inches.

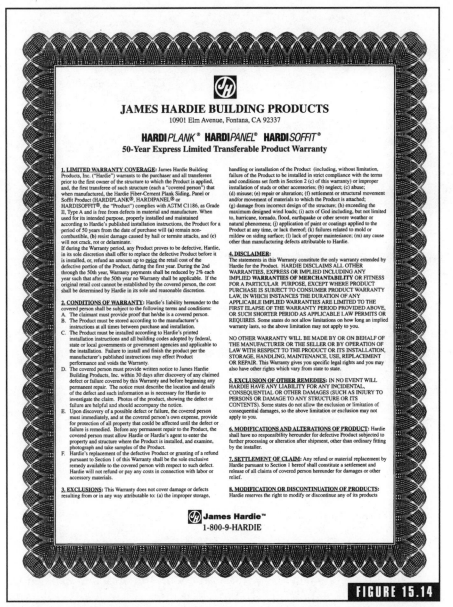

A typical product warranty on an engineered composite siding material. *(Courtesy of James Hardie Building Products.)*

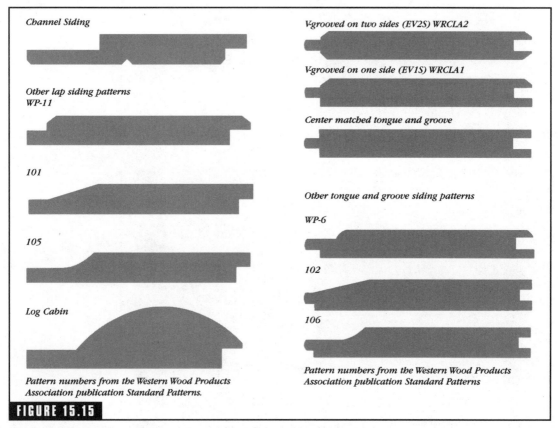

Channel Siding

V-grooved on two sides (EV2S) WRCLA2

V-grooved on one side (EV1S) WRCLA1

Other lap siding patterns
WP-11

Center matched tongue and groove

101

Other tongue and groove siding patterns

WP-6

105

102

Log Cabin

106

Pattern numbers from the Western Wood Products
Association publication Standard Patterns.

Pattern numbers from the Western Wood Products
Association publication Standard Patterns

FIGURE 15.15

Standard siding profiles. *(Courtesy of Western Red Cedar Lumber Association.)*

- *Dolly Varden:* This siding is similar to bevel siding, only thicker and with a rabbeted bottom edge that overlaps the top edge of the preceding board.

- *Log cabin:* This siding is designed to approximate the look of uniform individual logs. The boards have a curved face, with a flat lip on one face edge and a rabbet on the opposite back edge. They are installed horizontally with the rabbet overlapping the flat lip.

- *Tongue and groove:* These boards, of various widths and thicknesses, have tongue-and-groove edges. Most are installed horizontally, although some types can also be installed vertically.

House Wraps

House-wrap products, such as Du Pont's Tyvek, are installed over the exterior of the wall framing or sheathing to stop air leakage behind the siding. The material is vapor-permeable and is therefore not intended to act as a vapor barrier.

House wraps typically come in 10-foot-wide rolls, which contain enough material to wrap an average-size house. Begin installation at one corner of the addition or where the addition meets the house. Align the bottom of the roll so that it overlaps the top of the stem wall, and staple it in place. While one person slowly rolls out the material, a second person follows behind and staples it in place. Wrap the entire addition in one piece, if possible.

If the material needs to be seamed, as on a gable end or a two-story area, the upper sheet is lapped over the lower one and stapled on the seam. For a truly airtight barrier, use tape or mastic to seal the seams and the joint between the house wrap and the stem wall. At window and door openings, cut the material diagonally from corner to corner, fold it into the opening, and staple it to the framing.

Installing Siding Boards

Siding boards are almost always installed over wood sheathing in order to provide solid backing for the individual boards as well as lateral bracing for the framework of the house. Solid-wood siding should have a moisture content as close as possible to that of the region in which it's being installed in order to minimize the problems of shrinkage. If you bring in siding from another region, especially one with a vastly different humidity, keep it on the job site for several weeks before installation so it can adjust to the conditions there.

Cover the sheathing with an air-and-moisture barrier, such as kraft or felt paper or any of the new house wraps. Check with the building department for the exact requirements for your area. Apply the sheathing paper from the bottom up, with each succeeding layer overlapping the one below it by about 2 inches. Side laps should overlap by 4 inches.

In order to provide sufficient nailing support, additional blocking is required when installing siding boards vertically. Install blocking approximately 36 inches OC. Horizontal siding is adequately supported by the wall framing, and it can be nailed to the studs on 16-inch centers or with sheathing over studs on 24-inch centers.

Vertical siding is installed beginning at one inside or outside corner. Horizontal siding is always applied from the bottom up, similar to roofing, to ensure complete weathertightness (Figure 15.16). Bevel siding requires the installation of a starter ship under the bottom of the first course, beveling that course away from the wall to match the subsequent courses. Follow the manufacturer's recommendations for the size of the starter ship and for the amount of the overlaps between courses.

For the installation of horizontal siding, the use of a story pole (Figure 15.17) is a good idea. It speeds the layout and helps to ensure that all of the courses are the same on each wall. To make a story pole, measure the distance from where the bottom of the first siding board will be to the underside of the soffit, then cut a straight length of lumber to this length. Divide this length into spaces equal to the exposed face of the siding, marking these divisions on the piece of lumber.

Hold the story pole at each inside and outside corner of the building so that the top of the pole is against the bottom of the soffit, and transfer the marks from the pole to the wall. Repeat the procedure at

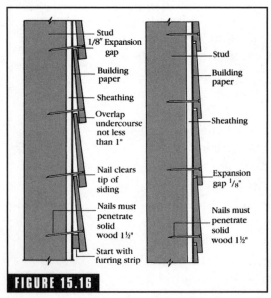

Stud
1/8" Expansion gap
Building paper
Sheathing
Overlap undercourse not less than 1"
Nail clears tip of siding
Nails must penetrate solid wood 1½"
Start with furring strip

Stud
Building paper
Sheathing
Expansion gap ⅛"
Nails must penetrate solid wood 1½"

FIGURE 15.16

Typical nailing procedure for two types of wood siding. *(Courtesy of Western Red Cedar Lumber Association.)*

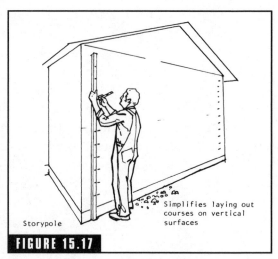

Simplifies laying out courses on vertical surfaces

Storypole

FIGURE 15.17

Use of a story pole for aligning horizontal courses of siding. *(Courtesy of Cedar Shake and Shingle Bureau.)*

both sides of each window and door opening. Finally, snap a chalk line between the marks to establish the level lines necessary to guide the siding.

For inside corners (Figure 15.18), horizontal siding is usually butted to a piece of 2 × 2 lumber and installed vertically in the corners, which provides a clean transition in the corner and eliminates a tremendous amount of cutting and fitting of the individual boards. For outside corners on either vertical or horizontal siding, two vertical corner boards are the most common choice.

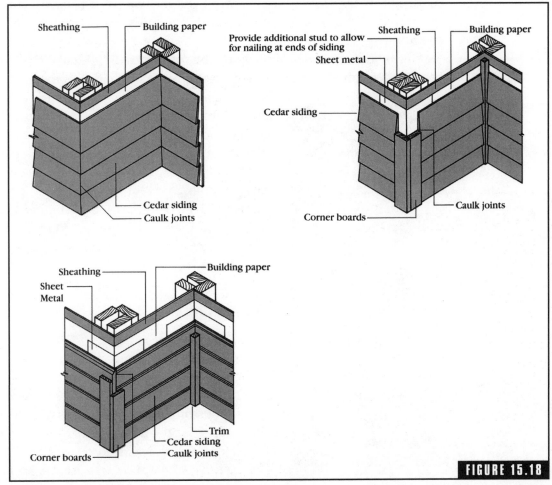

Different methods of dealing with inside and outside corners when installing horizontal wood siding. *(Courtesy of Western Red Cedar Lumber Association.)*

At windows, doors, and other openings, you can butt the siding directly to a trim board placed next to the opening or to the window itself—let the style of the home's existing trim be your guide for what looks best. Caulk the siding carefully where it butts against the inside corners and at all window and door openings.

Transitions

Where the new siding meets the existing house, take care to prevent the joints from being obvious (Figure 15.19). With vertical siding, carefully butting the new siding to the old is usually sufficient for a clean transition. If the last siding board on the old wall has been ripped down to fit the corner, be sure to remove it, allowing the transition to begin from a full-width board.

You should remove existing horizontal siding in individual courses back to an original joint, and then start the new siding run from there. Do one course at a time, tearing back the old siding, butting up the new, and completing that course for the length of the wall. If there are no joints in the old siding, or if too much siding would be wasted, cut random joints in the old siding as starting points for the new runs. Do not simply cut one vertical line of joints—such joints are hard to conceal and difficult to seal against the weather.

FIGURE 15.19

A transition between wood bevel siding and brick veneer.

Sheet Siding

The most common material for sheet siding has always been plywood, but, as with the board siding, OSB and other composite products are becoming increasingly popular. It's important to select a style of sheet siding for the addition that matches the existing siding as closely as possible— this includes the thickness, groove size and spacing, and surface texture of the sheets.

Whether the sheets are plywood or one of the composite materials, common sheet sizes are 4×8, 4×9, and 4×10 feet. If possible, always select a sheet length that allows you to cover the entire height of the wall with no seams.

Installing Sheet Siding

Siding sheets are installed vertically, either over sheathing or directly on the studs. Some patterns may also be installed horizontally. Apply a covering of paper first, as with the siding boards.

Begin the installation from the same corner that you started your stud layout to ensure that the panel edges fall directly over the studs. With shiplap panels, start so that the edge of the panel that is rabbeted on the back face is at the corner. The other edge of the panel will cover almost the entire stud, which is fine—when the next panel is put in place, the shiplap rabbets will overlap. When you nail along the edge of the second panel, the nails will be in the center of the stud.

Usually, a ⅛-inch space is recommended at all panel edges to prevent distortion from swelling. Nails should be placed 6 inches OC along the edges and 12 inches OC at the intermediate supports.

If the sheets are not long enough to cover the entire height of the wall, such as on a gable end where horizontal joints are unavoidable, a special galvanized sheet-metal flashing—called *Z-bar or Z-metal*—is used to seal the joint. The flashings are available in 10-foot lengths and in various leg dimensions to fit the different thicknesses of siding. Side-lap the flashings by 2 to 4 inches when you are making up longer lengths.

Because of the size of the sheets, cutting accurately mitered corners or butting cut edges around openings is extremely difficult, so wood trim is used at the outside corners and around openings. Inside corners simply butt to each other and are then caulked. Caulk all window and door openings also.

Transitions

Sheet-siding transitions are done like the transitions for vertical-siding boards. With shiplap edges, the last original panel will need to be torn out to get back to its rabbeted edge. Avoid the temptation to simply butt the panels together and then cover the joint with a piece of wood trim—this is easy but is the least visually appealing method and is a dead giveaway to where the addition joins the house.

FIGURE 15.20

Wood shingles used on a second-floor gable end and two shed dormers.

Other Siding Materials

A variety of other materials are used for siding purposes, including shingles, stucco, stone, and brick. As always, unless you are re-siding the entire home, you should match the existing material.

Shingles

Shingles, of either wood (Figure 15.20), fiber-cement, or other materials, can be used as an exterior siding. They offer fairly easy installation over sheathing, old sheet siding, or furring strips.

Shingles are installed in much the same manner as any horizontal siding. They need to be applied over a solid subsurface, usually sheathing, which has been papered first. You can use a story pole to align the courses from wall to wall and to speed the layout of the horizontal chalk lines.

As with roofing shingles, install wall shingles from the bottom up (Figure 15.21). Install a starter strip first at the bottom of the wall in order to bevel out the first course. Install each subsequent course to overlap the course below it, carefully maintaining the correct weather exposure and keeping the bottom of the shingles level.

Stucco

Stucco is a mixture of cement, sand, lime, and water that is applied wet over a prepared surface in a series of coats (Figure 15.22). Stucco is very durable and weather-resistant, although it is prone to cracking over time. It can be painted with most types of paint, or the final coat can be colored with powdered cement for a permanent color coating.

Stucco is mixed on-site, in quantities that can be applied within a relatively short time. Stucco is a fairly labor-intensive siding to apply and should be left to an experienced subcontractor—request the names of previous clients and examine some of the workmanship before hiring a sub.

INSTALLING STUCCO

Proper backing, usually solid sheathing such as plywood, is required to support the stucco. After the sheathing is in place, cover the walls with 15-pound felt, lapped the same as for roofing felt, and apply a layer of stucco netting (which resembles chicken wire) using special furring nails.

Special corners manufactured from wire mesh are used to form and strengthen the outside corners. On horizontal surfaces, such as the underside of a soffit, use expanded metal lath in place of the netting to provide a stronger backing. Wooden stucco molding is usually used around windows, doors, and other openings—the molding has a deep, rounded groove along one edge, allowing the wet stucco to flow into the groove and form a good bond against the wood to minimize cracking.

Apply the stucco in several coats, using a trowel. Press the first layer solidly against the netting, allowing it to flow through the netting and bond with it. As it dries, the layer is evened out and roughened to provide a good bond surface for the subsequent coat. The final coat is typically textured using a variety of hand- or machine-applied methods.

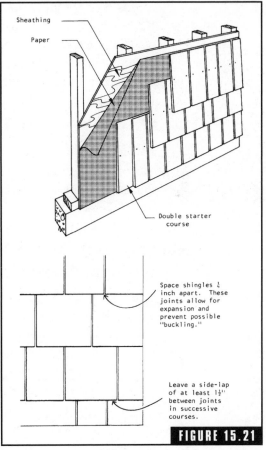

FIGURE 15.21

Installation procedure for wood shingles used as a siding material. *(Courtesy of Cedar Shake and Shingle Bureau.)*

TRANSITIONS

For a good transition with stucco, break the existing stucco away from the house/addition intersection with a hammer in a random line that obscures the exact line where old and new meet. Remove all of the loose stucco from the netting, and leave the netting intact. If possible, undercut the old stucco so that the new material can be worked under it, minimizing the chances of a crack forming along the seam.

Interweave the new netting with the old as much as possible, using galvanized wire to tie the two together.

The stucco is troweled over the intersection in the netting, and the second coat is feathered out slightly onto the old material. When texturing, pay particular attention to the seam area between the two surfaces, applying the texture in a pattern that matches the existing stucco and hides the seam as much as possible.

Masonry Siding

Masonry is another common siding material, and the type and style of masonry varies in different parts of the country. This type of siding can be bricks or stone, either in the form of solid masonry walls or, more commonly, a masonry veneer. Masonry veneers are one unit thick over a base of plywood or sheathing boards.

INSTALLING MASONRY

Concrete is usually poured at the base of the wall to serve as a level, weight-bearing platform from which the veneer is started. Individual courses are laid up one at a time, with L-shaped ties inserted at regular intervals to secure the masonry to the sheathing.

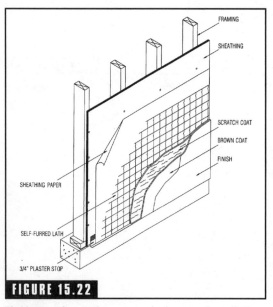

FIGURE 15.22

The layers that make up a typical stucco installation.
(Courtesy of Northwest Wall and Ceiling Bureau.)

FIGURE 15.23

The careful interweaving of courses of brick between an addition (right) and the existing house.

TRANSITIONS

Brick veneer must be broken back into alternating courses (Figure 15.23), and the new bricks are started from the end of each old course. Extreme care must be taken to align the course and keep the size of the new mortar joints consistent with the size of the old ones. The transition for stone is done in much the same way, with enough old stone being removed to provide a random seam for starting the new material.

To blend properly, stone and brick transitions require a solid knowledge of masonry installation. Mortar composition, brick and stone type and color, joint size, and many other factors influence how well a transition blends in, so this project should be left to an experienced mason.

Plumbing Systems

Every house, no matter what the age, has two complete and separate plumbing systems: the hot- and cold-water system, which supplies potable (clean) water to the building for normal cooking, cleaning, and similar uses, and the drain, waste, and vent (DWV) system, which removes nonpotable water and solid waste from the building and conveys it to a disposal site.

When constructing an addition, it often becomes necessary to tie in to and extend both of those systems to meet the needs of the addition. This typically involves the connection of a variety of dissimilar materials, but the nice thing is, once the tie-ins are complete, the addition can make use of all the newest materials and technology with no further regard for matching up to what's existing.

Hot- and Cold-Water Systems

Water is supplied to the home via a main supply line from the source, whether it's a municipal water system or a private well. A main shut-off valve, located on the main line just before or after it enters the house, is used to close off the supply when work on the home's plumbing system becomes necessary.

After the cold water enters the home, it branches off into smaller-diameter lines to feed various fixtures. Typically, the main water supply line is of a fairly large diameter, usually 1 or 1¼ inches. It drops down to ¾ inch for the main branch feeder pipes that go to various parts of the house and decreases further to ½-inch pipe for the lines that actually supply the fixtures. These diameters will vary with the water pressure, the number of fixtures being fed from the line, and the distance the line has to run.

One ¾-inch branch line will be taken off to supply cold water for the water heater, and a second ¾-inch line comes off the hot side of the water heater. From there, the hot line splits off into various ¾- and ½-inch branch lines—typically running parallel with the cold-water lines—that supply hot water to the various fixtures.

In planning any additions to the plumbing system, the plumber will take the time to study the existing plumbing layout to determine what the lines are, what they feed, and whether they are large enough for the intended purpose. Tapping into a ½-inch line, for example, might be adequate for a short run to supply a garden faucet, but a bathroom addition will require that a new branch line be taken off a ¾-inch or even a 1-inch cold-water line in order to supply enough volume of water.

Hot Water

When planning a bathroom addition, if the proposed room is a long distance from the existing water heater, or if a fairly substantial increase in hot-water capacity is needed, the addition of a second water heater might be necessary. This would require a ¾-inch cold-water supply line and a fuel source—typically electricity for a remodeling, because it eliminates the need for gas lines and flue vents. The second water heater can be placed next to the original one to simplify the plumbing, or it can be placed directly in the new addition.

If only a marginal increase in capacity is required, you can also consider removing the old water heater and replacing it with a new, larger-capacity model with improved energy efficiency and faster recovery time.

Another method of increasing the efficiency of a hot-water system is through the use of a recirculating pump. These small electric pumps attach directly to the water heater and greatly increase the speed with which hot water circulates through the system and out to the various fixtures. Faster delivery time is obviously more convenient for the user—especially in a two-story house—but it also cuts down on heat loss from water standing in the pipes. For most efficient operation, the pump can be controlled by a 24-hour or 7-day timer that activates the pump only during times of highest hot-water demand.

Drain, Waste, and Vent (DWV) Systems

The other plumbing system in the house is the DWV system (Figure 16.1), a carefully designed series of interacting pipes that allow for the

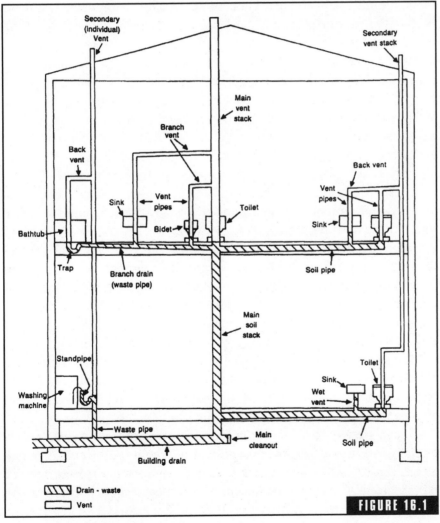

A typical drain, waste, and vent system.

removal of liquid and solid waste. Once again, knowing what the lines are and where they go is essential before tapping into one.

Drain Lines

Drain lines are the ones that connect directly to a sink, bathtub, shower drain, washing machine, or other fixture containing only liquid waste. Drain lines are usually 1¼, 1½, or 2 inches in diameter, and are intended to carry liquid waste only, never solids.

Individual drain lines run from the fixture, through a trap, and into the main drain and waste system. A small amount of water is always held in the curved section of the trap, which is below the level of the drain line. This standing water, called the *trap seal,* prevents gas and odors from the sewer from entering the house through the fixture.

Waste Lines

Waste lines, typically 2- and 3-inch diameter pipes, are designed to carry both liquid and solid waste. They are connected directly to toilets and kitchen sinks, and also serve as collectors for the liquid waste coming from the drain lines. The waste lines then discharge into a 4-inch line, called the *main building sewer* or *house sewer,* which conveys the waste out of the house and discharges it into a septic tank or municipal sewer system.

While the water lines are under pressure and can flow in any direction, the drain and waste portions of the DWV system operate on nonpressurized gravity flow to remove waste from the building. Each line, starting from the fixtures, is angled down slightly off of level. This angle, called *fall* (Figure 16.2), is usually equal to ⅛ to ¼ inch of fall per 1 foot of horizontal run. The angle of fall needs to be consistent throughout the system—too little fall and the waste won't move smoothly; too much fall, and the liquid waste will drain much faster than the solids, creating the risk of the solids becoming lodged in the line.

Fall is a critical consideration in the placement of new fixtures and lines. Each new line must be placed so that it can drain down into an existing line, which can present problems in some additions. As a last resort, if it proves to be impossible to achieve the necessary amount of fall, electrically powered sewage pumps can be used to force the waste uphill.

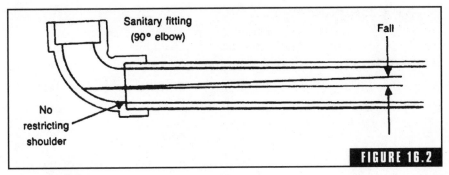

Fall in a drain pipe.

Adding to a building's DWV system takes careful study and planning to ensure that both the new system and the existing one will function properly. When a new plumbing run is added, it is necessary to tap into a waste line or a main sewer line, not a drain line. Drain lines are intended to serve one fixture only, and they cannot be doubled up. Also, the line you tap needs to be large enough to handle the intended load. A toilet, for example, needs to drain into a 3- or 4-inch line—code will not allow it to empty into anything smaller. A sink, on the other hand, can empty into any line 2 inches or larger.

Vent Pipes

Vent pipes make up the third portion of the DWV system. Vent pipes begin at a level above the drain and waste lines, and they are not intended to carry waste of any sort. Extending up through the roof, vents provide the atmospheric pressure necessary for the drain and waste system to operate.

In some installations there is a main vent stack—one large pipe, usually 3 inches in diameter, extending up through the roof from a central waste line, called the *main soil stack*. Other vents from other fixtures connect to the vent stack and vent through it, eliminating the need for several penetrations of the roof. In other types of systems, a single fixture vent may extend through the roof on its own, or two or more individual vents—called *secondary vent stacks*—will intersect in the wall or attic, allowing a single pipe to penetrate the roof. As long as the vent pipes are properly sized, any of these methods is fine.

Septic Systems

Many homes in more rural areas are not served by a municipal sewer system. They use a private, on-site sewage disposal system instead. In days past, that system may have been a cesspool, which received the solid and liquid waste from a building, allowing the liquid to seep out while retaining the solids for later removal. Cesspools, now illegal because of a variety of health and safety reasons, have been replaced exclusively by septic systems.

A septic system consists of a watertight concrete, metal, or fiberglass box, called a *septic tank* (Figure 16.3), along with a series of liquid disposal pipes. The septic tank receives all the waste from the building via the main sewer line. Solids settle to the bottom of the tank, where they are broken down by bacterial action. The liquids pass through a solid line at the other end of the tank into a distribution box and from there into a series of perforated drain lines. These drain lines are laid out in carefully spaced gravel-lined trenches, called a *leach* or *disposal field* (Figure 16.4). The liquid waste drains slowly out of

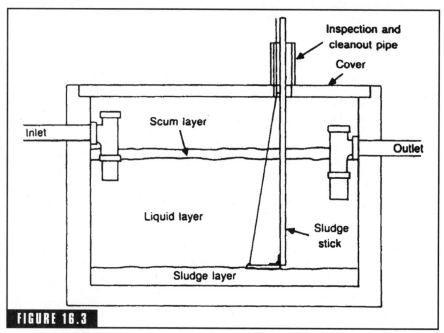

FIGURE 16.3

A typical septic tank, also showing the "sludge stick" used to check how full the tank is.

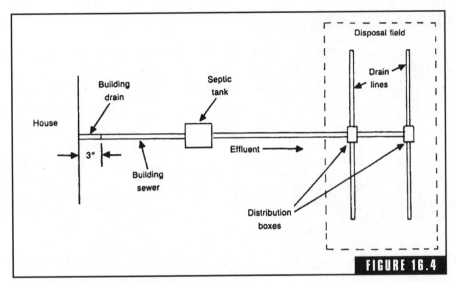

FIGURE 16.4

A typical drain-field configuration.

these lines to be filtered by the gravel as it disperses down into the soil.

Septic systems are rated by their capacity in gallons, which is an indicator of the volume of waste they can handle. The plumbing codes rate the size of a house by the number of bedrooms it has, and relates that to the capacity of the septic tank. For example, a one- or two-bedroom house requires a septic tank with a minimum capacity of 750 gallons, a three-bedroom house requires 1000 gallons, and a four-bedroom house requires 1200 gallons. An additional 150 gallons of capacity is required for each additional bedroom.

When adding onto a house with an existing septic tank, the plumbing or building department might wish to verify that the size of the septic tank and the length of the drain lines are adequate to handle the increased load imposed by the addition. You should discuss and verify this with the proper authorities early on. If expensive additions to the septic system are required, you'll want to incorporate this into your estimate.

Plumbing Materials

As mentioned previously, unlike other parts of the addition, the materials you use for any new plumbing do not have to be the same as the

FIGURE 16.5

Copper pipe (center, left to right) used for water lines. Also note the threaded steel pipe being used for a gas line (right, top to bottom).

existing materials. There are a variety of code-approved transition fittings that allow the change from old materials such as cast iron to new materials such as plastic pipe, so the materials chosen for the addition's plumbing are a matter of choice, not necessity.

Water Lines

For new water lines, the most common choice today is copper pipe (Figure 16.5). Copper does not rust or corrode like galvanized pipe; it's lightweight, relatively inexpensive, and easy to work with. Connections and direction changes are made with slip fittings, which are attached by soldering. No threading is required, and alterations to the system can be performed quickly and easily.

Copper pipe is found in four basic types, each carrying a letter designation and a color-coded stripe on the pipe's side for easy identification:

- *Type K.* Thick-walled pipe, color-coded green; used primarily for underground installations.

- *Type L.* Medium-walled pipe, color-coded blue; used in some underground installations and in aboveground locations where higher water pressures might be encountered.

- *Type M.* Thin-walled pipe, color-coded red; the most common residential pipe. It is intended for aboveground installations only, and is commonly limited to water pressures of 100 psi or less.

- *Type DWV.* Larger-diameter, medium-walled pipe, color-coded yellow; sometimes used in drain, waste, and vent installations.

In addition to these four rigid pipes, called *hard-supply pipes,* types K and L are also available as soft-supply pipes, meaning they are soft-tempered and can be bent, allowing the use of fewer fittings. Type K is used for aboveground and some belowground installations, while Type L is for aboveground use only. Color coding of the soft-supply lines is the same as for hard-supply pipe.

The old standard for water lines was galvanized iron pipe, and it's still widely used today, although primarily for gas lines instead of water. This type of pipe requires the use of threaded fittings, and each piece of pipe must be individually threaded after being cut to length.

Plastic pipe for water lines has also been around for a while, but, while widely used in mobile and manufactured homes because of its low cost, it is still not very common in standard residential construction. Plastic pipe is very easy to cut and join and is extremely lightweight. It requires more support than rigid metal pipes, and some of the compatible plastic valves and fittings have still not reached the high level of quality and reliability that metal fittings have. Only certain types of plastic pipe, such as polybutylene, are rated for both hot- and cold-water use in a residence.

DWV Lines

Plastic pipe for DWV use, specifically pipe formulated from acrylonitrile-butadiene-styrene (ABS) (Figure 16.6), is the most widely used pipe for residential and most light commercial construction. ABS is a rigid, black plastic, sold in 20-foot lengths in 1½-, 2-, 3-, and 4-inch diameters. It is joined with special ABS slip fittings (Figure 16.7), which require no threading and are secured and sealed with liquid solvent cement. ABS pipe is quite light compared to other DWV pipe, is extremely easy to cut and join, and requires no special tools. Alterations to it are easy, involving only cutting the pipe and gluing in a new fitting.

Cast-iron pipe was used for many years in residential work and, like galvanized iron pipe, is still widely used today. The older style of cast-iron pipe was joined using special cast-iron fittings that were flared out on each end to receive the pipe. The end of the pipe was inserted into the flared hub on the fitting, and the joint was

FIGURE 16.6

ABS pipe and fittings used for a waste line.

FIGURE 16.7

ABS pipe and fittings alongside copper water lines.

lined with oakum or other packing material, then sealed with molten lead. Today, most cast-iron pipe and fittings are joined using no-hub connectors, which consist of a neoprene sleeve and a screw-activated clamp.

For smaller-diameter drain pipes, copper or galvanized iron pipe was sometimes used. Galvanized pipe for DWV use is cut and threaded exactly like water pipe, and is joined with threaded fittings. Copper DWV pipe—a very durable, corrosion-resistant but relatively expensive larger-diameter pipe—is cut and soldered like copper water lines.

Transitions and Connections

Fittings for making the transition between different sizes and/or types of pipe are very readily available through a variety of outlets. These transition fittings are inexpensive and easy to use and, being specifically designed for these applications, are the only type of fittings that should be use to ensure safe, problem-free connections.

Water Line Transitions

Probably the most common water line transition encountered in constructing a room addition is the need to join new copper pipe to existing galvanized pipe. If the connection is done incorrectly, a chemical reaction will take place between the copper pipe and the zinc used in the galvanizing process, causing the joint to be slowly eaten away until it finally fails.

Basically, there are two ways to correctly join copper pipe to galvanized pipe. The first is to make the transition through a third material—brass—that will not react adversely to either the copper or the zinc. There are a variety of ways to use brass, depending on the particular installation. You can, for example, solder a copper slip-to-female fitting onto the end of the copper pipe, screw a threaded connector onto the end of the galvanized pipe, then connect the two with a brass nipple.

The second and more common transition method entails the use of a special fitting called a *dielectric union* (Figure 16.8). One-half of the union has a female slip fitting end that is soldered to the copper pipe, while the other half has a threaded female end for connection to the galvanized pipe (Figure 16.9). A thick rubber washer fits between the two halves, keeping the dissimilar materials separated while still forming a tight seal between them. A nylon washer inside the locknut separates the copper side of the union from the locknut itself for further protection. Installation is quick and easy, and you have the added benefit of a union fitting at the connection point in case disassembly of the pipes ever becomes necessary.

If a dielectric union is installed on a cold-water line that is being used as a ground for electrical, telephone, or other equipment, the rubber washer inside the union breaks the pipe's ground continuity. To prevent this situation and to keep the pipe's grounding capabilities continuous, it is necessary to attach a standard electrical ground clamp to the pipes on either side of the union and run a piece of #6 bare or green-jacketed copper wire, called a *jumper* or *bond wire,* between the clamps. This precaution is also necessary anytime a water pipe is broken up by a nonmetallic object, such as a water filter with a plastic casing.

A variation on the use of brass to make a safe connection between copper and galvanized pipe is the flexible water line (Figure 16.10). Constructed of copper, it

FIGURE 16.8

A dielectric union, assembled.

FIGURE 16.9

A dielectric union, disassembled to show the parts. The flanged sleeve (left) is soldered to the copper pipe, while the threaded sleeve (right) is screwed onto the threaded galvanized pipe. The locknut and washers (center) hold the union together and seal it against leaks while keeping the copper and galvanized pipes separate.

FIGURE 16.10

A flexible copper water line.

has a brass locknut with an insulating nylon bushing inside. It is useful for installing devices such as water heaters or water softeners, because the pipe's flexibility greatly simplifies alignment of the connections.

To adapt plastic pipe to copper or galvanized pipe, slip-to-thread adapters are used. The threaded female end of the adapter fitting is attached to threaded galvanized pipe—or to a threaded fitting soldered onto the copper pipe—and then the female slip end of the fitting is glued onto one end of the plastic pipe. Be certain the fitting is compatible with the type of plastic pipe being used.

For copper pipe, a wide variety of transition and adapter fittings are commonly available. Slip-to-thread fittings, either male or female, adapt the copper pipe for use with threaded fittings, allowing the transition from copper to plastic or to brass plumbing fixtures. Reducing couplings are used to join two pipes of different diameters, and reducing bushings will slip into a fitting such as a T to adapt it to a smaller pipe size. T fittings for use with two different-diameter pipes are available in several sizes and outlet combinations.

Galvanized pipe adapters are also available in several different sizes and styles. Female-threaded bell reducers will connect two different sizes of pipe, while male/female-threaded bushings are used to adapt a larger-size fitting to a smaller-diameter pipe. Reducing Ts and elbows are also available in a variety of size combinations.

Always be certain that the correct type of glue or thread sealer is being used for the type of connection being made. Read the label for the manufacturer's specific instructions and recommended applications.

Soil Line Transitions

A very common situation created by remodeling is the need to connect ABS soil pipes to cast iron, clay, Transite, or whatever other type of pipe was used in the house originally (Figure 16.11). For this purpose, a band clamp similar to that used with no-hub cast-iron pipe is used. A band clamp is simply a metal sleeve with two worm-drive or screw clamps and an inner sleeve made of rubber. If needed, rubber transition gaskets of various thicknesses can be inserted into the inner sleeve to make up the difference in the outer diameters of the pipes being joined.

To adapt ABS to galvanized pipe, slip-to-thread adapters are used. One end of the fitting is designed to either slip over the end of the ABS pipe or be inserted into a fitting and then glued into place. The other end of the fitting has a female or male thread to make the connection to the threaded pipe. Use Teflon tape or a Teflon-based joint compound as a sealant on the plastic threads, because other thread-sealing compounds are petroleum-based and may cause deterioration of the plastic over time.

A variety of adapters are available for changing from one diameter to another in pipe of the same material. For straight runs, adapter bushings can be inserted into a coupling or other fitting to step down the pipe diameter. For direction changes, elbows and Ts are available with outlets in different sizes.

FIGURE 16.11

An ABS waste line exiting a house and transitioning to another pipe. The wooden block holds the line at the proper fall until backfilling is complete.

To make a transition between two pipes of different diameters and different materials, a band clamp is used with the appropriate adapter gaskets for connecting the dissimilar materials. After that transition is made, the pipe is then stepped down to the appropriate size as described previously.

A special fitting, called a *split-case adapter,* can be used to tap a threaded pipe from an existing ABS line without cutting the pipe. The two halves of the heavy plastic case are placed around the existing pipe and secured in place with two worm-drive clamps. Next, a hole is drilled through the threaded side opening in the case and into the pipe. The clamps are tightened to compress various rubber O-rings in the case to ensure a watertight seal, and the new pipe is screwed into the case's side opening.

Plumbing Procedures

Every remodeling project can create a number of different plumbing situations, each of which needs to be analyzed and solved as it arises. The tools and procedures are basic to every application, requiring only the selection of the proper materials and fittings for the specific situation.

The plumber will typically complete the work on the addition first, using copper and ABS pipe and simply treating the work as a new-construction plumbing installation. The location of the tie-ins will be figured out in advance, and all of the new work will proceed from the addition toward those connection points. Remember that the connections will need to be made with the proper pipes in the proper locations to ensure adequate water pressure and the proper fall for the drain and waste lines.

If the addition has a crawl space, the rough underfloor plumbing is typically completed prior to installing the subfloor. This simplifies the installation—and is required by code in many areas. Framing work for the floor system is completed first, and 2 × 4s or other temporary boards can then be tacked to the top of the floor joists as needed to indicate the exact location of interior plumbing walls. In the case of a slab floor, all of the underslab plumbing needs to be in place, tested, and inspected before the slab is poured. After all of the slab or underfloor inspections are complete and the wall and roof framing is done (Figure 16.12), the remainder of the rough plumbing is completed.

FIGURE 16.12

Copper water lines and an ABS drain line coming up through the bottom plate of an interior wall. Tape on the drain line (center) keeps debris out of the line until final connections are made.

The plumbing inspector will typically require that all new DWV lines be tested before they are enclosed or covered in any way. To perform this test, a test ball is inserted in the lowest end of the new line, and all other outlets are closed off with caps or test plugs. One of the vent lines is extended all the way up through the roof, and a garden hose is placed in the end of the vent. Using the hose, the system is filled with water, and all joints are checked carefully for leaks.

Working with ABS Pipe and Fittings

ABS pipe can be cut with any fine-toothed handsaw or with a hacksaw. The pipe must be cut square, not at an angle, and the small burrs around the cut end are then brushed or filed off so that they don't interfere with the pipe's insertion into the fitting.

When measuring the pipe for cutting, allow for the fittings. First, measure the total length from the centerline of one fitting to the centerline of the next fitting. Then measure the distance from the centerline of the fitting to the inside of the shoulder where the pipe will seat on both ends. Subtract these measurements from the overall length of the run, cut the pipe to length, and dry-fit to check for accuracy.

ABS pipe and fittings are joined with ABS cement, which is a thick, black liquid available in cans, with a small brush attached to the inside of the lid. Using the brush, coat both the inside of the fitting and the outside of the pipe with cement, and seat the pipe fully into the fitting with a slight twisting motion to distribute the glue. The entire procedure must be done quickly, because the cement sets within a few seconds.

Installing DWV Lines

Drain, waste, and vent lines are usually installed first, because it is easier to work the smaller-diameter water lines around the DWV pipes than it is to do it the other way around. For a large plumbing installation such as a bathroom, it's common to run a 3-inch line (Figure 16.13) directly from the location of the toilet and tie the other drain lines into it.

A fitting called a *closet bend* is used at the floor to start the turn from the toilet into the waste line, and then a closet flange is attached to that. The closet flange contains two or more slotted holes for the insertion of the toilet bolt—the toilet will

FIGURE 16.13

An ABS waste line. Note the plastic strapping used to secure the line at the proper fall.

be attached to this flange, so it's important that the top of the flange be even with the eventual level of the subfloor and that the centerline of the flange be the correct distance away from the wall framing (usually 12 inches).

From the flange, the closet bend turns back toward the wall behind the toilet and enters a special fitting that resembles an elbow. It has a 3-inch inlet and outlet, and a second, 2-inch outlet at the curve of the elbow, from which the vent stack is removed. From the bottom of the elbow, another 90° elbow is added, facing the line in the direction of the tie-in with the existing house.

Bathtub, shower, and sink lines are added next. Sinks are usually installed with a fitting called a *sanitary T,* which resembles a standard T except that the side inlet flows into the fitting in one direction only. Since the third side of the T becomes the start of the vent, this fitting allows water from the drain to flow only into the waste line, not into the vent. The bottom side of the T points toward the underfloor, and piping is taken off of it to tie into the main waste line installed earlier. All connections to the main waste line are made with sanitary Ts to keep the flow going in one direction only.

Tubs and showers extend directly down through the floor, then enter a trap. For slab floors or second-floor installations where the ceiling below the tub will be inaccessible, a fixed trap with solid joints is used. For crawl-space applications, removable traps are used in case it becomes necessary to clear obstructions.

Vents are extended from the top of each T fitting. The vents can be taken through the roof individually, or they can be tied together into the vent stack that comes off the toilet. Use sanitary Ts to connect the vents to the vent stack, remembering that the direction of flow for the side outlet of the elbow is always in the direction that the waste will flow.

Working with Copper Pipe and Fittings

Copper pipe can be cut with either a hacksaw or a tubing cutter, although tubing cutters are preferred because they leave a square end. After cutting, the burr is removed from inside the cut end of the pipe, using a small, fold-down reamer that's attached to the tubing cutter.

It is extremely important to thoroughly clean the pipe and fittings where they will be joined, because solder will not stick to dirty or oxidized pipe. Use emery cloth, steel wool, or a special wire brush made for copper pipe to polish the end of the pipe until it is bright and shiny. Then clean the inside of the fitting in the same manner, and check both the pipe and the fitting to be sure they are round and free of dents.

Using a small brush, apply a generous coating of paste flux to the polished end of the pipe. The flux prevents the pipe from oxidizing during heating and allows the solder to flow more easily. Then insert the pipe into the fitting, and support the joint so that it remains together and correctly aligned while soldering.

Heat the joint with a propane torch to the point where it is just hot enough to melt the solder, but do not overheat. If the joint is properly heated, when the tip of the solder is touched to it, the solder will be rapidly drawn into the joint—do not use the flame itself to melt the solder. Before the solder hardens, wipe the joint with a cloth to cool it and remove excess flux.

When repairing or adding to an existing run of pipe, shut off the water at the main supply and drain the line. This can usually be done by opening the lowest faucet in the house, typically an outside hose bib, and allowing the lines to drain. Having the lines drained free of water is crucial in repair work, because water in the lines will prevent the pipe from reaching the temperature necessary for soldering.

Prepare and solder all the joints in a fitting at one time (for example, at both ends of an elbow or all three ends of a T). This helps prevent the heat you're applying to one joint from loosening one of the others. If it's not possible to solder all the joints at once, it may be necessary to wrap the other joints with a wet cloth to protect them.

Joints can be disassembled with heat as well. The torch is used to heat the joint until the solder becomes liquid and the pipe can be rotated slightly within the fitting; then the fitting is gently tapped off with a hammer. Previously soldered pipes and fittings need to be cleaned thoroughly before reusing them.

Electrical Systems

As with the plumbing system, the amount of work involved in adding onto or altering the electrical system depends primarily on the age and condition of the existing wiring and other components. Adding onto a relatively new house having a large-capacity electrical panel and standard electrical cable is considerably easier than adding onto one with an old fuse panel and no grounding system.

An electrician who is qualified and experienced in remodeling and room additions should check and evaluate the system at the outset of the project. He or she can give you an accurate allowance for your estimate and can let you know just how involved the remodeling will be from an electrical standpoint.

Be aware that faulty electrical wiring is one of the leading causes of residential fires, and for that reason the building inspectors will be looking very closely at the existing (as well as the new) wiring and service equipment. If any component of the existing system is thought to be dangerous—and this almost always includes older panels with glass fuses—the inspector will require that it be changed before the addition can proceed.

How the Electrical System Works

Even if you're not doing any of the wiring yourself, it's important to know something about residential electrical systems before undertaking a room addition. Again, as with the plumbing system, understanding the various parts of the system and how they interrelate can help you oversee your electrician's work and avoid costly—and potentially dangerous—mistakes.

Volts, Amps, and Watts

Three terms are commonly used when referring to the current flowing through a home's electrical system: *volts, amperes,* and *watts.* To understand the terms, it helps if you visualize the flow of electricity through the wires as if it were water flowing through a pipe.

The volt is a measure of electrical potential, which is probably better understood as electrical pressure. It is this pressure that causes the current to flow. Just as the water pressure in a pipe would be measured in pounds per square inch, electrical pressure is measured in volts. You will typically hear volts, or voltage, associated with total potential pressure in a circuit or device (for example, a 120-volt circuit or a 220-volt appliance).

An ampere (amp) is a measure of how much current is flowing through a wire or electrical device, just as gallons are used to express how much water is flowing through a pipe or a faucet. Individual circuits and devices are rated in amps to indicate the largest amount of current that the circuit or device is intended to handle, and the current flow should never exceed the amperage rating.

A watt is a unit of measurement of electrical power, which can be determined by a simple formula:

$$\text{Volts} \times \text{amps} = \text{watts}$$

Many devices, from lightbulbs to electric furnaces, are rated in watts. By knowing the wattage of a particular device, you will know how much electricity that device is consuming when it's in use.

Electrical Usage

The watt is also the unit used to measure a home's electrical usage for billing purposes. If you were purchasing water based on how much you used at any given time, it would be measured and sold by the number of gallons consumed. Similarly, electricity is measured and sold by the kilowatt-hour, or kWh. One kilowatt is 1000 watts, and 1000 watts used for 1 hour is equal to 1 kilowatt-hour.

For example, suppose you are using a small heater that is rated at 2000 watts. If you use the heater for 1 hour, you would consume 2000 watts of electricity per hour, or 2 kilowatt-hours of electricity. If you are paying 8 cents per kilowatt hour, using the heater for 1 hour would cost you 16 cents.

An Electrical Circuit

In order for electrical current to flow, it must have a complete, continuous path from its beginning—which is the source of the power—through the device using the power, such as a lightbulb, and then back to where it began. This complete path is called a *circuit.* No matter how confusing a set of wires might look, this principle remains the same: the current goes out and comes back.

In today's residential wiring, a three-wire cable is commonly used. The common outer jacket contains two individually wrapped wires, called *conductors,* plus a third wire that is bare or wrapped in green. As prescribed by the National Electrical Code (NEC), the two wrapped conductors are color-coded; one conductor is black, and the other is white or gray. The black wire is always hot, meaning it carries the current. The white wire is neutral, and it provides the return path for the current, thus completing the circuit.

Grounding

The NEC requires that all new circuits be grounded, and that's the purpose of the bare or green-wrapped conductor. The ground wire is a safety device, independent of the neutral wire, and during normal operation of the circuit it does nothing. It comes into use only when a problem occurs.

If the hot wire in the circuit were to become dislodged, or if its insulation were to wear or break away, the bare hot wire could come into contact with metal components within the circuit (e.g., a metal box or the trim on a light fixture). In that event, the entire metal part would become charged with electricity, and anyone touching the metal would receive a shock.

The ground wire connects all the metal parts of the circuit through to the neutral bus bar in the service panel, and from there to the earth, usually through a ground conductor connected to a cold-water pipe or metal grounding rod. In the event of a problem with the hot conductor, the potentially dangerous current is carried harmlessly to the earth.

Including the ground wire in the cable with the hot and neutral wires makes grounding the entire system quite simple. Within each box, the ground wires are tied together to make the ground continuous, and they also are connected to whatever device is installed in the box, such as a receptacle. Grounded receptacles (Figure 17.1) have a ground screw, colored green, which is provided for the attachment of this wire. That screw is in turn connected to a third opening on the face of the receptacle. When a tool, appliance, or other electrical device having a grounded plug is plugged into the receptacle, the grounding protection is conveyed to the tool. Should a wire come loose within the tool and touch the metal case, the user is protected against shock.

Alternating Current

Alternating current (ac) is electrical current that regularly reverses its direction of flow, flowing first in one direction, then reversing to flow in the other direction, then reversing back, with a short period between each reversal when no current is flowing at all. This alternating of current flow originates at the power source, and it is done to allow the electricity to be transmitted over long distances.

Each two reversals of direction is called a *cycle*, and the number of cycles per second is referred to as the *frequency* of the current. The unit of measurement for electrical cycles is hertz (Hz), and 1 hertz is equal to 1 cycle per second. Household current in the United States is

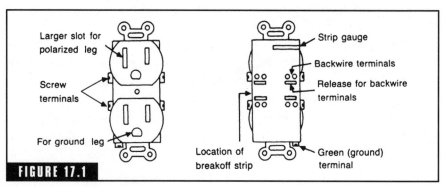

FIGURE 17.1

A grounded electrical outlet.

60-cycle, meaning the current makes two complete reversals of direction 60 times each second. The speed of these reversals makes the current appear to be continuous.

Residential Wiring System

Electricity originates at power-generating stations and is transmitted to electric utility companies for sale and distribution to the utility's consumers. The utility erects and maintains power transmission lines, extending wires from its lines to service each individual building. That service might be from overhead, which is probably the most common type or, in a growing number of cases, especially in residential subdivisions, from underground (Figure 17.2).

Overhead service conductors drop down from the transmission lines to connect with the home's service entrance conductors, which extend up within a piece of conduit that passes through the roof. Underground service, which is more expensive to install but eliminates the unsightly overhead wires, has conductors that extend in a conduit down one of the utility poles from the transmission lines, or they may be brought to the site completely underground, buried in a trench. They are then brought up through a conduit to enter the service panel from underneath. In both cases, the utility company provides the lines up to the service panel, after which all of the wiring and equipment is provided and maintained by the home's owner.

The service is also described as being *two-wire* or *three-wire*. Two-wire service, which is no longer being installed but which you may encounter on some older homes, has one 120-volt hot conductor and one neutral conductor. This type of service provides only 120 volts of power to the house.

In all new and remodeling installations, a three-wire service is used, providing two 120-volt hot conductors and one neutral. This type of service gives the house the potential for 240-volt power, which is needed for many of today's appliances.

The Service Panel

After the electrical current arrives at the house, it passes first through an electric meter, which is provided, installed, and sealed by the utility company (Figure 17.3). The meter measures and records the num-

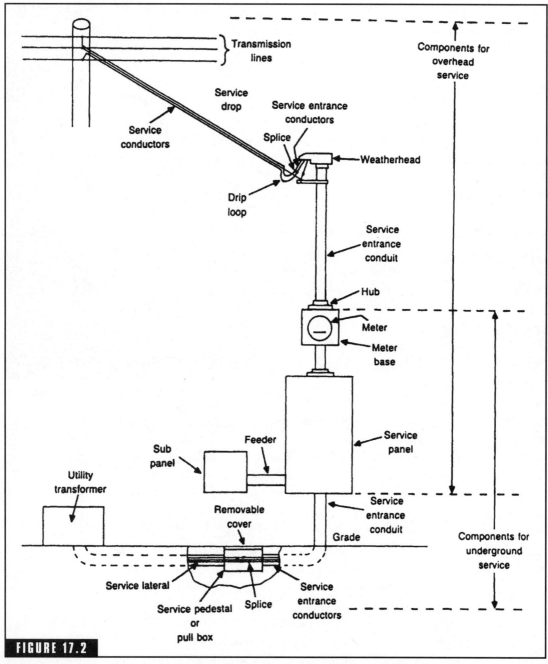

FIGURE 17.2

The various components in a typical overhead and underground residential electrical service.

ber of kilowatt-hours of electricity being consumed by the home, which is the basis for the utility company's monthly billing.

From the meter, the electricity enters the service panel itself (Figure 17.4), which might be incorporated into the meter or separate from it. The service panel takes the incoming current and distributes it to each of the branch circuits in the house. A main disconnect switch, which today is usually a circuit breaker but in older homes might be a large handle or a pullout fuse block, controls all of the current entering the panel. Closing this switch shuts off all power to the house at one time.

The main disconnect switch is rated in amperes, which indicates the total capacity of the entire service panel. Service panels are usually available in 100-, 125-, and 200-amp sizes. Today, most homes are equipped with a 200-amp service panel, even if that is more capacity than they need at the time, because it will accommodate additional load in the future if the need arises.

FIGURE 17.3

An electrical meter and main service disconnect for a 200-amp service.

From the main disconnect switch, the current travels down two metal bars, called the *hot bus bars.* Individual circuit breakers are snapped onto these bars to route the electricity into the various branch circuits.

Each hot bus bar carries 120 volts. For a 120-volt circuit, a single-pole circuit breaker is used, which connects to only one of the bus bars. A double-pole circuit breaker is used for 240-volt circuits, which contact both bus bars. The hot wires for the individual branch circuits are connected to the screw terminals on the circuit breakers.

The service panel also contains a neutral bus bar, which is connected to a service ground. The ground source might be a metal cold-water pipe in the home's plumbing system, a steel rod driven into the ground (Figure 17.5), or a piece of reinforcing steel set in the building's foundation. Some states require a double service ground that utilizes

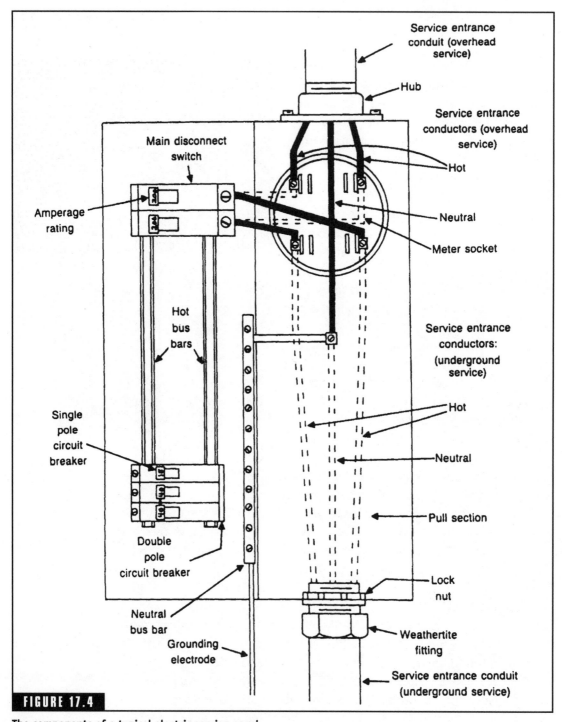

Service entrance
conduit (overhead
service)

Hub

Service entrance
conductors (overhead
service)

Hot

Neutral

Meter socket

Main disconnect
switch

Amperage
rating

Hot
bus
bars

Service entrance
conductors:
(underground
service)

Hot

Neutral

Single
pole
circuit
breaker

Double
pole
circuit breaker

Pull section

Lock
nut

Neutral
bus bar

Grounding
electrode

Weathertite
fitting

Service entrance conduit
(underground service)

FIGURE 17.4

The components of a typical electric service panel.

two ground wires—one connected to a ground rod and the other to a cold-water pipe. The neutral bus bar contains a series of holes and screws that allow for the connection of the neutral and ground wires in each of the branch circuits.

Capacity of the Service Panel

If your new addition requires a number of new circuits, especially appliance circuits that draw a lot of current, the existing service panel might not have the capacity to handle the increased load. The compo-

FIGURE 17.5

A grounding rod, ground clamp, and attached service-panel ground wire.

nents within a service panel are all sized to the panel's maximum capacity, which is usually reflected in the amperage rating of the main service disconnect switch and is stamped on that breaker.

In some cases, the panel might be rated for a higher capacity than the size of the main circuit breaker. In this event, the capacity of the panel to handle additional circuits can be increased simply by changing out the main breaker.

If the panel and the main disconnect are rated the same, which is usually the case, then the only way to increase the capacity of the electrical system is to change the entire service panel. For this procedure, the utility company must disconnect the service conductors that feed the old panel and, after the change-out, reconnect them to the new panel. All of the existing circuits then must be transferred to the new panel, and new circuits added as needed.

Calculating Load

To accurately determine the total electrical load on the system, most electricians perform a simple mathematical load calculation. All of the calculations are based on the wattage requirements of each circuit, and the total wattage requirement is then divided by the voltage of the service to determine the service panel's required amperage.

Some circuits are simply assigned an average wattage for calculation purposes, while others are determined by the wattage rating listed on an appliance's nameplate. The following example is based on a typical electrically heated home having a combined area for the house and addition of 2500 square feet.

First, the general lighting and receptacle load is figured at 3 watts per square foot:

$$2500 \text{ square feet} \times 3 \text{ watts} = 7500 \text{ watts}$$

Next, a minimum of two kitchen appliance circuits and one laundry circuit are figured in at 1500 watts each:

$$1500 \text{ watts} \times 2 \text{ kitchen circuits} = 3000 \text{ watts}$$

$$1500 \text{ watts} \times 1 \text{ laundry circuit} = 1500 \text{ watts}$$

Dedicated (individual) circuits for major appliances are added in next, based on their nameplate rating. (The nameplate rating is the actual wattage the appliance consumes. It is calculated by the manufacturer, and is stamped on a nameplate that is attached directly to the appliance.)

$$\text{Range} = 12{,}000 \text{ watts}$$

$$\text{Dryer} = 5500 \text{ watts}$$

$$\text{Water heater} = 2500 \text{ watts}$$

$$\text{Central furnace} = 20{,}000 \text{ watts}$$

$$\text{Air conditioner, wall mount, 2 @ 1500 watts each} = 3000 \text{ watts}$$

$$\text{Total} = 55{,}000 \text{ watts}$$

Because it can reasonably be assumed that not all of the circuits will be at full capacity at any one time, only the first 10,000 watts are calculated at full load. The remaining watts are calculated at 40 percent of capacity:

$$\text{First 10,000 watts @ 100\%} = 10{,}000 \text{ watts}$$

$$\text{Remaining 45,000 watts @ 40\%} = 18{,}000 \text{ watts}$$

$$\text{Total load} = 28{,}000 \text{ watts}$$

$$\frac{28{,}000 \text{ watts}}{230 \text{ volts}} \text{ (actual voltage supplied to the house)} = 121.73 \text{ amps}$$

Therefore, in order for the service panel to handle the load of the existing house and the anticipated load of the addition, an electrical service panel having a capacity of approximately 122 volts is required. A 125-amp panel would work, but just barely. A much better choice would be to install a 200-amp panel, which would easily handle the current load requirements and also allow for future expansion.

These simple calculations give you an idea of how to rate an electrical panel for a typical installation. Remember that all calculations are subject to approval by the building department and may vary in different areas and installation applications.

Transitions and Connections

As with plumbing, there are a number of components and materials on the market that simplify the wire-to-wire connections and transitions involved in remodeling. Use only approved components for connecting wires, and never attempt any wiring work that you are not fully qualified and licensed to perform.

Wire-to-Wire Connections

Of obvious importance is how to properly join two wires. For connections involving wires of the same material, such as copper to copper or aluminum to aluminum, the wire nut is probably the easiest and most secure connection method. Wire nuts are available in a variety of sizes, depending on the gauge of the wire and the number of wires being joined.

Insulation is stripped from the ends of each of the conductors, and the bare ends of the wire are twisted together lightly with a pair of pliers. The proper-sized wire nut is then placed over the wire ends and twisted firmly into place. No bare wire should be visible after the wire nut is attached.

For joining copper and aluminum wires together, care must be taken to keep the two wires from actually touching. The two most common methods are the split-bolt connector and the junction block.

A *split-bolt* is a special type of bolt with a long slot cut in the shaft. The wires to be joined are inserted into the slot and are kept separated by a small, sliding metal plate. Tightening a nut onto the shaft sandwiches the wires and the plate to make the connection, then the bolt is wrapped with several layers of electrical tape.

The *junction block* is simply a metal bar with holes and setscrews, similar to the neutral bus bar in the electrical panel. Wires are inserted into the holes in the block and secured with the setscrews. The blocks are designed so that the holes are separated by metal to keep the wires from touching. Both the split-bolt connector and the junction block are suitable for joining copper to copper or aluminum to aluminum as well.

When connecting aluminum wire to anything, be it a junction block, a terminal, or an appliance, it's important that the exposed wires be coated with a special compound to prevent oxidation. Most compounds are thick, greaselike substances and are simply spread on the wires by hand or brush prior to making the connection.

Grounding Connections

For making ground connections within an outlet box, the easiest method is to use a *crimp sleeve,* also known as a *bullet connector* because of its resemblance to a small shell casing. Two or more ground wires are slipped into the sleeve, and the sleeve is crimped down with a standard crimping tool to make the connection.

To ground a metal box, two methods are common. One is to use a ground clip (a simple spring steel clip that snaps over the side of the box), which traps the ground wire against the box for a positive connection. The second is to use a pigtail, a short, green-jacketed wire attached to a green screw. The screw is secured into a threaded hole on the back of the box—typically labeled "gr"—and then the other end of the wire is tied in with the rest of the grounds in the box.

For attaching a ground wire to a galvanized or copper water pipe, a special ground clamp is available. The two serrated jaws of the clamp are placed on either side of the pipe, then secured with the two attached screws. The ground wire is inserted into a hole on the top of the clamp, and a setscrew is used to hold it in place. Two sizes of ground clamps are commonly available: small, for ½-, ¾-, and 1-inch pipe, and large, for 1¼-, 1½-, and 2-inch pipe.

A different ground clamp is used for securing a ground wire to a rod that has been driven into the earth. This type of clamp is merely a metal ring with an attached bolt, which is slipped over the rod. The wire goes between the rod and the ring, and both are held in place by tightening the bolt.

To provide grounding protection for threaded, rigid-metal conduit, bonding bushings are available. These bushings have an attached grounding screw—the bushing is screwed onto the end of the conduit above the locknut, then a ground wire can be run from any convenient ground source to the screw terminal on the bushing. Bond bushings are commonly used on the underground feeder conduit that is connected to a service panel.

Conduit and Cable Connectors

The number of connectors and fittings designed for use with the various types of conduit and electrical cables is extensive, and the choice can vary considerably with the requirements of each individual installation.

Cable connectors, also known as Romex connectors or wire looms, provide a means of entering an electrical or junction box without having the wire contact the rough sides of the knockout hole, and they also provide a clamp for securing the cable to the box. One type is secured to the box with a lock ring and has a small screw clamp to hold the wire, while another type is secured to both the box and the wire by crimping the connector with pliers. A variety of sizes are available to accommodate different knockout and cable sizes.

Several types of conduit are available for use in electrical wiring applications. Here are some of the most common: PVC, which is similar to plumbing pipe, but thicker, and treated to be sunlight-resistant (for easy identification, electrical PVC is gray, as opposed to white for plumbing PVC); electromechanical tubing, commonly known as EMT or thinwall, which is a type of galvanized metal tube; flexible conduit, which is a metal conduit made up of interlocking wrappings that allow it to be flexible; and Sealtite, a type of flexible conduit that is coated to be waterproof. Each type has its own specific connectors that use setscrews or lock rings to secure the joints or, in the case of the PVC, a cement that solvent-welds the joints together.

Adding a New Circuit

In most cases, installing new circuits is a fairly straightforward procedure. New circuits extend from the electrical panel to the point of use, and both the wire and the circuit breaker must be properly sized for the intended amperage use of the circuit.

Wire

Wire size and type are important considerations when installing a new circuit, so a working knowledge of how wire is described will be helpful. An individual wire, called a *conductor,* is rated by its diameter, or gauge, according to American Wire Gauge (AWG) standards. The larger the gauge number, the smaller the wire.

When two or more conductors are grouped together in a common outer jacket, they form a cable. Cables are designated by the gauge of the conductors, the number of conductors grouped in the cable, and the insulation type. Earlier cables also had a designation regarding whether or not they contained a ground wire, but all cables are now equipped with a ground wire automatically.

Generally speaking, most 120-volt circuits will require three wires: one hot (black), one neutral (white), and one ground (green or bare). A 240-volt circuit usually will need an additional hot wire (commonly red). In recent years, these combinations of individual conductors have been grouped together into cables and bound by another layer of thermoplastic insulation for ease in handling and more resistance to damage. Technically named *nonmetallic sheathed cable,* or type NM, you will often hear it referred to by the trade name Romex (Figure 17.6). The cable is designated simply by the wire gauge followed by the number of conductors, such as "12/2."

FIGURE 17.6

Running nonmetallic sheathed cable for electrical wiring. Engineered I-joists such as these have knockouts to eliminate having to drill holes. *(Courtesy of Trus Joist MacMillan.)*

Circuit Size

The first thing to determine is how big the circuit must be in terms of amperes. General lighting and plug circuits are usually 15 amps, and kitchen circuits are 20 amps to handle higher-wattage appliances such as toasters, electric frying pans, and the like. As previously discussed, if a dedicated circuit is required, such as one for a specific tool or appliance, you can determine the circuit size from the manufacturer's specifications. If the amperage is not given but the wattage is, use the following formula:

$$\frac{\text{Watts}}{\text{Volts}} = \text{amps}$$

The proper circuit breaker and gauge of wire are the next considerations. Circuit breakers are rated and labeled according to the maximum amount of amperage they can be used with, and they are commonly found in 15-, 20-, 30-, 40-, 50-, and 60-amp sizes for branch circuit use. The circuit breaker needs to be as close to the amperage requirement of the circuit as possible, but no smaller. Therefore, a circuit requiring 12 amps would use a 15-amp breaker, but a circuit of 16 amps would need a 20-amp breaker.

The amperage of the circuit breaker determines the size of the wire:

15-amp circuit	14-gauge wire
20-amp circuit	12-gauge wire
30-amp circuit	10-gauge wire
40-amp circuit	8-gauge wire
50-amp circuit	6-gauge wire

Note: These gauges are for standard, thermoplastic-insulated copper wires.

Conduit and Cable

How the wire will get from the panel to the end use will determine the type of wire to use. In general, there are three different ways in which you can get a wire from one place to another. If the cable will be concealed from weather and abrasion, the easiest and least-expensive method is to use the Type NM cable described earlier.

If the wire must be installed outside or in a place where normal activities might subject it to damage you must encase it in conduit, and the type of conduit chosen is dependent on where it will be used. For areas where a high degree of support or impact resistance is needed, use rigid-metal or PVC conduit; burial and some outdoor uses require PVC only; flexible metal conduit can be used in areas where a number of bends or angles will be encountered; and Sealtite is used for flexible applications outside or in wet locations.

For short runs of conduit or for transitions, such as running cable exposed in the attic and then entering conduit to come down a wall, Type NM cable can typically be used inside conduit—the thickness of the outer jacket, however, limits the number of conductors that can be run within a given conduit diameter. For longer runs, it is more cost-effective and much easier to pull the wires through the conduit using individual conductors, which eliminates the bulk of the cable's outer jacket. The most common type of wire for this use is Type TW (thermoplastic weather-resistant), which is available in the same gauges and colors as the conductors used in Type NM.

The third method is direct burial. Depending on local frost and soil conditions and any building code restrictions, you can bury rigid-plastic conduit or directly bury the cable. A special sunlight- and weather-resistant cable is made for this application—Type UF (underground feeder), in which the conductors are encased in solid plastic.

In remodeling work, a combination of two or three of these methods is often necessary. Your considerations include the easiest and most direct route to the panel and how you will enter the panel itself once you get there.

Installation Procedures

Type NM cable can be run in the walls, attic, underfloor, or any other protected area. When running the cable through wood framing, the holes need to be located so that the wire is far enough back from the edge of the framing member to protect it from being damaged by nails from the siding, drywall, or other sources. If this is not possible, you must install metal safety plates on the framing to protect the wire.

In the attic or under the floor, cable staples are used to secure the cable neatly along the joists, out of the way of potential contact. Most building codes require that cables installed in attics be run in areas with 3 feet or less of headroom to prevent possible damage from footsteps. Leave at least 6 inches of excess wire where cable enters a box to allow for hookups, and secure the cable within 8 inches of the box.

For a typical new circuit installation, run wire from the addition back to the electrical panel. Remove a knockout of the appropriate size from the panel box, and install the proper type of cable connector or conduit fitting. Then snap the new circuit breaker onto the bus bars.

After routing the cable into the panel box, strip the outside jacket from the cable. Route the hot wire(s) to the breaker and attach them to the screw fitting—a single-pole, 110-volt breaker will have one screw for the single hot wire, while a double-pole, 220-volt breaker will have two screws. Route neutral and ground wires to the neutral bar, and secure them under any of the unused screws on the bar. Remember to use great care with aluminum wires so that they don't get nicked during the stripping and installation process. Dip the exposed wires in a corrosion inhibitor before securing them under their respective screws.

Finally, remove the appropriate knockout from the panel cover to accommodate the new breaker. Remember to indelibly label the panel to identify which circuit the new breaker controls.

Preparing for Electrical Inspections

Because of the health and safety issues involved, electrical codes and inspections are typically the most strict that you'll have to face. Remember that the electrical inspectors are there to ensure the safety of the house and the occupants, so learn to work with them.

The following checklist will help you prepare for the rough wiring inspection and minimize any mistakes.

FIGURE 17.7

An electrical meter base. The base has been installed, wired, and inspected (note inspection tag), but the meter has not yet been installed.

__ Exterior walls are enclosed on the outside, and insulation is not yet installed (Figure 17.7).

__ The roof structure and roofing are complete.

__ On the common wall between the house and the garage, all penetrations are properly sealed.

__ Receptacle outlets are provided as follows: within 6 feet of the start and finish of any wall and at least one every 12 feet thereafter; on any usable wall space 2 feet wide or greater; on counter spaces 12 inches wide or greater in kitchens and dining rooms; in bathrooms adjacent to the sink; outside (at least one); in the basement and attached garage; and in the laundry area.

___ Separate branch circuits are provided as follows: 20-amp for laundry; 15-amp lighting circuit for each 500 square feet of floor area or fraction thereof; 20-amp for dishwasher and/or garbage disposal; 20-amp for microwave; minimum 15-amp for furnace motor; 30-amp for clothes dryer; minimum of two 20-amp small-appliance circuits for receptacles in the kitchen, pantry, breakfast room, and dining room, with the receptacles divided evenly between the two circuits.

___ A separate branch circuit is provided for whirlpool bathtubs, and the circuit is protected by an approved GFI outlet or breaker.

___ Nonmetallic sheathed cable is supported within 8 inches of the boxes and at intervals not exceeding 4½ feet.

___ Outlet boxes are of sufficient size to provide free space for all conductors.

___ At each box, 6 inches of free conductor is provided for connections.

___ Ground fault interrupter (GFI) receptacles are installed as needed in kitchen, bathroom, garage, and exterior outlets.

Although the information in this chapter is fairly generic regarding the requirements for most jurisdictions and for most installations, remember to read the specific codes for your area and your application, and check with your local electrical inspectors for other specific rules and requirements.

Always disconnect electrical circuits prior to working on them. To prevent the circuit from being inadvertently reactivated, place a piece of tape temporarily over the circuit breaker, and include a warning that the breaker must remain in the off position because of ongoing work on the circuit.

Finally, electrical repairs and the installation of new wiring and electrical equipment should be done only by a qualified, experienced, and licensed electrician.

Heating, Ventilating, and Insulation

The heating, ventilating, and air-conditioning systems within a home, known collectively as the HVAC system or simply as the mechanical equipment (which includes all the air-handling and air-conditioning equipment) can vary widely from house to house. The HVAC system includes the furnace, permanent room heaters, ducts, fans, vents, filters, humidifiers, and other related equipment.

Heating and cooling systems fall into two broad categories: *central* and *zonal*. Central systems have one or, in larger homes, more than one centrally located furnace and/or air-conditioning unit that supplies conditioned air to the entire home through a series of air ducts. Zonal systems have several individual, independently controlled units, which treat the air in different rooms or areas of the house separately. The type of HVAC system you choose for the addition depends primarily on the size and type of the existing heating system and the size of the addition.

Central Systems

The furnace (Figure 18.1) currently being used in the home will be fueled by electricity, natural gas, propane, heating oil, coal, or wood.

FIGURE 18.1

An example of a gas-fired central furnace.

The fuel is supplied to a central furnace unit and consumed to heat the air within the furnace, which is then fan-forced or gravity-fed into the rooms through ducts. Cool air is taken in from within the house (Figure 18.2) and returned to the furnace for reheating, ensuring a continuous supply and cycle of heated air (Figure 18.3).

Central air-conditioning is electrically powered, and most commonly uses a split system, with an indoor evaporator unit located in the furnace plenum and an exterior condensing unit, connected by two large, flexible copper tubes. A refrigerant is circulated through the system via the tubes. The refrigerant enters the evaporator as a liquid, where it is allowed to expand and change state into a gas. The expansion process draws heat from the surrounding air, and the resulting cooled air is blown into the house through the ducts. The refrigerant leaves the house as a gas to enter the outdoor unit, where a compressor compresses it back into a liquid. The compression process causes the refrigerant to give off its heat, and a condenser distributes that heat to the surrounding outside air. As a liquid again, the refrigerant passes back into the house to repeat the process. Heat pumps (Figure 18.4) use the same process in reverse to heat the house, drawing heat from the outside air and distributing it to the interior of the home.

If the existing home is equipped with a central heating system of adequate capacity, the simplest method of heating the addition is to extend new ducts from the existing system as needed. This method requires no expensive new equipment, and the new duct runs are a fairly simple matter. In the event of a very large addition, say one of over 1000 square feet, a whole new central system dedicated to the addition would be the best choice.

FIGURE 18.2

A ceiling-mounted return-air grill. This type has a filter built into the grill housing.

Duct Systems

There are two types of duct systems commonly employed in residential installations: the *radial* or *perimeter system* and the *extended plenum system.*

A radial system (Figure 18.5) consists of registers placed around the building's outside walls, usually under a window so that the warm air can counteract the natural convection currents around the cold glass. Each register is served by a duct that extends directly off the plenum chamber— the warm-air distribution box attached to the outlet side of the furnace—or off of one large duct extending out from the plenum and branching into two smaller ducts for individual registers.

In the extended plenum system (Figure 18.6), a large rectangular duct extends off the plenum, usually in a straight line that

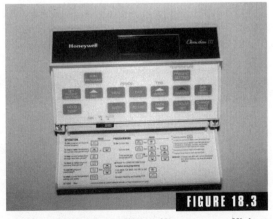

FIGURE 18.3

A clock thermostat, which offers energy-efficient automatic control for a central furnace.

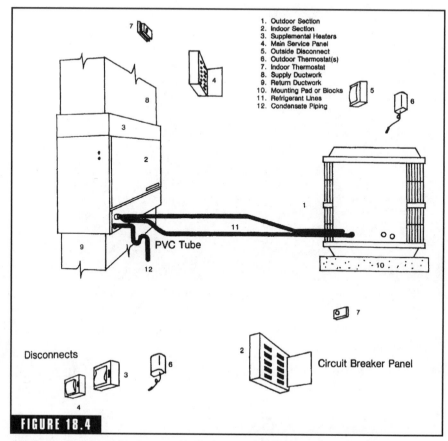

1. Outdoor Section
2. Indoor Section
3. Supplemental Heaters
4. Main Service Panel
5. Outside Disconnect
6. Outdoor Thermostat(s)
7. Indoor Thermostat
8. Supply Ductwork
9. Return Ductwork
10. Mounting Pad or Blocks
11. Refrigerant Lines
12. Condensate Piping

PVC Tube

Disconnects

Circuit Breaker Panel

FIGURE 18.4

A typical split-system heat pump, with indoor section (left) and outdoor section (right) connected by two refrigerant lines.

runs the length of the building. Individual ducts extend off this main plenum duct to serve each register. This type of system offers less resistance to airflow and easier arrangement of the registers, and it is more common in larger buildings with greater heat requirements.

Hydronic Systems

In some systems, water takes the place of air as the heat-delivery medium. The furnace heats the water and delivers it through a series of closed pipes to individual radiators in the rooms or distributes it through a series of pipes in the floor.

Some types of hydronic systems have the capacity to be extended. If you are considering adding to an existing system, be aware that the

system is very carefully sized and balanced, and any additions must be very
carefully designed.

Zonal Heating Systems

For a room addition, a workable alternative
to installing new ducts is to use room
heaters. Individually installed and controlled, these heaters allow one room or
area of the addition—called a *zone*—to be
heated independently of the others. Zone
heaters are easy and convenient to install,
and they provide only the heat that's necessary for that zone. In addition, they are
quite inexpensive compared to a whole
new central system.

Electric Systems

The most commonly used zone heaters for
remodeling situations are electric. They
are easy to install, requiring the running of
only a single electrical cable, and they
require no special ducting. There are several forms of electric heaters, each suited
to a particular application.

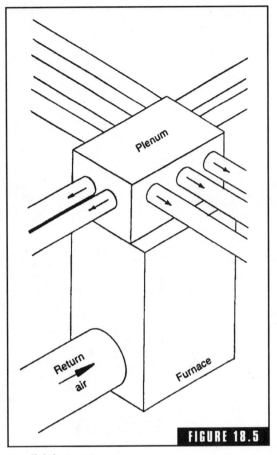

FIGURE 18.5

A radial duct system.

- *Baseboard heaters.* A long radiant strip heater, ranging in length
  from 2 to 8 feet. Several units can be joined end to end for longer
  runs. They are attached to the wall at floor level, like a baseboard. Some types have a thermostat built into the heater; other
  types are wired through a wall thermostat that operates on either
  low or line voltage. Split systems for heating and cooling are also
  available.

- *Wall and ceiling heaters.* Wall heaters (Figure 18.7) are small
  square or rectangular units, available in a wide range of sizes and
  wattages. They consist of a resistance coil heater with a small fan
  that blows over the coil to distribute the heat, and they have

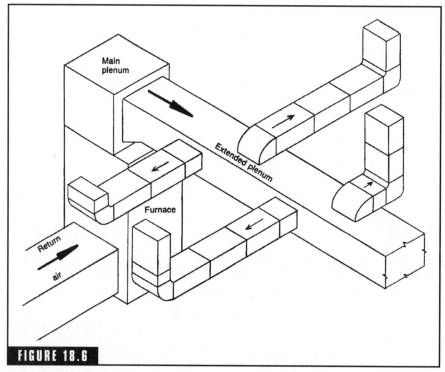

FIGURE 18.6

An extended plenum duct system.

either an attached or a separate thermostat. Ceiling heaters are small, fan-forced units recessed into the ceiling, especially in bathrooms. Some types are made up in combination with a light or an exhaust fan.

- *Radiant heaters.* Radiant heaters take the form of either cables placed in the ceiling or decorative wall- or ceiling-mounted panels. They rely on the natural radiation of heat from a warm surface to a cold one, and provide a very gentle, silent source of heat. Their disadvantage is that anything blocked from a direct line of sight to the heater will not be warmed.

Hydronic Zonal Systems

Hydronic heaters offer another alternative when considering zonal heating. Available primarily in baseboard or wall-mounted units, they tap the home's hot-water plumbing system as a source of heat. Hot water passes through coils within the unit, warming a series of heat exchanger fins, and a fan blowing across the fins extracts the heat and forces it into the room.

For a typical installation, a T is placed into a regular, potable hot-water system at any convenient location and a line is run to the heater. The return line ties into the home's cold-water line where it enters the water heater. A check valve is installed on the return line to prevent cold water from being drawn into the heater when it's not in operation. Remember that adding this type of heater places some additional demand on the hot-water system, and the water heater may need to be upgraded accordingly.

An electric fan-forced wall heater.

Fireplaces and Other Heat Sources

Besides the more conventionally thought-of zonal heaters such as an electric wall heater, there are other options. Fireplaces, woodstoves, and a whole new generation of gas stoves offer some additional alternatives.

Wood Heat

For most homes, wood heat is typically thought of more as a secondary system than a primary one. It is mostly used as a backup to take some of the load off the main heating system, and it's also a good zonal system for heating one or more individual rooms, such as a living room or a family room. And few things can replace the warm ambience of a wood fire.

The traditional wood-burning device has always been the fireplace (Figure 18.8). For appearance and atmosphere, it can't be beat. For efficiency as a heat source, however, it leaves a lot to be desired.

Fireplaces draw in room air as a necessary oxygen source to support the combustion of the wood, and the smoke is exhausted up the

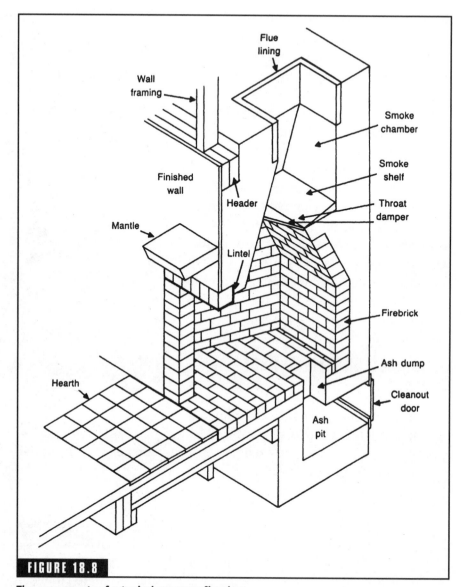

FIGURE 18.8

The components of a typical masonry fireplace.

chimney. As much as two-thirds of heat energy produced by burning the wood is lost directly up the chimney. In addition, the constant need for combustion air causes a slight and often uncomfortable draft across the floor of the room—and that air being used for combustion is usually room air you've already paid to heat. For that reason, many traditional fireplaces are being converted to airtight inserts (Figures 18.9 and 18.10).

A popular alternative to the fireplace is the woodstove (Figure 18.11). Airtight and with a large metal surface area, these units make much better use of the heat energy in the wood. Fires burn longer, and much more usable heat is obtained. A tremendous variety of styles are available to suit any decor, and a popular option is the glass door, which provides energy efficiency while not sacrificing the traditional enjoyment of watching the burning wood.

Woodstoves must be installed on a noncombustible surface, such as a brick or

FIGURE 18.9

An airtight wood-burning insert that's been retrofit into an existing masonry fireplace.

FIGURE 18.10

Fireplace inserts require that the masonry chimney be retrofit with a flue pipe and cap.

FIGURE 18.11

An airtight woodstove, in this case one that burns wood pellets.

FIGURE 18.12

A woodstove in a vaulted ceiling installation, with flue pipe.

synthetic hearth pad, and specific clearances must be maintained from walls and other combustibles. Special pipe (Figure 18.12) is used for venting, and you'll need to take great care to provide the necessary clearances from wood framing. Woodstove installations, like any mechanical equipment, require a building permit, and the main thing the inspector will be looking for is the type of flue pipe and adequate clearances.

Gas and oil stoves, burning natural gas, propane, or heating oil, are an alternative to wood. Installed and vented in a similar manner to a woodstove, a gas stove is piped into the home's gas system or to a propane or oil tank. Most of these heating devices are thermostatically controlled like a furnace, offering much better control over the heat output than a woodstove, and many of the newer models throw off a surprisingly realistic flame over ceramic logs.

Zone Cooling

Homes with central heating systems can have an air-conditioning unit added fairly inexpensively, because the duct system and part of the mechanical equipment are already in place. For other homes, the cost of adding on central cooling to a zonal heating system may be impractical. The alternative is a zonal cooling system.

The most common example of zonal cooling is the room air conditioner. Individual air conditioners can be installed in a window, but you should be aware of several drawbacks. A window installation will block up to half of the natural light coming through the window, and it also eliminates that window as a source of fresh air and ventilation. Even more important, installing the air conditioner in a bedroom window may eliminate the room's only means of egress, which is a serious safety hazard.

An alternative is to install the unit directly into the wall. A hole of the appropriate rough opening is cut and framed, either between two studs or, for larger installations, with a headered opening like the type used for a window. The unit is fit into the opening and trimmed out so that just the face grill shows—the remainder of the unit is outside the wall, supported by platform or metal brackets.

For a house that gets warm and stuffy in the summer but not warm enough to justify air-conditioning, a whole-house fan is worth considering, either for use by itself or to supplement a central air-conditioning system on days when air-conditioning isn't really needed.

The fan is recessed into the ceiling in a central location and covered by an unobtrusive white shutter panel (Figure 18.13). Any time the outside temperature is lower than the temperature inside, simply activate the fan and open the windows. The powerful fan will draw in cool outside air and push it up into the attic and then out through the roof vents, flushing and cooling the entire home, including the attic, in a very short time.

Several manufacturers offer these fans in kits that are designed to simplify installation. The most common sizes are 30 and 36 inches, and all are 120 volts for easy wiring. The 30-inch fans have a rating in

FIGURE 18.13

The ceiling louver for a whole-house fan. The suction of the fan draws the louvers open automatically.

the 5100- to 5500-cubic-feet-per-minute (cfm) range, and these are adequate for homes of up to about 1800 square feet. The 36-inch fans, at 6800 to 7000 cfm, will handle homes of about 2300 square feet. Multiple units in different areas might be required for larger homes. The fans can provide a complete change of air in the house in as little as 10 minutes, but the air movement, especially on low speed, resembles no more than a gentle breeze.

Energy Conservation

Even though the room addition might represent only a small portion of the total square footage of the house, insulation and energy-conservation measures cannot be overlooked. In fact, while the addition is under way is an excellent time to talk with your clients about upgrading existing insulation and taking care of other weatherization needs (Figure 18.14).

To help your clients with their energy needs, it's helpful to understand how heat moves and how it is lost from a seemingly solid structure.

The Basics of Heat Transmission

Heat is a form of energy created by the movement of molecules. Heat will always travel in one direction—from a warm surface to a colder surface—and it does so in one of three ways: convection, radiation, or conduction.

CONVECTION

When a gas such as air takes on heat, it expands and becomes lighter, causing it to rise. As it rises it cools, becoming more dense and heavy until it falls again. This natural rising and falling is called *convection.* If the heated air is confined to a relatively small area, these natural air movements take on a circular pattern, called a *convection current.*

RADIATION

Every heated object gives off energy in the form of infrared waves, which will travel naturally from the heat source to an object having a lower surface temperature. This is *radiated heat,* an example of which would be the warmth you feel on your body when you are standing in front of a hot stove or in direct sunlight.

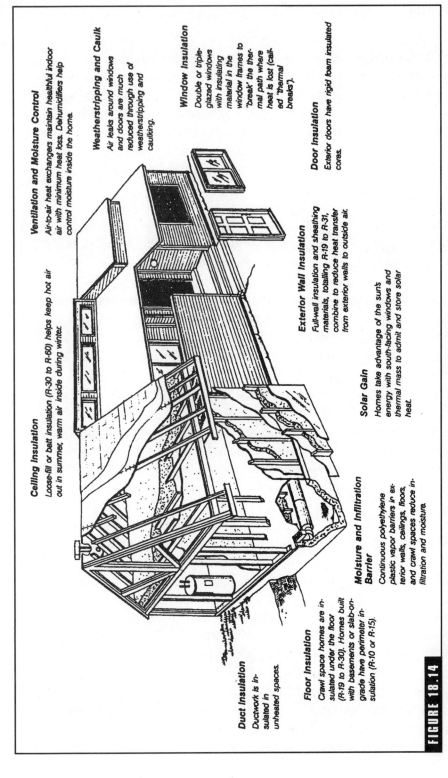

Ceiling Insulation

Loose-fill or batt insulation (R-30 to R-60) helps keep hot air out in summer, warm air inside during winter.

Ventilation and Moisture Control

Air-to-air heat exchangers maintain healthful indoor air with minimum heat loss. Dehumidifiers help control moisture inside the home.

Weatherstripping and Caulk

Air leaks around windows and doors are much reduced through use of weatherstripping and caulking.

Window Insulation

Double or triple-glazed windows with insulating material in the window frames to "break" the thermal path where heat is lost (called "thermal breaks").

Door Insulation

Exterior doors have rigid foam insulated cores.

Exterior Wall Insulation

Full-wall insulation and sheathing materials, totalling R-19 to R-31, combine to reduce heat transfer from exterior walls to outside air.

Solar Gain

Homes take advantage of the sun's energy with south-facing windows and thermal mass to admit and store solar heat.

Duct Insulation

Ductwork is insulated in unheated spaces.

Floor Insulation

Crawl space homes are insulated under the floor (R-19 to R-30). Homes built with basements or slab-on-grade have perimeter insulation (R-10 or R-15).

Moisture and Infiltration Barrier

Continuous polyethylene plastic vapor barriers in exterior walls, ceilings, floors, and crawl spaces reduce infiltration and moisture.

FIGURE 18.14

A look at the various components that go into making up an energy-efficient house.

Radiated heat is line of sight. For example, if you stand facing a campfire on a cold night, the front of you, which is at a lower temperature than the fire and which is directly exposed to the fire's heat, feels warm. The heat is moving from the warmer surface, the fire, to the colder surface, your body. The back of you, sheltered from the fire but still at a higher temperature than the surrounding air, feels cold as the heat from your body moves to the cooler surrounding air.

CONDUCTION

While convection and radiation involve the transference of heat through the movement or disruption of the surrounding air, *conduction* is the movement of heat between molecules within a solid object, or within air or liquid, without such disruption. As the molecules are heated, their speed of movement increases, and they give off energy. This energy causes adjacent molecules to heat and move faster. This process is repeated until, given enough time, the entire object will achieve the same temperature. An example of conduction is a frying pan on a stove—heat from the stove warms the pan to cook the food, but eventually that heat expands out into the metal handle as well.

This concept is of primary importance in construction, because conduction causes heat inside a building to pass through the walls, floor, and ceiling to the cooler areas on the other side. Thermal insulation is incorporated into a building in order to minimize this heat transfer, called *conduction loss*.

The Four Values of Heat Resistance

Every material has some resistance to heat flow. This is known as its *resistance value* or *R-value*. How resistant a material is depends primarily on the number of air cells it contains. These minute cells resist all three forms of heat transfer. Transfer by convection can't occur efficiently because the air space is too small to allow movement. Transfer by radiation is resisted because very little of the heat striking the dead-air space is transmitted to the opposite surface. Transfer by conduction is lessened because continuity of the molecules within the material is broken up by the dead air.

Four values are used to evaluate and measure how different materials act as thermal insulation. Two of them, U-values and R-values, are used all the time in construction.

K-VALUE

This is the basic measurement of heat transfer, dealing with a uniform size and thickness of material. It is the number of Btu's of heat that will pass through 1 square foot of a material 1 inch thick in 1 hour at a temperature difference of 1°F between the surfaces. The lower the K-value, the less heat will pass through that material, and the better it is as an insulator.

C-VALUE

Because not all materials can be tested at a uniform thickness of 1 inch, C-value is used as a measurement of heat movement through standard thicknesses such as ½-inch drywall or ¾-inch plywood. It is defined as the number of Btu's that will pass through 1 square foot of a material of actual standard thickness in 1 hour, again at a 1°F temperature difference between the two surfaces. The lower the C-value, the better the material is as an insulator.

U-VALUE

Because some objects are made up of several different materials having different heat-transfer characteristics, such as windows, doors, or entire walls (Figure 18.15), U-value measures the heat movement through the combined materials in a building component or section. U-value is defined as the number of Btu's that will pass through 1 square foot of a combined building component or section at a temperature difference of 1°F between the surfaces.

The lower the U-value, the more effective is that component in resisting heat flow. U-value is used almost as much as R-value in construction, and you will often see windows and doors rated by the manufacturer in U-values instead of R-values.

R-VALUE

The most common of the terms, R-value measures a material's resistance to heat flow. The higher the R-value, the better the material will be as a thermal insulator. Since R-value measures how well a material *stops* heat flow, it is the opposite, or *reciprocal,* of the C-, K-, and U-values, which all measure how well a material *permits* heat flow. Therefore, you can use the following conversion formulas:

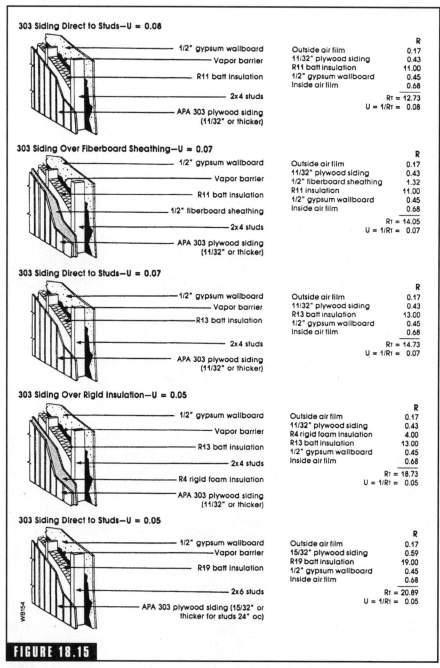

303 Siding Direct to Studs—U = 0.08

- 1/2" gypsum wallboard
- Vapor barrier
- R11 batt insulation
- 2x4 studs
- APA 303 plywood siding (11/32" or thicker)

	R
Outside air film	0.17
11/32" plywood siding	0.43
R11 batt insulation	11.00
1/2" gypsum wallboard	0.45
Inside air film	0.68
$R_T = $	12.73
$U = 1/R_T = $	0.08

303 Siding Over Fiberboard Sheathing—U = 0.07

- 1/2" gypsum wallboard
- Vapor barrier
- R11 batt insulation
- 1/2" fiberboard sheathing
- 2x4 studs
- APA 303 plywood siding (11/32" or thicker)

	R
Outside air film	0.17
11/32" plywood siding	0.43
1/2" fiberboard sheathing	1.32
R11 insulation	11.00
1/2" gypsum wallboard	0.45
Inside air film	0.68
$R_T = $	14.05
$U = 1/R_T = $	0.07

303 Siding Direct to Studs—U = 0.07

- 1/2" gypsum wallboard
- Vapor barrier
- R13 batt insulation
- 2x4 studs
- APA 303 plywood siding (11/32" or thicker)

	R
Outside air film	0.17
11/32" plywood siding	0.43
R13 batt insulation	13.00
1/2" gypsum wallboard	0.45
Inside air film	0.68
$R_T = $	14.73
$U = 1/R_T = $	0.07

303 Siding Over Rigid Insulation—U = 0.05

- 1/2" gypsum wallboard
- Vapor barrier
- R13 batt insulation
- 2x4 studs
- R4 rigid foam insulation
- APA 303 plywood siding (11/32" or thicker)

	R
Outside air film	0.17
11/32" plywood siding	0.43
R4 rigid foam insulation	4.00
R13 batt insulation	13.00
1/2" gypsum wallboard	0.45
Inside air film	0.68
$R_T = $	18.73
$U = 1/R_T = $	0.05

303 Siding Direct to Studs—U = 0.05

- 1/2" gypsum wallboard
- Vapor barrier
- R19 batt insulation
- 2x6 studs
- APA 303 plywood siding (15/32" or thicker for studs 24" oc)

	R
Outside air film	0.17
15/32" plywood siding	0.59
R19 batt insulation	19.00
1/2" gypsum wallboard	0.45
Inside air film	0.68
$R_T = $	20.89
$U = 1/R_T = $	0.05

WB154

FIGURE 18.15

U-values for various types of wall construction. *(Courtesy of American Plywood Association.)*

$$\frac{1}{K} = \text{R-value per inch of a uniform material}$$

$$\frac{1}{C} = \text{R-value of the standard form and thickness of a material}$$

$$\frac{1}{U} = \text{R-value of a combined building component or section}$$

$$\frac{1}{R} = \text{U-value}$$

Vapor Barriers

The other element in effective insulation is the vapor barrier (Figure 18.16). Warm, moist air trying to escape the inside of a building will collide with cool, dry air trying to enter. This collision takes place within the insulated area and results in condensation. This condensation wets the insulation, substantially reducing its insulating value, and also becomes a potential source of damage to the wood framing.

Placed on or over the side of the insulation that faces the heated area of the building, the vapor barrier prevents moist air from passing through it. This moist air, turned back into the building, helps the building to retain its heat, while also retaining needed humidity.

In residential construction, vapor barriers are commonly achieved through the use of insulation that is faced on one side with asphalt-impregnated paper or with reflective foil. Unfaced insulation is also used to fill the wall, floor, or ceiling cavity, then covered with a continuous layer of polyethylene (plastic sheeting) to act as the vapor barrier.

Vapor barriers are also used on the outside of the building, underneath the siding. Should moisture pass through the siding material, either as airborne water

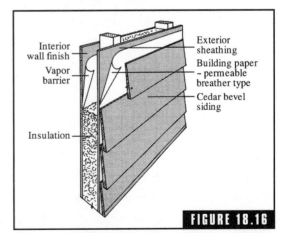

FIGURE 18.16

Cross section of a typical wall, including interior vapor barrier and exterior house wrap. *(Courtesy of Western Red Cedar Lumber Association.)*

vapor or as an actual liquid, the outside moisture barrier helps stop the underlying sheathing and framing from being damaged.

Insulation Materials

Insulation is commonly available in several different materials and in three basic forms, depending on its intended application.

Batts and Blankets

Batts and blankets are flexible strips of insulation designed to fit between structural members. Batts are sold in precut lengths, usually 4 or 8 feet, primarily for use in wall and floor cavities, while blankets are sold in long rolls. Both types come faced with kraft paper or foil, to be held in place with staples, or unfaced, to be held in place by friction against the framing members on each side. Batt and blanket insulations are sold in two widths: 15 inches for use with framing on 16-inch centers, and 23 inches for 24-inch OC framing.

Insulation in this form is used in unfinished wall cavities, in ceilings, and in underfloor areas. It is also commonly used for wrapping pipes and ducts. Remember that the paper facing on batt and blanket insulation is combustible, and it should not be left exposed. The following are common batt and blanket materials:

- *Fiberglass:* These are long filaments of spun glass, loosely woven and cut into various widths and thicknesses. The R-value of fiberglass in batts is approximately 3.1 per inch.

- *Rock wool and slag wool:* This is granite rock or furnace slag that has been melted at temperatures between 2500 and 3000°F and processed into a thick, wool-like material. It has an R-value of approximately 2.9 per inch.

Loose Fill

Loose fill is any of a variety of insulation materials that are provided in loose, bulk form, usually in bags, to be poured, blown, or placed by hand into walls or attics. Common loose-fill materials include the following:

- *Fiberglass:* This is the same material that is used in batts, but it's left loose, in small clumps. It is placed by blowing, using a special, high-power blower and a large-diameter hose. The R-value of fiberglass as a blown material drops to about 2.2 per inch.

■ *Cellulose:* Paper products, primarily recycled newsprint or wood fibers, are shredded and milled into a fluffy, low-density material and then treated with fire-retardant chemicals, usually boric acid. Cellulose can be blown in using commercial blowers like those used for fiberglass, or it can be blown in using do-it-yourself machines, which can be rented or borrowed through some retail distributors. Cellulose is also commonly used for blowing into closed, uninsulated wall cavities. Its R-value is around 3.7 per inch.

■ *Rock wool:* The same material as that used in batts, but left loose for blowing. The R-value is approximately 2.9 per inch.

■ *Perlite:* A volcanic material, expanded 4 to 20 times by heating to produce a light, cellular material in pellet form. It is placed by pouring and then raking level to the desired thickness. Its R-value is about 2.7 per inch.

■ *Vermiculite:* A material having numerous thin layers that expand under heat in accordion-like folds, producing light-weight pellets. It can be used alone, as a poured, loose-fill insulation, or can be mixed in plaster or concrete. It has an R-value of approximately 2.2 per inch.

Rigid Boards

Rigid board is thermal insulation in the form of rigid sheets, with either square or tongue-and-groove edges, for use on roofs, wall surfaces, stem walls, and under slabs. The sheets are usually 2 × 8 or 4 × 8 feet, available in several different thicknesses. Several different materials are used in producing rigid boards, and virtually all of them are combustible and should not be left uncovered.

■ *Extruded polystyrene:* Polystyrene beads are fed into an extruder and melted into a thick fluid, which is then injected with a mixture of gases to foam the fluid into a mass of bubbles. Heat and pressure are applied, and the mixture is shaped by the extruder into a solid board. It has an R-value of about 5.2 per inch, and is suitable for below-grade and underslab use. Above grade, it should be protected from constant exposure to sunlight.

■ *Molded or expanded polystyrene:* In this process, polystyrene beads are poured into a mold, then heated. The beads swell to fill the mold and fuse together into a solid form. Because it is lower in density and its cells do not contain gases, it has a lower R-value, about 3.6 per inch, and is more brittle than extruded polystyrene. This material is often referred to as *beadboard,* and is also commonly used in such items as ice chests and coffee cups. This type of insulation should not be used in below-grade applications.

■ *Polyurethane and polyisocyanurate:* These are plastic polymers that are formed into boards using a process similar to that for extruded polystyrene, but using somewhat different chemicals. The resulting foam sheet contains a number of gas-filled cells, and it offers a high R-value. Polyurethane insulation is rated around R-6 per inch, and polyisocyanurate is approximately R-7.5 per inch.

Installing Insulation

There are several areas of the addition, and of the existing house if possible, that should be well insulated. They include the ceiling, floor, walls, water pipes, and ducts.

You will need only basic hand tools to install blanket insulation: a tape measure, utility knife, staple gun, and portable lighting. Temporary floorboards installed across the ceiling joists will give you a more comfortable and stable working platform when insulating an attic, and lessen the risk of damaging the ceiling.

You should always wear protective clothing, particularly when you are working with fiberglass. Wear long pants, a long-sleeved shirt, gloves, and some sort of respirator to avoid breathing in the tiny floating fibers. If you are particularly sensitive to fiberglass, take the added precaution of wearing a shirt or sweatshirt with a hood to prevent fibers from finding their way in around your neck, and use duct tape to tape the area between your shirt sleeves and your gloves. There are also some new fiberglass insulation products—just introduced into the construction market—that greatly reduce floating fibers and substantially lessen irritation.

Ceiling Insulation

Of all the areas you'll be insulating, the ceiling is where most heat is lost, so the levels of insulation there will be the greatest. Most codes now require R-38 in ceilings having an accessible attic above.

For attic insulation, the typical choice is blown fiberglass. It is uniform in its coverage and offers a good R-value per inch. It needs to be installed by a professional who has the right type of blowing equipment, because part of the insulating value comes from the loft that's obtained by the act of air-blowing the insulation into place.

Before installing the insulation, you'll need to do some preliminary work. First of all, you need to protect the soffit or frieze vents with insulation baffles so that they won't be covered with insulation (Figure 18.17). Simply place a piece of plywood, drywall, heavy cardboard, or other material across the rafters wherever there is a vent, extending the baffle down to the plate line and up to approximately 2 inches above the finished level of the insulation. Place a similar wood or cardboard dam around the attic access hatch.

Any fixtures or flues that produce heat, including ceiling fans, ceiling heaters, recessed lights, doorbell transformers, chimney flues, flues for combustion appliances, and other similar objects, need to be protected from being covered by insulation. If they are covered, a tremendous amount of heat can build up under the insulation, creating a high risk of fire.

Using thin-gauge sheet metal, which can be purchased in rolls at most lumberyards, construct a dam around each of these fixtures and flues. The dam should be of a sufficient size to provide at least 3 inches of clearance around the fixture, and it should extend at least 4 inches above the insulation level. Secure the dam to the ceiling or to the rafters to prevent it from being knocked loose during the insulation process.

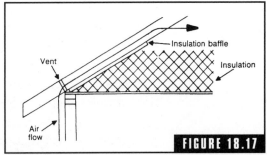

FIGURE 18.17

Vent baffles to protect attic vents from blown insulation.

FIGURE 18.18

An electric exhaust fan with sockets for two lamps. Fans such as this must be vented to the outside.

Check to see that all exhaust fans (Figure 18.18) are vented completely out of the attic. Exhaust fans draw moisture from inside the house, and this moisture can cause a number of problems if it is allowed to enter and remain in the attic. In addition to wetting the insulation, which drastically reduces its effectiveness, attic moisture can stain ceilings and cause serious damage to wooden structural members.

Vent all fans through the roof to the outside, using rigid metal duct and fittings or flexible pipe. Terminate the vent with an approved, weatherproof flashing and cap. Follow this procedure for bath fans, laundry-room fans, kitchen range hoods and fans, clothes-dryer vents, and any other fans that vent into the attic.

The other alternative in the attic is blanket insulation, which can be done without any type of special installation equipment. After preparing the attic as described previously, simply roll out the insulation between the ceiling joists, vapor-barrier side down. No other fastening is necessary.

You can use R-38 batts, which speed up the installation but leave a cold spot at each one of the joists. The alternative is to install an R-19 blanket between the joists, then lay a second R-19 blanket over the first, but perpendicular to it—the overlap of the two directions gives more complete insulating coverage. Remember to use unfaced insulation for the second layer to avoid doubling the vapor barriers.

Wall and Vaulted-Ceiling Insulation

For unfinished wall cavities, batt or blanket insulation is the common choice. Most new-construction codes call for R-21 in the walls, which will fit into a standard 2 × 6 stud cavity. For greater convenience, you can use precut batts if their length suits the height of the wall cavities, or else cut blanket insulation to the proper length. Cut the insulation by placing it, vapor-barrier side down, on a scrap of plywood or drywall and then compressing it with a board along the line of the cut.

Using the board as a guide, cut through the compressed insulation and the vapor barrier with a sharp utility knife.

Press the insulation between the studs, with the vapor barrier facing the heated side of the room. Unfold the stapling flanges, and secure the insulation by stapling through the flanges into the face of the studs, creating a continuous vapor barrier across the face of the wall. Take care that the insulation flanges do not wrinkle and bunch up over the face of the stud, which can cause slight bulges in the drywall.

When all of the full-width stud spaces have been filled, cut narrow strips as necessary to fill in the other spaces. You won't have stapling flanges to work with here, so cut the insulation a little wider than the space so that friction will hold it in place.

Where you encounter electrical wiring running through the walls, separate the insulation near the center, and work part of it behind the wire while leaving the rest to cover the front. This procedure prevents the insulation from bunching over the wire, which could cause a bulge in the finished wall, and ensures a uniform thickness of insulation on both sides of the wire. Trim the insulation neatly around electrical boxes; don't just compress it around the boxes, which causes uninsulated gaps. Work carefully around any plumbing, filling in around the pipes as thoroughly as possible.

An alternative method is to use unfaced insulation, which is held in place by friction, and then cover the wall with plastic sheeting. This creates a much more uniform and effective vapor barrier, and the stud faces remain visible to simplify installation of the drywall.

Vaulted ceilings are insulated in the same manner as the walls, by pressing the proper blanket insulation between the rafters. Code in most areas requires an R-30 in a vaulted ceiling, and in some high-moisture areas, a continuous plastic-sheeting vapor barrier is the only method that's allowed.

Floor Insulation

Underfloor insulation is most effective when it is placed directly up against the underside of the subfloor (Figure 18.19). An easier option is to simply insulate the stem walls, but this still allows a tremendous amount of heat to be lost through the floor into the crawl space. Remember to insulate the floors over garages, unfinished basements,

FIGURE 18.19

Underfloor batt insulation placed between floor joists and held in place by strips of wood lath.

and other unheated spaces. In most areas, R-19 to R-25 is required by code.

To begin, cover the ground in the crawl space with a vapor barrier. The vapor barrier prevents ground moisture from dampening the insulation and also prevents heat absorption by the soil. By installing the ground cover first, you also provide yourself with a cleaner place to work.

Place 6-mil black plastic sheeting directly on the ground, allowing it to lap up the stem walls approximately 6 inches. For best results, glue the plastic to the stem wall with a compatible adhesive, or hold it against the wall with bricks. Lap it up the sides of the piers, but do not allow the plastic to touch any wood members—condensation that sometimes forms on the underside of the plastic could rot the wood members. Side and end seams in the plastic should overlap by 6 inches.

There are several options for holding the insulation in place, depending on the framing. A simple and inexpensive method favored by many contractors is to friction-fit the insulation in place between the joists, then nail thin wood strips, such as lath sticks, to the underside of the joists. Use galvanized nails, and place the lath approximately 18 inches OC. Remember that the vapor barrier must be up against the underside of the subfloor—always facing the heated space.

Roof and Slab Insulation

Two areas of the home that are difficult to insulate using conventional methods are concrete slabs and roofs having no rafter spaces, as in the case of an open-beam ceiling. Rigid insulation is the proper choice for both of these applications. However, since only extruded polystyrene is moisture-resistant, it should be used under the slab. It also has the necessary strength and denseness to handle the load imposed on it by the weight of the concrete.

For a slab with a separate stem wall, you can insulate the inside of the stem wall before you put the fill material in place, or you can insulate the outside of the stem wall. A more effective alternative is to insulate under the entire slab and also the area between the stem wall and the edge of the slab. For monolithic slabs, place the insulation under the entire slab area, and insulate the outside of the footing as well. Be sure to consult with the specific underslab insulation requirements for your area.

Roof insulation is placed after the decking has been completely installed (Figure 18.20). Nail furring strips, equal in thickness to the thickness of the insulation boards, to the decking on 24-inch centers. Cut strips of rigid insulation to fit between the furring, and cover the entire area with plywood sheathing before you apply the roofing. Some codes limit the total thickness of the furring and therefore the total amount of insulation, so you'll want to check with local building officials first.

Pipe and Duct Insulation

Ducts (Figure 18.21), water pipes, and hydronic pipes should not be overlooked, either under the floor or in the attic. Because attics and

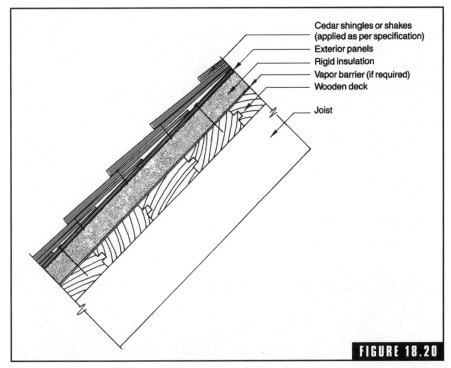

Cedar shingles or shakes
(applied as per specification)
Exterior panels
Rigid insulation
Vapor barrier (if required)
Wooden deck

Joist

FIGURE 18.20

A cross section of a typical roof-insulation situation, using rigid insulation boards on top of the ceiling decking. *(Courtesy of Cedar Shake and Shingle Bureau.)*

FIGURE 18.21

An insulated flexible duct installed under a floor.

underfloor areas remain considerably colder than the temperature of the water or the heated air in the pipes and ducts, convection heat loss is considerable.

Wrap heat ducts with a layer of unfaced R-11 blanket insulation. Before insulating, check to see that all of the joints are securely taped with duct tape. Starting at the plenum, tie the end of the roll around the duct, using wire or string. Continue to wrap the insulation spirally around the entire length of the duct, abutting or slightly overlapping the edges. Secure the insulation with spirally wrapped string or wire as necessary. Insulate all the plenums, ducts, and boots in the entire system, and don't forget any exposed ducts or plenums in the garage, basement, or other unheated areas.

Wrap water pipes in the same manner, using an R-11 blanket that has been separated into two half thicknesses (Figure 18.22). An alternative is to use preformed hollow foam tubes, manufactured specifically for water pipes (Figure 18.23). Purchase these tubes according to the outside diameter of the pipe being wrapped, and install them by opening the lengthwise slit in the tube and placing it over the pipe.

FIGURE 18.22

A water pipe that's been insulated with spirally wrapped fiberglass insulation, held in place with thin wire.

FIGURE 18.23

A foam insulation jacket for water pipes.

Air Infiltration

Air infiltration—the movement of air into and out of the house through a myriad of tiny cracks and gaps—can be a substantial source of heat loss. In leaky older buildings, it can account for as much as 40 percent of the home's heat loss.

There are a number of ways to minimize leakage, both during construction and on the finished house and addition. Caulking is the primary weapon against air infiltration; in fact, it has been estimated that a truly tight house can use as much as five times as much caulk as a conventional house.

Areas to Seal

During construction, it is easy to caulk a number of areas that would be difficult or impossible to reach after the addition is complete. Keep a caulking gun and several tubes of good-quality caulk or sealant available during construction.

During the framing stages, be sure to seal the area between the sill plate and the stem wall, using either caulking or a foam-sheet sill sealer. Seal the subfloor to the joists with construction adhesive, which not only will stop air from coming up from the crawl space, but also helps prevent squeaks. Caulk underneath the rim joist where it sits on the sill plate and below the bottom exterior walls by applying a bead to either the plate or the subfloor just prior to raising the wall. Repeat the caulking process for the rim joist, subfloor, and exterior wall plates at each subsequent floor.

In addition to caulking under the nailing flange on the windows, you will need to seal the space between the finished window trim and the rough framing, as well as any gaps between exterior door frames and the wall framing.

Depending on the size of the gaps you encounter, you can seal these areas using fiberglass insulation, foam backer rod, or expandable foam in spray cans.

When the rough plumbing and electrical wiring is complete, it's important to seal all of the penetrations through the upper and lower wall plates on both the interior and exterior walls to prevent airflow through the wall cavities. If you are having an insulation contractor do the wall insulation, sealing all of the window, door, and wiring gaps is usually included as part of the insulation package.

On the exterior, caulk the areas between the bottom of the siding and the lowest framing member to prevent air from working its way up behind the siding. Caulk the top siding board against the framing in the same manner. Caulk carefully around window and door trim and between any openings in the siding.

Plaster and Drywall

For many years, plaster was the standard interior finish material. Plaster is a hard, smooth, and highly fire-resistant mixture of portland cement, lime, sand, and water, often with gypsum and other materials added. It is site-mixed and applied wet over a base material that's attached to the interior framing.

Until about 1950, wood lath strips were the standard base material, applied horizontally with small spaces between them. When the wet plaster was applied, it would ooze between the cracks and dry, locking the lath and plaster together. In more recent construction, gypsum lath panels, usually 16 or 24 inches wide and 48 or 96 inches long, took the place of the wood. Regular perforations in the lath panels acted in the same manner as the spaces between the wood lath to bond the wet plaster to the base sheet.

A base coat was applied over the lath by spray or with a hand trowel and allowed to dry. Then one or two finish coats were applied. It was essential that a uniform thickness be maintained and that the final coat be completely smooth.

With the advent of perforated gypsum lath panels, it became a logical time- and money-saving step to simply make the panels solid, and then just finish off the joints between the sheets. This process became known as *drywalling,* because the interior finish was achieved with dry sheets instead of wet plaster. While interior plastering is still done for its hard, smooth finish (Figure 19.1), drywall has become the most widely used interior wall and ceiling material for almost all residential and light commercial construction.

Drywall

Drywall serves as a base for almost any finish material you choose to apply, including paint, prefinished paneling, wallpaper, ceramic tile, and wood or masonry veneers. About the only exception would be solid wood or wood panels in thicknesses over ½ inch, which can be applied directly over the studs if desired.

Drywall sheets, known variously as *wallboard, gypsum board, gypsum wallboard, plasterboard,* and by the common brand name Sheetrock, are constructed from a continuous layer of gypsum wrapped with heavy paper on the two faces and the two long edges. There are three commonly available thicknesses: ⅜, ½, and ⅝ inch. Common sheet sizes are 4 × 8 and 4 × 12 feet.

Most sheets have beveled edges along the two long edges. When the sheets are installed, the beveled edges form a recess, which makes it easier to conceal the taped seams. The short edges of the sheets are not beveled.

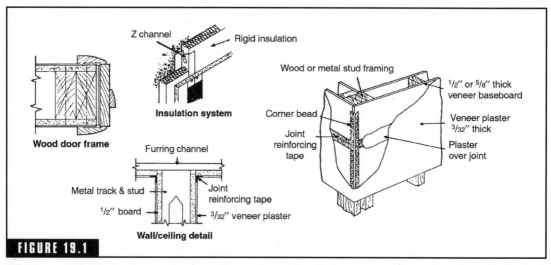

FIGURE 19.1

A look at some of the elements of a modern residential or light commercial interior plastering system. *(Courtesy of Northwest Wall and Ceiling Bureau.)*

Another common drywall designation is Type X, which you might see called out specifically on your plans in certain areas. Type X drywall has fiber added to make the sheets fire-resistant, and ⅝-inch Type X will give the 1-hour firewall protection required in some construction applications. The building codes typically require 1-hour firewall protection on garage walls that are common with living spaces, on the underside of interior stairways, between separate but connected living spaces such as apartments, and in various other locations.

Installing the Drywall Sheets

Drywall sheets are typically installed with the long dimension perpendicular to the studs and joists, and they must be cut so the ends fall over the center of the framing member. Depending on the dimensions of the area to be covered, the use of 12-foot sheets might eliminate some of the end-to-end seams and speed up the finishing process.

Cutting

Use a sharp utility knife to cut the drywall, changing the blade as often as it becomes dull or dirty. Using a drywall T square as a guide, score the face side of the sheet with the blade, cutting through the paper and slightly into the core. Snap the sheet away from the cut to break the core, then cut through the back paper to separate the piece. For small cuts of 1 inch or less, cut through both faces before you try to snap off the piece.

After snapping, the gypsum at the core of the piece is usually somewhat ragged. It's a good idea to smooth this edge to allow for a clean fit between the sheets and to simplify the finishing. You can use a Surform plane, made by Stanley tools, or a rasp, a piece of metal lath around a block of wood, or even coarse sandpaper on a wooden block, although this tends to clog quite quickly.

For cutting outlet holes and other small openings in the sheet, use a drywall saw. Similar to a keyhole saw, a drywall saw has a series of coarse teeth and a pointed end with a wooden or plastic handle. Place the point against the face of the sheet within the area of the cut and tap the handle to drive the saw into and through the sheet; then cut out the opening. An electric drill with a hole saw or wood-boring bit will also work. Remember to cut from the front side to avoid tearing the face paper.

Hanging

You can install drywall sheets using either screws or nails. Special flathead drywall screws are made for this purpose, and these are the only type you should use. The screws should be installed with a drywall screw gun—the gun has an adjustable clutch that regulates how deep the screw is driven, and you should set it so that the screw head is just below the surface of the sheet but does not tear through the paper face.

Screws offer the advantage of better holding power, virtual elimination of "nail pops," and somewhat increased installation speed over nails. They are especially recommended for ceilings that have a floor above them.

If you are using nails, use only drywall nails specifically manufactured for this purpose. The nails are coated to prevent staining from the joint compound, and they have a slightly cupped head that holds the joint compound and makes them easier to conceal.

It is very important to drive the nails straight into the sheet to the proper depth without tearing the face paper. Using a hammer with a crowned (slightly convex) face, the last blow should set the nail head slightly below the surface of the sheet. The hammer creates a slight concave depression, called a *dimple* (Figure 19.2), which receives the joint compound and allows the nail head to be concealed and finished off flush with the surrounding sheet. If you drive the nail too deep, you will tear the paper, making the holding power of the nail practically nil. If you do not drive the nail deep enough, you will leave the head exposed, preventing it from being concealed during the taping process.

For ½-inch drywall, use 1¼-inch-long nails, and use 1½- or 1⅝-inch fasteners for

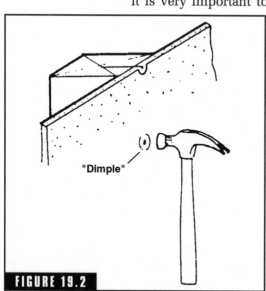

"Dimple"

FIGURE 19.2

"Dimpling" a drywall nail, which allows the nail to be covered with joint compound and concealed.

⅝-inch material. Install the fasteners 8 inches apart on walls and 7 inches apart on ceilings.

Install the drywall sheets on the ceilings first, where their edges can be supported by the wall sheets. Mark the location of each ceiling joist on the wall plates first, which simplifies finding the joists for nailing after they have been concealed by the drywall sheets.

Begin at one corner, working out in a line perpendicular to the joists. Measure from the wall to the center of the joist closest to but less than 8 feet from the corner (or 12 feet for 12-foot sheets). Cut the sheet ¼ inch shorter than this measurement to allow for framing irregularities.

Drywall is heavy—about 1.8 pounds per square foot, or almost 58 pounds for a 4- by 8-foot, ½-inch-thick sheet. In addition to its weight, the size of the sheet and its flexibility make it awkward for one person to handle. For those reasons, hanging drywall is a two-person job. Provide short benches, scaffolds, or ladders for each person, adjusted as necessary to allow people of different heights to comfortably reach the ceiling and nail off the sheet.

Make sure the sheet is facedown, then lift it into place and push it against the ceiling joists. Check to see that each end is squarely over the center of a joist. Brace the sheet against the joists, drive enough nails to secure it in place, and finish off the rest of the nailing pattern for each joist. Always nail off the entire sheet before you move on to the next one.

If working alone is a necessity, you'll need to rent a drywall jack. Place the drywall sheet facedown on the arms of the jack, turn the lifting wheel to raise the sheet to within about an inch of the ceiling, and maneuver the jack until the sheet is properly positioned. Finish raising the jack until the sheet is in contact with the ceiling, then let the jack hold it in position while you secure it.

If you laid out your framing correctly, the sheets should go up with no cutting until you reach the opposite wall. For the second row, start at the same wall and measure to the center of the joist closest to but less than 4 feet from the wall. Begin the third row with a sheet cut to the same length as the first one. Staggering the joints in this manner makes them easier to conceal and provides a smoother finished ceiling.

When the ceiling is completely done, begin on the walls. Install the sheets horizontally on the upper half of the wall first, perpendicular to the studs. Use the same techniques of measuring, cutting, and securing as for the ceiling. Staggering the seams is not necessary, since the joints are much less obvious on the walls, and staggering the sheets will make the vertical seams more time-consuming to finish. Install the full sheets and large pieces first, setting aside all of the smaller scrap. Use the scraps as you go along to fill in the smaller areas.

Do not end a sheet directly against the edge of a door or window. This method places the seam directly above the jambs, where the repeated opening and closing of the door or window will eventually crack it. Instead, span the opening with a sheet and then cut out the opening later, or if a joint is necessary, butt the sheets above the center of the opening instead of at the edge.

Outside corners should be finished off with metal corner beads, which are available wherever you purchased your drywall. Trim and smooth the drywall at the corners for a good fit with no protrusions or gaps, then seat the bead over the corner joint. Nail the bead in place carefully, alternating nails from one side to the other so as not to distort it; you want to maintain a nice, straight line on the corner.

For curved corners (e.g., those over an archway), use flexible corner-bead material that can conform to the irregular shape. One of the popular looks in drywall today is the round corner, which is done with corner bead that is curved along the edge rather than straight.

Taping and Topping

Finishing drywall is not particularly difficult. It just requires a little patience and practice to learn the techniques (Figure 19.3).

Joints are finished off with a paper tape that's embedded in joint compound, a thick, soft material specifically intended for drywall applications. Joint compound is available in all-purpose, taping, and topping formulas and as dry

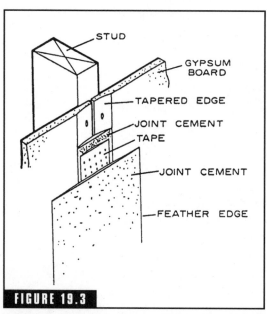

STUD

GYPSUM BOARD

TAPERED EDGE

JOINT CEMENT

TAPE

JOINT CEMENT

FEATHER EDGE

FIGURE 19.3

The various steps in taping and topping a drywall joint. Note the tapered edges in the drywall, which simplify concealing the joint.

mix or premixed. Most professional finishers use the premixed material, using the all-purpose compound for taping and embedding nails and corner metal and the topping compound for the subsequent top coats.

Joint tape is a heavy, nonadhesive paper tape that's 2 inches wide. It has a slight ridge down the center, enabling it to be creased easily for taping corners. As a rough estimate, each 150 square feet of drywall will require 2 pounds of compound and 120 feet of tape, but the amount can vary widely depending on the installation.

Tape the flat seams first, beginning with the ceiling, and then do the corners. Apply a layer of joint compound to the seam with a 6-inch-wide taping knife. Hold the blade at a fairly flat angle to the ceiling, leaving a nice layer of joint compound that is not too thick. This is the bedding coat, into which the tape will be placed.

Be certain that the entire seam is coated with compound and that there are no dry spots. Keep the knife and pan clean and free of debris at all times; don't scoop up any dropped compound and put it back in the pan. If the compound becomes dirty, discard it, since small bits of dirt and other debris will prevent you from getting a smooth coat.

Start at one end of the seam and press the end of the tape into the compound. Unroll the tape along the seam, pressing it lightly into the compound every 2 to 3 feet to hold it in place and keep it centered over the seam. Use your taping knife as a straightedge, and tear the tape off cleanly when you reach the end of the wall.

Return to the starting point and use the 6-inch blade to embed the tape into the compound. Hold the blade at about a 45° angle to the face of the drywall, and apply enough pressure to smooth the tape and work out all of the bubbles. Continue to scrape your blade along the edge of the pan to remove excess compound.

Finally, apply a skim coat of compound over the tape. Don't worry about trying to completely conceal it; that step will come later. Keep the compound smooth, scraping off the excess and returning it to the pan.

When all of the flat seams are taped, do the corners. For inside corners, apply about a 4-inch-wide layer of compound to each side of the corner, then crease the tape between your fingers and place it in the corner. Use the 6-inch blade to smooth it into place as you did for the flat seams, keeping the tape centered in the corner. Special corner trowels are also available that smooth both sides of the corner at the same time.

For outside corners, no tape is necessary. Simply cover the metal corner bead by resting one corner of your knife edge on the bead and the other on the wall. Let the knife ride along the bead and the wall, filling in the area beneath the blade with compound. Covering corner metal consumes a lot of compound in relation to the other seams, so keep your knife and mud pan full.

After you do the corners, you'll want to cover the heads of the fasteners. Scoop up some joint compound on one corner of the knife and run a bead over a line of about four to six nails at one time. Then, again holding the blade at a 45° angle, simply scrape off the excess, filling in each of the dimples.

Allow the compound to dry for at least 24 hours, or as recommended by the manufacturer. You will need to maintain a temperature of at least 50°F in the room in which you're working, using heaters if necessary. The compound is water-based, so be certain it is not allowed to freeze or the joints will fail. Make sure the compound is completely dry before you apply the next coat.

Apply the second coat, which can be either all-purpose or topping compound, with a wider taping knife, usually a 12-inch. Use the blade at a low angle to spread on a layer of compound over the entire seam; then, with the blade more vertical, go back over the seam and smooth it out. Remember that each time you lift or twist the blade, you move the compound beneath it, causing slight irregularities. For the smoothest results, try to cover as much of the seam as possible in one continuous movement.

Keep scraping your blade clean on the edge of the pan, and keep scraping excess compound off the walls to minimize sanding. Top the inside and outside corners, and go over the nail heads again. By the time you are finished with the second coat, none of the tape or metal should be visible.

After the second coat has dried, sand it as necessary. Rubber-backed drywall sanding pads work quite well for this step, and they offer the advantage of precut, easily changed sandpaper. A pole-mounted version with a swiveling head is available for sanding ceilings and the upper parts of walls, and for sanding the lower wall areas without stooping.

Sanding drywall compound produces a very fine dust, so you should wear an approved face mask while you are sanding. Also, be sure to hang plastic sheeting as needed to contain the dust and protect the home's contents, and close off the heater grills to keep out the dust.

Apply the third coat in the same manner. Feather-out the third coat as much as possible to blend the seam into the surrounding area and to minimize sanding. If the seam you are finishing is one where two tapered edges meet, it is sufficient to merely fill in this recess with compound; extending it farther onto the surrounding sheet will just necessitate further sanding later.

For untapered butt joints, it is necessary to build the compound up to a somewhat greater thickness, allowing the seam to be sanded in such a way that the compound is feathered out onto the sheet without cutting into the underlying tape. Don't overdo it, however; remember that the ultimate goal is a flat seam that blends in totally with the surrounding sheet.

Finish off the outside corners a third time also, applying the compound as you did for the first two coats. The inside corners and nail heads are usually all right with two coats, unless you notice obvious deficiencies while you are sanding. When the final coat is dry, sand it as necessary, concentrating on blending the edges into the surrounding wall area.

Transitions

Here again, room addition construction means that you'll have to deal with the transition between old and new wall and ceiling surfaces. In newer homes, where ½- or ⅝-inch drywall was used, the transitions shouldn't present any problem. Simply butt the new material carefully to the old, then tape the resulting seam. You may need to shim the drywall slightly to get the faces as even as possible, and slight irregularities at the transition line will probably require several coats of joint compound to smooth out.

If you are butting new drywall to existing plaster, the difference in the thicknesses can cause problems. Plaster usually was applied in a ¾-inch thickness, but in areas where the plaster was being used to even out irregularities, it could be considerably thicker or thinner than that.

Take the time to carefully measure the thickness of the lath and plaster at several points along the transition line, and write the measurements on the wall or ceiling at the point they were taken. This will give you a guide for matching the new material smoothly to the old.

Probably the easiest way to make the transition is to use ⅝-inch drywall. If the plaster measurements are fairly consistent at ¾ of an inch, tack a layer of ⅛-inch shim material to the stud or joist at the transition point to bring the two surfaces level. Wood veneer, paneling, linoleum strips, or any other material of the proper thickness will work fine.

If the thickness of the plaster varies widely, the lath might have pulled away from the underlying framing. Try reattaching it by nailing or screwing through the plaster, recessing the heads of the fasteners as much as possible. Recheck your measurements afterward to see if the problem has been corrected. As a last resort, you might need to place individual shims of varying thicknesses at different points along the transition in order to align the surfaces.

It's very common for the brittle plaster to break away along the transition line as a result of damage sustained during the tear-out. These areas need to be filled in prior to taping the transition line, using patching plaster to fill the gaps and to ensure the plaster and the drywall surfaces are level with one another as much as possible.

After the patches are dry, you can tape the joint with regular joint compound and joint tape. Apply as many coats of joint compound as necessary to get a smooth blend, feathering each coat farther out onto both surfaces. Texturing, wallpaper, or other surface coverings will further hide the transition.

FIGURE 19.4

Texturing applied to a drywall ceiling.

Texturing

If the drywall is to be painted later, application of a texture coat is a very common practice (Figure 19.4). Texturing covers minor imperfections in the taping and topping and, because of its hiding power, speeds the finishing process. Applying a texturing over the transition between old and new walls and ceilings can blend the two surfaces together, obscure the transition lines, and cover cracks and deficiencies in the old-wall surfaces.

In addition, texturing gives the finished walls and ceiling a nicer look, providing an interesting blend of light and shadow that's a visual relief from a stark, flat wall surface. It can create different moods in the rooms or can add contrast between different areas or between the walls and the ceiling.

There are many types and styles of texture, limited only by your imagination. As with all other aspects of the addition, however, you will want to match the new texture to that of the existing house.

If you have a lot of drywall area to cover, the texture is usually applied by spraying with a special-purpose texture gun. Machine-sprayed texture creates an attractive, uniform surface texture, and it's great for blending the new drywall with the existing surfaces of the house.

For hand-texturing, there are a variety of methods you can try:

- Apply a light sand finish simply by blending a texture additive into paint.

- Dip a stiff brush in thinned joint compound, then run a stick or a piece of pipe across the end of the bristles to spray the compound on the wall.

- Trowel a thick layer of joint compound on the wall, then swirl it with the end of a paintbrush.

- Apply random splotches of joint compound with a heavy sponge, crumpled wax paper, a brush, or other objects.

- Apply stiff, heavy peaks of texture in a Mediterranean style, using commercially available texturing compounds.

- Add coarse sand to joint compound that has been thinned to the consistency of paint, then apply it with a heavy paint roller for a sand texture.

- Use a carpet roller to apply thickened paint or thinned joint compound, creating a light texture commonly known as *stippling*.

Flooring and Finish Carpentry

One of the most enjoyable and satisfying aspects of a room addition is the interior finish work. All of the framing, roofing, and other rough work is behind you, the walls and ceilings are enclosed, and now the addition really begins to come together.

Much of the finish work in the addition will be dictated by what's been done in the rest of the house. You certainly don't want to use a contemporary 2¼-inch baseboard if the rest of the house had been done with solid 1 × 4.

The old adage for finish work is "measure twice, cut once," and it's well worth remembering. Trim material is expensive compared to framing lumber, and almost all of the joints you make will be visible. Take your time, measure carefully, then take a moment to verify your measurements before you cut.

Materials

A tremendous number and variety of materials are available for use as interior trim. You can combine materials or cut your own if you need a special piece. Closely study the style and material used in the rest of the house, and let that be a guide in selecting materials for the addition.

Most molding patterns are available in both hardwood and soft-wood, and a growing selection is available in medium-density fiberboard (MDF) as well. For stain-grade applications, select clear grades of solid wood. In some cases, depending on the quality, No. 1 material might work as well as clear and save you some money, if you don't mind working around some small imperfections.

For paint-grade applications, fingerjointed softwood molding (small scraps of clear lumber that are connected with a series of interlocking joints, like fingers) is commonly available. The joints are strong and the moldings are well milled, offering you good savings while still providing you with an excellent trim for painting. MDF, which is dense and very smooth with no surface imperfections, is also great for painting and is less expensive than wood.

There is usually a fair amount of waste with trim, because of the miter cuts and the number of odd-length pieces that need to be cut and fit around the windows, doors, baseboards, and other areas. Depending on the size of the material and the number and type of cuts you'll be making, allow anywhere from 10 to 20 percent waste when ordering.

Tools and Equipment

The vast majority of finish carpenters today use power miter saws and air-operated nailers. These tools will greatly speed up the trim process and create joints that are clean, well-fastened, and easier to finish.

A variety of manufacturers offer 10-inch power miter saws at very affordable prices. Relatively new on the market are the next generation of compound and compound slide saws (Figure 20.1), which offer a remarkable range of features for cutting trim and a variety of other materials. The compound saws, which cut angles and bevels at the same time, are marked with combinations of angle and bevel cuts that greatly simplify such complex installations as crown moldings.

Air-operated finish nailers (Figure 20.2) and finish staplers (Figure 20.3) are also well worth the investment. They require a fairly low airflow, allowing the use of relatively small and lightweight air compres-

FIGURE 20.1

A compound slide saw, which allows cutting on an angle, a bevel, or both at the same time.

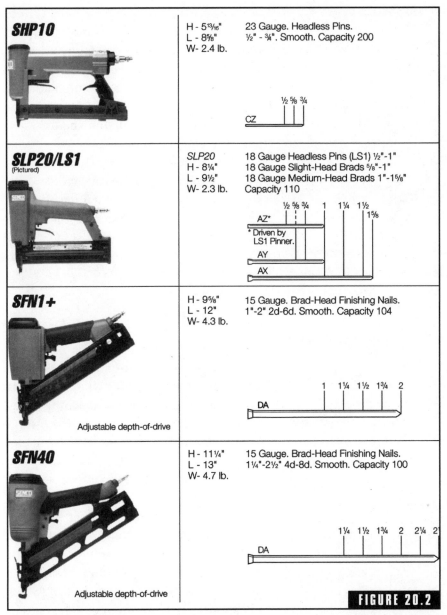

Model	Dimensions	Fasteners
SHP10 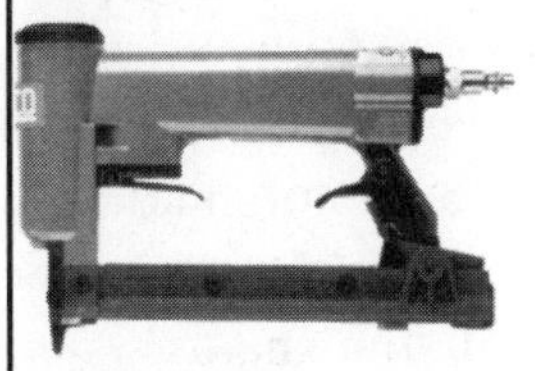	H - 5 13/16" L - 8⅝" W- 2.4 lb.	23 Gauge. Headless Pins. ½" - ¾". Smooth. Capacity 200 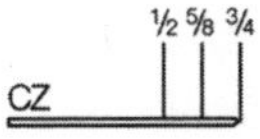 ½ ⅝ ¾ CZ
SLP20/LS1 (Pictured) 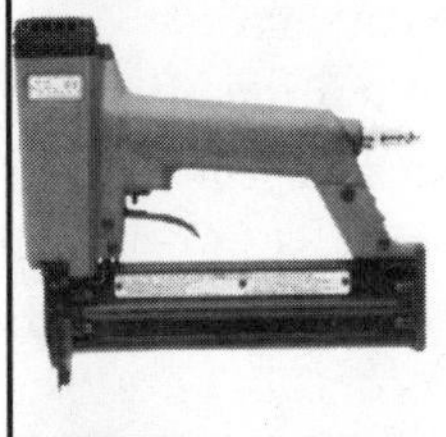	*SLP20* H - 8¼" L - 9½" W- 2.3 lb.	18 Gauge Headless Pins (LS1) ½"-1" 18 Gauge Slight-Head Brads ⅝"-1" 18 Gauge Medium-Head Brads 1"-1⅝" Capacity 110 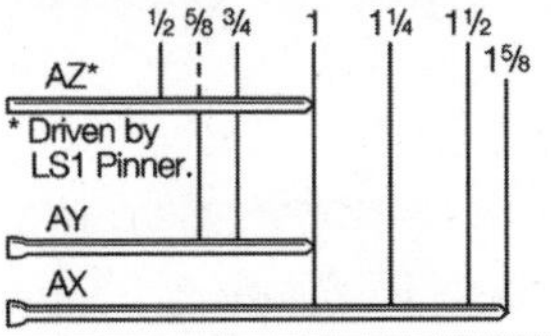 ½ ⅝ ¾ 1 1¼ 1½ 1⅝ AZ* * Driven by LS1 Pinner. AY AX
SFN1+ 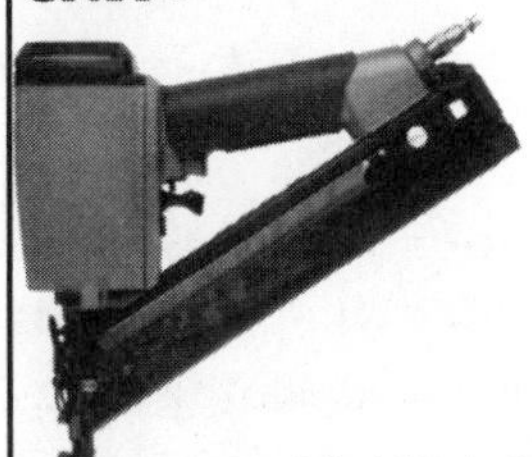 Adjustable depth-of-drive	H - 9⅝" L - 12" W- 4.3 lb.	15 Gauge. Brad-Head Finishing Nails. 1"-2" 2d-6d. Smooth. Capacity 104 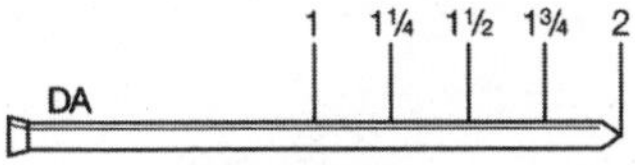 1 1¼ 1½ 1¾ 2 DA
SFN40  Adjustable depth-of-drive	H - 11¼" L - 13" W- 4.7 lb.	15 Gauge. Brad-Head Finishing Nails. 1¼"-2½" 4d-8d. Smooth. Capacity 100 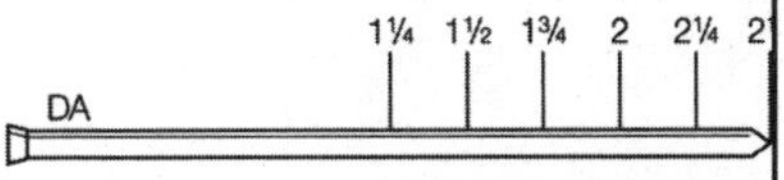 1¼ 1½ 1¾ 2 2¼ DA

FIGURE 20.2

A selection of air-powered pin guns and finish nailers, along with the various fasteners that they shoot. *(Courtesy of Senco Products.)*

FIGURE 20.3

A small, lightweight finish stapler, used for a variety of trim and cabinet installations. *(Courtesy of Senco Products.)*

FIGURE 20.4

Using an air nailer to install door casing.

sors. The guns allow you to fasten a variety of hardwood and softwood moldings and other trim without predrilling (Figure 20.4). Surface marring is virtually eliminated, the fasteners are automatically countersunk, and the resulting fastener holes on the surface of the material are small and easily concealed.

All of these tools obviously represent a sizable investment, and you should purchase only quality tools for long life and easy, accurate operation. For these reasons, you may want to rent some of the more specialized tools until you can afford to purchase them.

Wall Paneling

A popular choice for an interior finish, either for an entire room or just as an accent on one wall, is wood paneling (Figure 20.5). Wood paneling can take the form of wood strips or veneers, solid boards, or prefinished panels. Whatever your choice, install the wood paneling first, before baseboards, door and window casing, or any other trim. This will allow you to trim out the paneling at the same time as the rest of the room and will make the installation simpler and neater.

The wood paneling should be on-site a couple of weeks before you need it. Stack the paneling in the room in which you will install it, using small spacers to keep the pieces separated and to allow an even air-flow around them. This procedure allows the wood to dry and to become acclimated to the temperature and humidity conditions of its environment, which minimizes shrinkage and warpage after the material is installed.

Installing Individual Boards

If you are installing individual boards horizontally, you can attach them directly to the studs. Apply thin wood over a backing of drywall or other solid material to provide adequate support. Vertical boards will require horizontal blocking between the studs on 24-inch centers to provide a nailing surface, or you can attach 1 × 2 or 1 × 3 furring strips horizontally across the studs.

FIGURE 20.5

Individual tongue-and-groove boards installed diagonally as wall paneling.

Installing Prefinished Paneling

Prefinished paneling is commonly sold in 4- by 8-foot sheets. You can install sheets of ⅜-inch thickness or greater directly over studs on 16-inch centers, but you must apply thinner materials over a drywall backing.

Colors and face grains on prefinished paneling can vary considerably. It's a good idea to lean the panels up against the walls in the location where they'll be installed, then stand back and take a look at how they match up. Move the sheets around as necessary to create a pleasing flow of grain and color. When you're satisfied with the look, start at one corner and number each panel sequentially on the back as a guide for installing them.

Prefinished paneling can be installed with nails, panel adhesive, or a combination of both. For a nailed installation, install the nails into each stud, keeping them about 16 inches apart. Many types of paneling have vertical grooves or dark decorative areas on the face—drive the nails into these areas if possible for best concealment. If you're using panel adhesive, follow the manufacturer's specific instructions carefully.

Scribing

Quite often you will encounter the need to fit a straight surface against an irregular one. This could be a piece of paneling butting to the edge of a brick fireplace or a piece of molding being used against a wavy plaster corner. In these instances, you must scribe the board so that its contours match up to those of the irregular surface.

The easiest way to do scribing is with an inexpensive compass (the type that holds a replaceable pencil). Butt the straight piece—for example, a sheet of paneling—against the irregular edge. Be sure the sheet is plumb, and tack it to the wall if necessary to hold it in this position. Sight along the gap between the sheet and the corner, locate the widest point, and set the compass to this width.

Starting at the top, hold the steel point of the compass against the corner and place the pencil point on the paneling. Slowly move down the wall, keeping the compass point against the corner and the pencil point in contact with the paneling. Let the steel point follow each jog and irregularity in the wall corner, which will automatically transfer them in pencil onto the sheet.

Door and Window Trim

Once all of the paneling and other wood wall coverings are done, the next stage is to trim out the windows and doors. This should all be completed prior to installation of the baseboards.

Window Surrounds

If you're not using wood windows that came equipped with their own jambs, then the first project is to construct the window surrounds. The easiest method is to simply build a box and slip it into the window opening, similar to installing a prehung door frame.

Measure the distance from the face of the window frame to the face of the finished wall surface. Check this measurement in several areas to be sure it's consistent. Rip your jamb stock to the measurement, and sand the exposed edge and face. Cut two jamb legs to the height of the window opening minus ¼ inch, and cut the top and bottom jambs to the width of the window opening minus twice the thickness of the jamb material and minus ¼ inch. Assemble the four pieces into a box, slip the box into the opening, then shim and secure it as you did for a prehung door.

If the other windows in the house have a finished sill, also called a *stool,* you can make the box in pretty much the same manner. First, rip a piece of trim lumber to the desired width of the sill; then cut it to length. Some windowsills are made the same width as the window, while others have small "ears" on each side that overlap the edges of the window and give the casing legs something to sit on—for an addition, match the depth and length of the sill to the others in the house. Mark the ears if necessary and cut them out with a jigsaw. Now simply build and install the box in the same manner, using the sill as the bottom piece.

Some windows have drywall applied directly to the framing around the two sides and the top of the opening, and therefore use no jambs and casings. In this case, build a wooden sill as described previously and install it directly onto the rough sill of the window opening.

Casings

Casings are used to cover the gap between the door and window frames and the rough framing that surrounds the opening. Select a casing material that is compatible with the other moldings in the room and that is consistent with the rest of the house (Figure 20.6).

Begin by marking the reveal on the edge of the frame. The standard reveal is ¼ inch, but it can be adjusted to suit your own preference. Using a combination square, a marking gauge, or a rabbeted piece of wood, mark both jamb legs and the head jamb with a sharp pencil.

For a door or a window with a sill, set the end of one piece of side casing on the floor (or sill), in line with the marked reveal. If the finish flooring has not been laid and you are using linoleum, tile, or hardwood, place a scrap of the flooring down first, then set the casing on it. This procedure will leave a gap under the casing that the flooring can slide into, simplifying its installation.

Mark the casing at the point where it crosses the reveal line on the head jamb. Cut the casing on a miter at this point, then tack it into place with just a couple of nails, driven only partially in. Repeat the procedure for the other side. Measure the distance between the insides of the casings and cut the top casing to this measurement. Test-fit it, and finish nailing all three casings into place.

FIGURE 20.6

A beautiful door-casing installation, made up of a combination of several pieces of molding.

If the door frame is not square, you'll need to cheat a little on the top casing miters. Cut one end at the approximate angle needed (44 or 46°, for example) and test-fit it by holding the miter against the side casing and lining up the bottom of the casing with the reveal mark on the head jamb. When you have a good fit on one end, repeat the procedure on the other end, but leave the casing long. Test-fit this second cut, and when you have both angles correct, cut the piece to length. You can usually get away with cheating on the angle up to about 2°; beyond that the miters on the side casings also will need to be adjusted to prevent the finished joint from being noticeable.

There are many other methods for casing doors and windows, such as square-cutting the casing pieces and butting them into corner blocks or creating built-up casings from a combination of other moldings. Just be consistent with the look and style of the rest of the house.

Baseboards

Baseboards (Figure 20.7) are used to finish off the area at the bottom of the walls where they meet the floor. They are not essential, but they add a professional, finished touch to the room while protecting the wall from damage, and they are typically needed to match the style of the existing house.

FIGURE 20.7

Routed 1 × 6 baseboards and plinth blocks (bottom right) were used with the casing in Figure 20.6 to complete the door-trim installation.

If you are installing wall-to-wall carpet or hardwood floor, you will usually install the baseboards first, then butt the carpet to them. With other types of flooring, install the baseboards after you have laid the flooring—this simplifies the installation of the flooring and lets the base cover the area between the edge of the flooring and the wall.

In older homes, wide, square-topped material was sometimes used for baseboard, followed by a second, smaller molding on top called a called a *base molding* or *base cap*. With hardwood flooring, the base is laid first, then the flooring, and another molding, called a *base shoe,* is installed at the bottom of the baseboard to finish off the flooring installation.

Coped Joints

Most carpenters install baseboard simply by cutting the boards to length with a miter at each inside corner. The problem is that those wall corners are rarely 90°, and this creates a gap in the miter. An alternative method is to make a *coped joint,* which is a little more time-consuming, but the resulting joint is much cleaner. The only tool needed is a coping saw—a type of small handsaw with a deep throat and a thin, narrow, replaceable, fine-toothed blade.

For coped joints (Figure 20.8), install one entire wall of baseboard first, using square-cut ends. Cut the baseboard just slightly longer than is needed, bow out the center, place the ends of the board in the corners, and allow the center to spring back naturally against the wall, tightly pressing the ends of the board into the corners.

Cut the intersecting piece at a 45° angle, as you would for any mitered joint. Set the molding on a bench or worktable and hold or clamp it steady. Starting at the top of the board, use the coping saw to carefully cut along the face contour (darkening the corner where you'll be cutting with a pencil will make the contour easier to follow). The resulting cut will fit tightly against the other baseboard, even if the wall corner is not a true 90°.

Stairs

Stair construction represents a combination of both rough and finish carpentry (Figure 20.9). There are several types of stairways, and your choice will depend on the size of the area and the desired finished appearance.

In most instances, you will construct the rough carriages for the stairs during the wall-framing stage (Figure 20.10) and then finish them out with the rest of the trim.

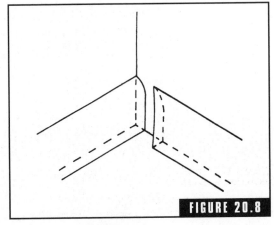

FIGURE 20.8

A coped joint in baseboard.

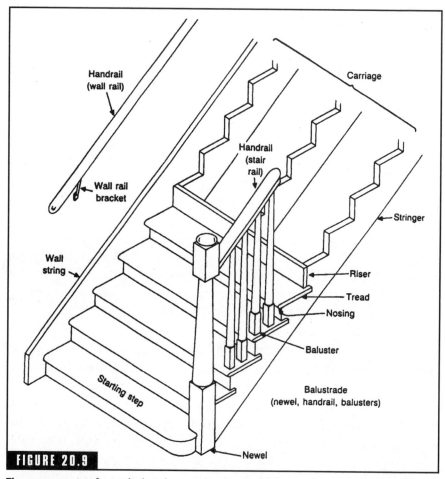

FIGURE 20.9

The components of a typical staircase, showing both the rough framing and finish trim portions of the installation.

You also can purchase stairways for special situations (e.g., a spiral staircase for a confined area) in off-the-shelf or custom sizes.

Ratio of Riser to Tread

If the sizes of the risers and treads are not already specified on your plans, you will need to make these calculations based on the existing conditions. It's important to maintain the correct ratio between the two, so that the stairway looks and feels right.

The ideal riser height is between 7½ and 7¾ inches, with a tread width of around 9½ to 11 inches. A variety of building codes affect

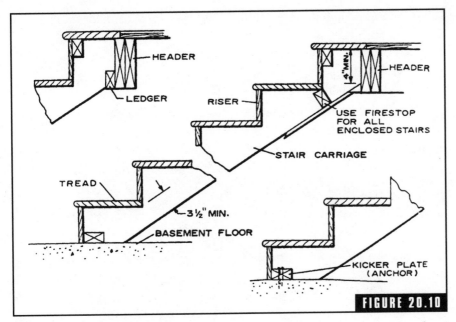

FIGURE 20.10

Rough stair carriage installation.

stair layout and construction, so be sure to check the applicable codes in your area.

As a rule of thumb, the tread width multiplied by the riser height should equal between 72 and 75. For example, a 9½-inch tread with a 7¾-inch riser would equal 74, and a 10-inch tread with a 7½-inch riser would equal 75. Both fall within the range of an ideal ratio. Another rule of thumb is that the tread width plus twice the riser height should equal approximately 25. In the two examples just given, both of the combinations would equal exactly 25 (9½ + 7¾ + 7¾ and 10 + 7½ + 7½).

Working from these ideal riser heights, you can calculate the number of steps between floors. First, measure the total distance from finished floor to finished floor—let's use 9 feet (108 inches) as an example. A common number of stairs for a main stairway is 14, so check your riser height by dividing 108 by 14. The result is 7.7 inches, which falls within the range of an ideal riser height.

The stairway will have one less tread than it does risers, so if the stairway has 14 risers, it will have 13 treads. If the tread width is 10 inches, the entire horizontal run of the stairs will be approximately

130 inches (10 inches × 13 treads). The finished widths for main stairs vary with the style of the installation, but 3 to 4 feet is common.

Stringer Layout

The stringers are laid out according to the number and size of the treads and risers. First you need to determine the length of the stringer, which is calculated from the Pythagorean theorem discussed earlier $(a^2 + b^2 = c^2)$.

In the previous example, the rise is 108 inches and the run is 130 inches:

$$108^2 = 11,664$$
$$130^2 = 16,900$$
$$11,664 + 16,900 = 28,564$$

The square root of 28,564 is approximately 169 inches, or just over 14 feet. That means you will need a 16-foot board for the stringer, usually a 2 × 12.

Next, cut a piece of straight lumber to exactly the same measurement that you calculated between floors, in this case 108 inches. Set a pair of large dividers to the calculated riser height, which in this example is 7.7 inches. Starting at one end of the board, use the dividers to lay off 14 risers of approximately 7.7 inches each. If the last space you lay off is not equal to all the others, adjust the dividers accordingly and repeat the procedure until the board has been divided into 14 equal parts. Measure the setting of the dividers at this point, which will be the exact height of the risers you'll use in the layout.

Select a straight No. 1 grade 2 × 12, 16 feet long (Figure 20.11). It should be as free of knots, splits, and other defects as possible. Set it out on a pair of sawhorses or other supports to make it easy and convenient to work on. Hold a framing square against the top edge of the stringer so that the height of the riser is shown on the tongue and the width of the tread is shown

FIGURE 20.11

A notched 2 × 12 stringer.

on the blade. Draw a line along the outside edge of the square to get the layout of the first tread and riser. Move the square to where the tread line meets the edge, and repeat the procedure. Continue along the board in this manner until you have laid out all of the treads and risers.

Finally, you will need to reduce the height of the bottom riser by an amount equal to the thickness of the material you'll be using for the treads. This reduction is to compensate for the tread thickness and to make the first step come out equal with the last. Using a handsaw or circular saw, carefully cut out the stringer. Using this stringer as a pattern, mark and cut two more to the same size. These three stringers will make up the stair carriage, which is installed during the rough framing stage (Figure 20.12). Temporary plywood treads are typically installed during framing as well, so that the stairway can be used for access (Figure 20.13).

Trimming the Stairs

You will install the stairway parts after you have finished installing the drywall in the stairwell. Cut and install the finished stringer, usually a 1 × 10 or 1 × 12, along both walls if the stairway is fully enclosed (Figure 20.14). A variation is to install the rough stringers directly against the wall, then finish off with a notched stringer. The layout of the notched stringer is the opposite of the rough stringer, and one can serve as a pattern for the other.

When the rough and finished stringers are in place, rip the riser material to width. Cut each piece for a snug fit, and install them so that the top of the riser is exactly flush with the top of the stringer notch. Cut and install the treads after the risers, again concentrating on a clean fit between the finished stringers and a good line against the riser.

FIGURE 20.12

The completed stringer installation, with a small landing that allows a 90° change of direction.

FIGURE 20.13

Temporary treads allow the rough stairway to be used during construction. *(Courtesy of Trus Joist MacMillan.)*

The material you select for the treads and risers depends on the finished floor covering (Figure 20.15). If the stairs will be carpeted, ¾-inch plywood treads are common, secured with glue and 6d or 8d nails or with screws. If the stairs are to be left exposed, select a clear hardwood or rugged softwood for both the treads and the risers—oak and clear fir are two common choices. Attach the pieces with glue and finish nails.

Several companies manufacture balusters, handrails, and other related stair parts and accessories (Figure 20.16). Secure a catalog from your lumberyard or home center, and select the appropriate style and size of parts for your particular application. They will come with all the necessary hardware for assembly, plus an instruction booklet.

Cabinets

If the addition includes a new kitchen, bathroom, pantry, or other areas requiring cabinetry, your clients need to select their cabinets far enough ahead so that you can order them well in advance of the trim-

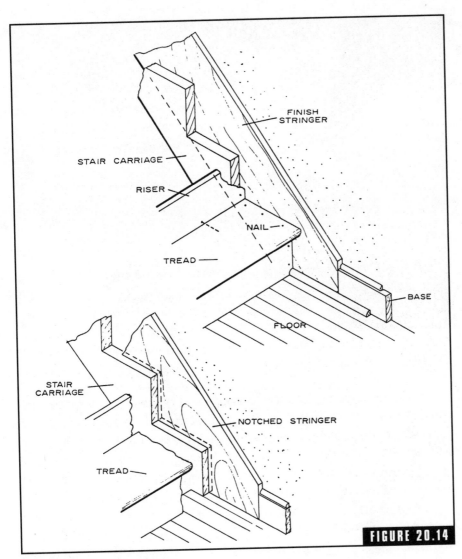

FIGURE 20.14

Two types of finished stringers.

out stage. Whether they are custom or modular, you can expect anywhere from 3 to 8 weeks lead time.

To install the modular cabinets discussed in Chapter 4 (Figure 20.17), double-check the established layout in the plans against the cabinets that were shipped to you. The actual installation begins with the wall cabinets, starting from one corner and working outward.

FIGURE 20.15

A combination of painted risers, stained oak treads, and carpeting make up this stairway.

FIGURE 20.16

Prefabricated stair parts—in this case, painted hemlock spindles and stained oak newel post, volute and handrail set on a curved starting stair—were carefully assembled to make up this stairway.

Wall Cabinets

If the wall cabinets do not go all the way up to the ceiling or to a soffit, you'll first need to mark the wall to identify where the cabinet tops will be. Nail a long, straight board to the wall at this point, making sure it's level. Remove all of the cabinet doors (marking where they go for reassembly), and set them aside in a protected area.

Place the first cabinet in the corner, sliding it up the wall until it meets the ceiling or the board, then check it for plumb and level. Locate the studs, and drill through the cabinet's nailing strip—the board inside the cabinet, against the back at the very top. While one person holds the cabinet in place, a second can attach the cabinet loosely to the wall with 3- or 3½-inch screws.

Set the next cabinet in place beside the first, and visually align the face frames. Again, loosely screw the cabinet to the wall, just enough to hold it. Be certain the screws are hitting the studs. Using bar clamps or C-clamps, align and clamp the adjacent face frames of the two cabinets together (Figure 20.18).

Carefully drill through the edge of the face frame of one cabinet into the face frame edge of the other cabinet. Countersink the hole with a countersink bit, then screw the face frames together. Place one screw near the top and another near the bottom, then one approximately every 12 inches.

Check the cabinets for both plumb and level in several areas. Working with two cabinets at once makes it easier to level them accurately. Using thin, tapered wooden shims, shim between the cabinet

FIGURE 20.17

Partially completed installation of a set of modular kitchen cabinets.

and the walls or ceiling as necessary. Be sure to check the cabinet against both walls of the corner. When the two cabinets are plumb and level, finish driving the screws, then double-check with the level to be certain that the screws didn't rack the cabinet.

Proceed around the room with the rest of the upper cabinets. Plumb and level each one, shimming as necessary, and screw them to the walls and to each other. If necessary, you can rip filler strips of matching wood to width and place them between the face frames, adjusting the width of the overall cabinet run to fit the length of the wall, or you can place two larger, equal-size fillers at each end of the run. Finally, screw through the bottom nailing strip, then replace the doors and adjust them for fit and appearance.

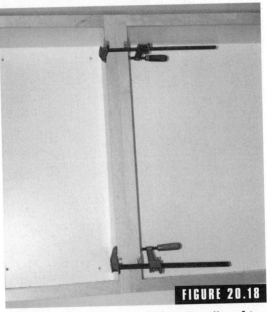

FIGURE 20.18

Small bar clamps are used to hold the stiles of two cabinets together until they are permanently fastened.

Base Cabinets

For the base cabinets, again start from a corner (Figure 20.19). Screw the first two cabinets together and set them in place. Shim between the cabinets and the wall (Figure 20.20) and floor (Figure 20.21) until they are plumb and level, then screw through the backs into the wall studs. Use filler strips as necessary. Continue in this manner, screwing the cabinets to each other and to the walls, until all the base cabinets on one wall have been installed.

Working out from the same corner, begin the adjacent run. Screw the cabinets to the wall and to each other, plumbing and leveling as you go. Next, check to see if the two cabinet runs form a 90° corner, using a 3:4:5 measurement. If not, loosen the wall screws and adjust the shims to "open" or "close" the corner, pulling the runs closer together or farther apart as necessary. For U-shaped kitchens, it's easiest if you install the run along the base wall of the U first, then square both side runs to the base run.

When all of the base cabinets are in, lay a long, straight board across any two adjacent runs. Set a level on the board, and

FIGURE 20.19

A blind corner cabinet that's been "pulled," or set away from the corner, to make up the odd inches in a run of modular cabinets.

FIGURE 20.20

A shim placed between the wall and the back of the cabinet to plumb the cabinet prior to attachment.

FIGURE 20.21

Shims placed below the cabinets to adjust for a slightly uneven floor.

check that the two runs are level to each other as they proceed around the room. Check in several places, and adjust the shims as necessary. Finally, tighten all the screws, adjust the doors, and cut off any exposed shims. Finish the job with matching moldings, as desired.

Flooring

One important consideration for the finish carpenter is the type of floor covering being installed in the addition. Different types of floor require different types of underlayment, and it's important to do your preparation correctly—the wrong underlayment, or the right underlayment improperly installed, will often void the manufacturer's warranty for materials such as vinyl flooring.

Underlayment

Hardwood flooring and carpet and pad installations are typically made directly over the plywood subfloor. For sheet vinyl, vinyl tiles, ceramic tiles, glue-down carpet and a variety of other flooring, the subfloor in the affected areas should be underlayed first. Underlayment ensures a clean, smooth surface to which the finish flooring can bond, and it also raises these thinner flooring materials to the level of the thicker hardwood or carpet.

For most floors except ceramic tile, particleboard underlayment is the most common choice—⅜-inch material is the thinnest you should use, and ½-inch particleboard is preferable. Plywood is also accepted by most manufacturers, as is the new generation of composite underlayment boards now on the market. However, most flooring manufacturers have a long and ever-growing list of things that will void their warranties, so before selecting and installing any underlayment material, be sure to get a copy of the underlayment instructions for the *specific* flooring being used.

The sheets should be laid so that their seams are staggered to one another and to the seams in the subfloor sheets underneath. There should be a slight gap between the sheets on both the edges and the ends to allow for expansion. Secure the underlayment sheets to the subfloor using nails or staples, but do not use glue (glued underlayment also voids some warranties). A narrow-crown, air-driven staple works best for most underlayment, and this method is fast and very secure. Set the air pressure to drive the staple head just below the surface of the sheet.

For ceramic tile, cement-board underlayment works best. The boards are made from a slurry of portland cement, reinforced with a vinyl-coated fiberglass mat. The sheets are smaller than plywood or particleboard—typically 3 × 4 or 4 × 4 feet—and can be cut with a circular saw equipped with a carborundum cutting wheel or by scoring and snapping the sheet. Install the sheets using drywall-type screws or galvanized roofing nails.

Vinyl Flooring

Most of today's vinyl flooring materials are very rugged and long-lasting. Installed correctly, they create a beautiful, low-maintenance floor. The key to a successful installation is proper underlayment, proper floor preparation, and the right adhesive.

After the underlayment is in place, your flooring installer will check to see that it's adequately fastened and will run a wide blade over the entire floor to make sure none of the fasteners are protruding above the surface—any that are will simply be hammered down. The underlayment is then covered with a thin layer of vinyl filler, which covers the indentations from the fasteners and also fills the seams and other irregularities.

Finally, the floor is carefully swept clean and the vinyl is installed. Verify with your installer that the exact adhesive required by the manufacturer is being used—gone are the days of the generic floor-covering mastic that worked for just about everything. Not to overstress this point, but the flooring warranties have become so restrictive that it doesn't take much to void them, and given the high

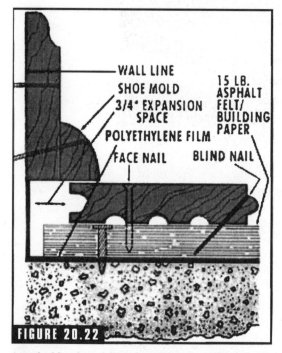

FIGURE 20.22

A typical hardwood floor installation on plywood over a concrete slab floor. The trim and shoe molding (left) allow expansion and contraction in the flooring while concealing the gap against the wall. *(Courtesy of the National Oak Flooring Manufacturer's Association.)*

cost of today's vinyl flooring, you don't want to be responsible for replacing a bad installation out of your own pocket.

Hardwood Flooring

Thanks to improvements in floor finishes and resulting easier maintenance, hardwood flooring is enjoying a new popularity. Although prefinished products on the market may speed and simplify the installation, the traditional method of laying individual unfinished boards and then sanding and finishing them in place is still preferred.

FIGURE 20.23

Installation of oak flooring strips, using a hand-driven flooring nailer. *(Courtesy of the National Oak Flooring Manufacturer's Association.)*

FIGURE 20.24

Using a drum sander to sand an oak floor installation. Arrows indicate the back-and-forth sanding pattern, always working in the same direction as the grain in the wood. *(Courtesy of the National Oak Flooring Manufacturer's Association.)*

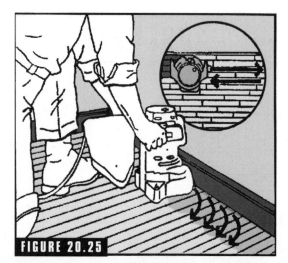

FIGURE 20.25

Using a rotary edge sander to reach along the edges where the drum sander can't effectively reach. The sander has small casters underneath to prevent gouging into the flooring. *(Courtesy of the National Oak Flooring Manufacturer's Association.)*

The flooring should be on-site at least a week before its scheduled installation and placed in the rooms where it will be used, allowing it to become acclimated to the temperature and humidity. The flooring can be installed directly over plywood subfloors. If you are laying hardwood over concrete, you can put down the flooring with adhesive or you can install wood furring strips first.

Installation begins along one wall with a long strip, leaving a gap along the wall (Figure 20.22). The first and last pieces are typically face-nailed where the nails will be covered by the trim; all of the other pieces are blind-nailed diagonally through the tongue. Lay out several rows of flooring first (Figure 20.23), prior to installation, to arrive at a desirable pattern of lengths and joints. Nailing is typically done with a special air-driven or manually operated nail gun.

Once all of the flooring is in place, the entire floor is sanded with a large drum sander (Figure 20.24). Along the edges where the drum sander can't reach, a special edging sander is used (Figure 20.25). Small areas that are otherwise inaccessible to either machine are finished by hand.

After sanding, the floor is carefully swept and at least two coats of finish are applied. Request specific maintenance and cleaning instructions from your flooring installer, and provide a copy of them to your client for future reference.

Sources

American Plywood Association (plywood
   and engineered panels)
P.O. Box 11700
Tacoma, WA 98411-0700

Cedar Shake and Shingle Bureau (roofing)
P.O. Box 1178
Sumas, WA 98295

James Hardie Building Products (siding)
26300 La Alameda, Suite 250
Mission Viejo, CA 92691

Jeld-Wen (windows and doors)
3250 Lakeport Blvd.
Klamath Falls, OR 97601-1099

Northwest Wall and Ceiling Bureau
   (wallcoverings)
1032-A NE 65th St.
Seattle, WA 98115

Senco Products, Inc. (air tools)
8485 Broadwell Rd.
Cincinnati, OH 45244

Trus Joist MacMillan (engineered lumber)
3166 Elder St.
Boise, ID 83705

Velux-America, Inc. (skylights; free guide
   available)
P.O. Box 5001
Greenwood, SC 29648-5001

Western Red Cedar Lumber Association
   (cedar lumber)
1100/555 Burrard St.
Vancouver, BC, Canada V7X 1S7

Wood Truss Council of America
   (manufactured trusses)
One WTCA Center
6425 Normandy Lane
Madison, WI 53719-1133